John Betjeman

A SHORT HISTORY OF
SCOTLAND

BY

ROBERT L. MACKIE

OXFORD UNIVERSITY PRESS
LONDON : HUMPHREY MILFORD
1931

OXFORD UNIVERSITY PRESS
AMEN HOUSE, E.C. 4
LONDON EDINBURGH GLASGOW
LEIPZIG NEW YORK TORONTO
MELBOURNE CAPETOWN BOMBAY
CALCUTTA MADRAS SHANGHAI
HUMPHREY MILFORD
PUBLISHER TO THE
UNIVERSITY

A SHORT HISTORY OF SCOTLAND

By

R. L. MACKIE

Complete in one volume, 5s.

Also in two parts

Part I   216 pp.   2s. 6d.

Part II   214 pp.   2s. 6d.

PRINTED IN GREAT BRITAIN AT THE UNIVERSITY PRESS, OXFORD
BY JOHN JOHNSON, PRINTER TO THE UNIVERSITY

PREFACE

THIS little book contains a survey of Scottish History from the time of the earliest human inhabitants of Scotland to the present day. I hope that it will serve as a useful introduction to more detailed studies of the subject. It embodies many of the results of recent investigation; Chapter II, for example, is based almost entirely on Sir George Macdonald's *Roman Wall in Scotland* and on his contributions to the *Proceedings of the Society of Antiquaries of Scotland* and the *Journal of Roman Studies*.

To Mr. Alan O. Anderson I am specially indebted, both for the help afforded by his two invaluable source-books, *Scottish Annals from English Chroniclers* and *Early Sources of Scottish History*, and for the generously proffered advice which guided me through many a dark place in early Scottish history. I am equally indebted to Mr. C. R. L. Fletcher, who read my manuscript, for his valuable suggestions and emendations. To his sympathy and encouragement I owe most of the pleasure that I have had in writing this book.

Finally, I must thank the Professor of Political Economy in Aberdeen University for permission to use a poem from *Gossip* as the prologue to my history. I wish that the soul of Scotland could be revealed in my prose as clearly as it is in Mr. Gray's verse.

R. L. M.

TRAINING COLLEGE, DUNDEE.
1930.

CONTENTS

List of Illustrations
Scotland, by Alexander Gray

PART I

CONTENTS

LIST OF ILLUSTRATIONS

LIST OF ILLUSTRATIONS

LIST OF ILLUSTRATIONS

LIST OF ILLUSTRATIONS

SCOTLAND

HERE in the Uplands
The soil is ungrateful;
The fields, red with sorrel,
Are stony and bare.
A few trees, wind-twisted—
Or are they but bushes?—
Stand stubbornly guarding
A home here and there.

Scooped out like a saucer,
The land lies before me;
The waters, once scattered,
Flow orderedly now
Through fields where the ghosts
Of the marsh and the moorland
Still ride the old marches,
Despising the plough.

The marsh and the moorland
Are not to be banished;
The bracken and heather,
The glory of broom,
Usurp all the balks
And the fields' broken fringes,
And claim from the sower
Their portion of room.

This is my country,
The land that begat me.
These windy spaces
Are surely my own.
And those who here toil
In the sweat of their faces
Are flesh of my flesh,
And bone of my bone.

Hard is the day's task—
Scotland, stern Mother—
Wherewith at all times
Thy sons have been faced:
Labour by day,
And scant rest in the gloaming,
With Want an attendant,
Not lightly out-paced.

Yet do thy children
Honour and love thee.
Harsh is thy schooling,
Yet great is the gain:
True hearts and strong limbs,
The beauty of faces,
Kissed by the wind
And caressed by the rain.

ALEXANDER GRAY.

CHAPTER I

THE BEGINNINGS

BEN VANE [1]

Of mica schist, in many a twist,
  The goodly frame began
By Lomond shore, some time before
  The Leven Water ran.

First there was heat; to find a seat
  Was inconvenient here,
And grievous then, in every glen
  Was many an atmosphere.

But, ages long, the fabric strong
  Had time enough to cool,
While ice and snow their virtue shew,
  In every furrow full.

At last yielding, one lovely spring,
  The winter shrank, and there
Beneath the face a resting place
  Was offered to the bear.

And woolly elephants, they tell,
  In Coiregrogan roamed;
Still on the bank you find the fank
  Where they were clipped and combed.

Then, withering fast, the glaciers passed,
  And there at length arrayed
With waters sheen and mosses green
  The mountain was displayed.   W. P. KER.

I T is a strange land, white and silent; a land of snow and
ice washed by a leaden sea. Strange yet curiously familiar;
that cold, glittering barrier, rising from the featureless wastes
of snow, might be the Grampians; that ice-choked estuary
might be the Firth of Tay. But there is no sign of human
habitation, nor does any stranger ever make his way to these
desolate shores.

---

[1] There is more than one version of this poem : that here printed is by
kind permission of the Scottish Mountaineering Club, taken from their
Journal (1912, vol. xii, p. 46).

Years, centuries, pass, and with the march of the years the brief summer grows longer, the winter cold less intense. The green of the mosses and low arctic shrubs, at first visible only in the valleys, creeps higher and higher up the mountain sides; to these low shrubs succeed trees, till the whole land—all but the highest mountain peaks—is covered with a great forest of silver birches.

One generation of forest trees succeeds another, and makes way for a third; still no hunter's foot presses the fallen leaves in these lonely woods, no human voice sounds under the branches. Then the pendulum swings back; the snows lie longer in spring; the summer, when it comes, is cold and wet; glaciers appear in the higher valleys and creep slowly downwards; the great forests disappear; the land is once more in the grip of winter.

It is a winter to be measured not in weeks or months but in years, in centuries; but at last it comes to an end. The forest returns; not only the plains and valleys, but the mountains up to three thousand feet above sea-level, are covered with dense masses of the red-stemmed Scots fir.

Again the pendulum swings: the centuries of long genial summers are ended; the second great forest shrinks to the lower slopes of the mountains. But the cold is not as intense as it was before; only on the highest mountains does the snow lie all the summer through. And bleak and inhospitable as this melancholy land would appear to us, men have chosen to make their homes here, in caves on the mountain-side that hitherto have been occupied only by the bear and the wolf. A starved and meagre existence they lead, these first of Scotsmen; they have no dwellings except these damp and noisome caves; they cannot till the ground, but live on the flesh of the reindeer, for herds of reindeer haunt these frozen wastes; they are ignorant of the use of metal, and so have to make their tools and weapons of bone or of roughly chipped stone.

In time the climate becomes milder again; the snow disappears from all but the highest peaks. This strange country has become very like the Scotland that we know to-day.

Very like, but not quite the same. In these far-off times—twelve thousand years ago at least—the seaward cliffs lay lower in the water, some twenty-five or thirty feet below their

FLINT SPEAR-HEAD   ADZE OF CHIPPED FLINT

The spear-head was found in the eighteenth century in Ayrshire; the adze in 1860, also in Ayrshire. Scales ½

present level; the climate was colder and wetter; great lakes and marshes covered what is now fertile cornland; and though the trees had vanished from the mountains, the low-lying country was covered with dense forests of birch, oak, and fir.

Though the wolf and the wild boar remained, the reindeer had disappeared. The human inhabitants—some of them at least—kept near the shore, living in caves or rock-shelters a little above high-water mark. They had advanced a little beyond the point reached by their predecessors, the men of the Early Stone Age—these cave-dwellers who were the first inhabitants of Scotland. They could not till the soil; for food they depended largely on shell-fish, which they detached from the rocks with little gouges of bone or stone. They caught crabs in traps, killed seals and fish with harpoons of bone, snared sea-birds, and hunted the red deer and the wild boar. They knew nothing of the use of metals; the only stone tools that have been found near their dwellings, except the chisels or gouges, are round stones that they used as hammers for breaking large shells, and little flakes of flint. With these flint scrapers, however, they fashioned pins and borers, and their beautifully polished harpoons. They clothed themselves in skins; large shells were their only drinking-cups, and the only animals that they succeeded in taming were the cat and the dog.

This is all that we can find out about these early inhabitants of Scotland, for they left no written records behind them, only their shell mounds and shell-filled caves.

Slowly these men climbed up the ladder. As the centuries passed, after the land had risen to its present level, they acquired a greater mastery over the materials they worked with: their heavy stone axes and hammers were beautifully ground and polished; they fashioned their little flint arrow-heads so delicately that the medieval rustic who turned them up with the plough thought that they had been made in some fairy workshop. They were no longer content to dwell in caves, but made shallow circular pits, which they roofed over with branches; they learned to spin and weave; they grew wheat and barley in clearings in the forests; and they made round-bottomed bowls of earthenware. Their dead they buried in a little oblong chamber made of stone slabs, over which they piled a great oval-shaped mound of stones and earth. From the

remains that have been found in these cairns or barrows, we
know that these Neolithic men—men of the Late Stone Age—
must have been of comparatively small stature, five feet four or

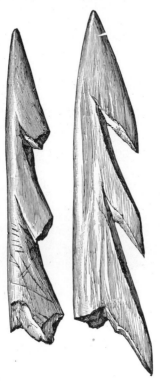

BONE HARPOONS FROM DRUIMVAIRGIE CAVE, OBAN
Natural size

five feet five inches, and that their heads must have been long
in proportion to their breadth, like the heads of the Scotsmen
of to-day.

Then, somehow or other, these primitive Scotsmen discovered the use of bronze. They may have learned the secret

BRONZE SWORD FOUND IN THE ISLAND OF SHUNA. Length 25⅝ inches, greatest breadth 1¾ inches.   Scale 3/16

from those adventurers from the other side of the North Sea who, many centuries before the birth of Christ, invaded and occupied the eastern coasts of Scotland. These new-comers were taller than the aborigines and their heads were shorter; they brought implements and weapons of bronze with them; they buried their dead in circular barrows, and in the grave they often put a tall, narrow-waisted earthenware vessel, the 'beaker', which gives these strangers the only name that they have to-day.

Of the names and deeds of their mighty men, of their religion, of their very language, nothing is known; all we can see plainly through the mist of the years is the craftsman, pouring his molten copper and tin from the crucible into the moulds of clay or stone. As the years pass his skill increases, the objects that he fashions —axe-heads, spear-heads, leaf-shaped swords, rapiers, and daggers—grow more and more beautiful, more and more cunningly adapted to their purpose, till he goes and another craftsman takes his place.

But stone did not go out of use altogether: the hunter's arrow was still tipped with flint; when the deer had been brought home the skin was cleaned with flint scrapers. In the same way, the new fashion of burning the dead and placing the ashes in a sepulchral urn did not find favour with every one; some people still buried their dead in the ancient way.

Just as the Stone Age was followed by the Bronze Age, so about the fourth century before the birth of Christ bronze yielded to iron;

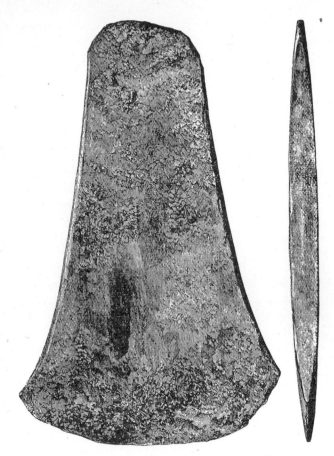

FLAT BRONZE AXE FOUND NEAR TURNBERRY CASTLE
Natural size

though just as bronze failed to oust stone completely, so iron failed to oust bronze. In fact, the craftsmen of the early Iron Age displayed far more skill in the working of bronze than their predecessors had done. The difference was that bronze was now used mainly for ornamental objects, like buttons, brooches, and pins, while from the harder metal were made swords and ploughshares, spears and pruning-hooks.

How did these old craftsmen discover the use of iron? The secret seems to have been brought from the Continent by a new set of invaders, the Britons, a Celtic people who had slowly drifted across Europe from Asia Minor, and, instead of settling in France like their kinsmen, the Gauls, had held on their course till they came to this island, then called Albion. We know nothing about the struggle between the invaders and the natives except that the Britons became masters of the island, and that the language of the conquerors was adopted by the conquered tribes. It was a language not unlike modern Welsh; modern Welsh is, in fact, the present-day form of this ancient British speech.

So the people who dwelt north of the Tweed in the first century of our era were far from being brutal and ignorant barbarians. Some of them at any rate dwelt in little towns, collections of wattled huts arranged in regular rows on some level hill-top; others lived in crannogs, artificial islands, or natural islands which they had enlarged by treading down earth behind a barrier of piles. They tilled the soil, cut the grain with bronze or iron sickles, and carried the sheaves to their hill-towns in carts drawn by horses.

They seem to have spoken a language very closely akin to, though not exactly the same as that spoken by the Britons south of the Tweed; in fact, the Romans called them Britons. Not till almost ten centuries after the coming of the Romans was the name Scotland given to the country between the Cheviots and the Pentland Firth. But though no barrier of

language divided the peoples of Scotland, they formed not a
united nation but a collection of tribes, keeping themselves to
themselves in time of peace, and reluctantly forming temporary
alliances in time of war.

But undisciplined valour was soon to be pitted against
organization. For thirty-seven years after the Roman occupation of southern Britain had begun the Romans left Scotland
alone, but in the summer of the year 80 the sound of the great
Roman war trumpet disturbed the silence of the Cheviots, and
over the empty moorland wound the legions and the auxiliaries,
cohort after glittering cohort, in seemingly endless procession.

THE CHEVIOTS NEAR THE FRONTIER

CHAPTER II

THE ROMANS IN SCOTLAND, A.D. 80–211

But his shield was picked up in the heather
And he never saw Rome any more !

KIPLING.

THE leader of the invading army was Julius Agricola, whom the Emperor Vespasian had sent to Britain as commander-in-chief two years before. Agricola seems to have thought that as long as any part of the island remained unconquered, the hold of Rome over the rest would be insecure. In the first summer that he spent in Britain he had subdued the turbulent tribes in North Wales, and now he had girt himself for a mightier task.

Agricola was a good general. He did not believe in showy victories, followed by undignified retreats; whatever Rome touched Rome must hold. So along the line of his northward march he built forts, cleverly designed to resist a surprise attack and containing provisions for a twelvemonth. Not one of his forts, his son-in-law Tacitus proudly tells us, was ever captured by the enemy. At the end of his first summer he had subjugated south-eastern Scotland; in his second campaign he occupied the isthmus between the Forth and Clyde and secured it by a line of forts; his third campaign saw him and his legions in the south-west.

These successes cannot have been easily gained, for the Britons of the north were hard fighters. In other parts of the Empire a single rampart and a single ditch were considered a sufficient defence for a fort; the officer who planned the defences of the fort at Ardoch found that he required seven ditches, while at Roughcastle another unusual device was employed: rows of pits in which pointed stakes were concealed were used to strengthen the ordinary defences.

Still Agricola was not satisfied. In the summer of 83 he resolved to carry the war into the country beyond the Forth—Caledonia he called it. He sent the fleet on ahead to skirt the east coast, to penetrate into all the bays and estuaries, and spread—as he hoped—doubt and terror wherever it appeared.

THE ROWS OF PITS AT ROUGHCASTLE

But the sight of Roman galleys in the Tay did not have the effect on the Britons that Agricola had expected. They saw now that unless they acted quickly the north of Scotland would pass into the control of an alien ruler just as the south had done. A common fear forced them into some sort of unity, and soon the garrisons of the isolated forts on the isthmus found that they were being assailed by overwhelming forces of the natives.

The more cautious of his officers advised Agricola to withdraw, but he resolved to risk his army among the hills and

trackless woods that loomed before him. Still, his troops
narrowly escaped a big disaster.

He had sent his army forward in three separate divisions.
The usual precautions were taken: when the soldiers halted
for the night they invariably surrounded the site of their camp

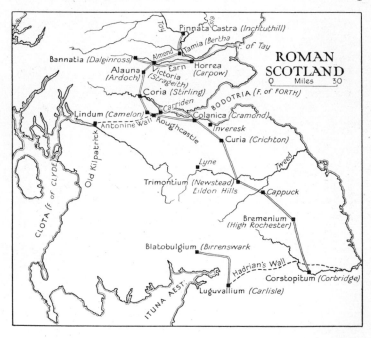

with a great ditch, the upcast from which they used to form
a rampart. Gaps, of course, had to be left in the middle of
each of the four sides to form entrances; otherwise the tents
and shelters, with the commanding officer's tent in the centre,
were completely enclosed by this double defence.

All these rules had been observed by the men of the luckless
Ninth Legion; sentinels had been posted, and were patrolling
the ramparts, envying their sleeping comrades, perhaps, or

gazing at the stars, the only familiar things in this unfamiliar land on the very edge of the world. Suddenly the stars that hung lowest in the sky were obscured by strange shapes, crouching black figures, and before the sentinels could give the alarm the Britons were upon them. Over the low rampart they rushed, in among the sleeping men, whom they hacked and stabbed to their hearts' content. Those of the Romans who survived the first onset fought where and how they could, without plan and without hope of success.

But the night soon passed—summer nights are short in Scotland—and at dawn a great shout was heard. The hard-pressed soldiers looked up and saw in the distance the Roman eagles glittering in the morning sun. Agricola had been warned by his scouts that the enemy were crowding in upon the track of the Ninth Legion, and he had sent forward a swift-moving body of cavalry and infantry to take them in the rear. En-couraged by this sight, the beleaguered garrison turned fiercely upon its assailants and step by step drove them towards the gates of the camp. Attacked now on three sides at once, the Britons were forced to retreat, but if Agricola had hoped to break them utterly he was disappointed; fighting behind the natural defences of woods and marshes, they were able to beat off their pursuers.

Nor were they cast down by this reverse. They knew how near they had come to success; give them more men, and victory would be theirs. But the legions marched steadily on, through Perthshire to the head of the Firth of Tay, on to Inchtuthill, near the junction of the Tay and the Isla, where a great fortified camp was built. It was the point of the spear, the last of the line of forts strung along the military road that led from what is now High Rochester in the north of England, by Newstead under the triple peak of the Eildons, on to Cramond and Stirling, and then from the valley of the Forth to the valley of the Tay. There was no need now for provisions to be brought to the troops by a tedious overland journey; the dwellers in the 'dun' or fortified hill—destined to be the nucleus of the town of Dundee—that rose steeply from the waters of the Firth of Tay, could now see the Roman galleys escorting the heavily laden provision ships to the new granaries at the mouth of the Earn.

In the summer of 85 the Romans continued their advance; while the fleet emerged from the Tay and sailed slowly up the east coast, plundering the settlements of the natives as it went, Agricola with his army plunged into the unknown country between the Firth of Tay and the Moray Firth. Somewhere in this region, on the slopes of a great hill called Mons Graupius, their numbers swelled to more than thirty thousand by warriors from tribes that had not hitherto faced the Romans, the Britons were waiting for Agricola. They were commanded by the chieftain Calgacus, the first native of Scotland whose name has been handed down to us.

Had the Roman soldiers not been Roman soldiers their courage might have been shaken as they looked across the plain at the heaving, surging masses of the Britons and listened to their fierce war-chants and frenzied shouting, or watched the war-chariots with their cargoes of spearmen dash along the ranks, or marked, high up on the hillside, another host waiting for the signal to descend. But they had little cause for fear; Agricola, in fact, proposed to use only the auxiliaries, troops drawn from the remoter parts of the Empire, and to keep the legions, the splendid regular Roman infantry, in reserve throughout the engagement.

The long line of the auxiliaries moved slowly forward to meet the mass of howling, shouting warriors that rushed towards them. Then the two lines halted a few yards apart; arrows rattled on the helmets and breastplates and great oblong shields of the Romans, while the heavy Roman javelins whirred through the air, to be caught on the small round shields

A ROMAN WARSHIP, MANNED BY LEGIONARY SOLDIERS

From a marble bas-relief

or parried dexterously by the swords of the Britons. For a time it seemed as if the auxiliaries were to be held up, but when the Batavian cohorts rushed forward, smashing at their opponents with the bosses of their shields, and running in under their guard and stabbing them with their short swords, the Britons began to recoil.   The cohorts to right and left of the Batavians now rushed up, and so the whole line moved forward once more.

But the Britons were not beaten yet; though they were now assailed not only by the Roman infantry but also by the horsemen, victorious in their contest with the charioteers, though riderless horses and masterless chariots shook their ranks, they fought on grimly and again held up the Roman advance. Observing this, their comrades on the hill-slopes moved down to the plain and began to work round the flank of the auxiliaries in an attempt to get between the Romans and their camp.

Agricola was ready for them; he launched four regiments of cavalry at the advancing Britons, who reeled back, broken and terrified.

The cavalry now wheeled round till they were behind the main body of the enemy and then charged a second time.   The Britons, shaken by the double onslaught, surged back to the woods that lay a little behind them; gaps opened in their ranks, gaps into which the triumphant horsemen poured, slaying or making prisoners at their pleasure; the gaps became wider, till the great army of a few hours before had melted away into a multitude of terrified fugitives.

They were not all terrified.   The Romans could not refrain from admiring those who refused to flee and fought on with blind and desperate fury.   And even the fugitives rallied when they reached the shelter of the woods and ambushed the foremost pursuers.   But they could not outwit Agricola.   Again he sent his cavalry forward, in a long continuous line that swept the woods like a drag-net.   Again the Britons fled, but this time they did not rally.

The Roman sentinels who paced the ramparts that night heard, away in the distance, a strange, unearthly sound, the wailing of women for their dead. When morning came they looked out beyond the ghastly débris of the battle-field to a silent and empty world. As the light grew clearer they saw on the horizon column after column of smoke rising into the air. Then they knew that their victory was complete: the Britons had fired their villages and were seeking other homes far from the track of the Roman eagles.

But the Romans never completed the conquest of Scotland. In the following year Agricola was recalled; about the same time one of the four legions that formed the backbone of the Roman army in Britain was transferred to Germany. The successors of Agricola contented themselves with defending what Agricola had gained. For another thirty years the trumpets sounded from the lonely forts that he had built on the Perthshire moors, waking the sleeping soldiers and the red grouse among the heather, and then they sounded no more. In 115 the tribes in Scotland and the north of England turned upon the Roman garrisons; fort after fort was assailed and captured; the luckless Ninth Legion marched northward to the relief of the beleaguered garrisons and was never heard of again. So serious did the situation become that in the year 122 the Emperor Hadrian himself came to Britain to restore order. He succeeded, but he decided that Scotland was not worth the trouble which it had given him, and that the line of stone forts which he had ordered to be built between the Tyne and the Solway should become the northern boundary of the province of Britain. A deep ditch, stretching from sea to sea, marked the exact position of the northern limit of empire; a year or two later the distinction between the peaceful south and the unconquered north was emphasized still further by a great wall of stone, joining up the hitherto isolated forts.

But it seemed to the Roman commanders that something

more was needed, some kind of breakwater or outpost line away to the north, where troops could be stationed to check a southward movement of the tribes before it had well begun. So in the reign of the Emperor Antoninus Pius, about the year 140, the legions, with Lollius Urbicus, the governor of the

The wall of the Emperor Antoninus Pius, on Ferguston Muir,
New Kilpatrick

Province, at their head, took the road once more. They were making for the line of deserted forts that Agricola had built across the isthmus of the Forth and Clyde. Along this line they now built a rampart of earth, ten feet high and six feet broad at the top, which stretched without a break for thirty-nine miles, from Carriden on the south side of the Firth of Forth to Old Kilpatrick on the north side of the Firth of Clyde.

Nineteen forts, each of them capable of containing at least
five hundred men, abutted on the wall. To the north a ditch
made access more difficult; on the south a broad road linked
up the forts. For the Romans did not intend to fight behind
the wall; it was to serve as a raised walk rather than as a

Inscribed slab, erected in honour of the Emperor Antoninus Pius by a
detachment of the Second Legion, the Sixth Legion, and the Twentieth Legion
—the three legions concerned in the building of the Antonine wall. This
slab was recovered from the bed of the River Tyne in 1903

barrier, along which the sentries would pace to scan the hills
and moors for any appearance of bands of hostile Britons.
Should the hostile force turn out to be more than the garrison
of a single fort could manage, or should the Britons launch a
surprise attack upon a fort, the trumpets would ring out,
beacons would send up their clouds of smoke into the air, and
the garrisons of the forts to right and left would race along
the road to reinforce their comrades.

When the legions had finished the wall they withdrew, leaving the forts to be manned by cohorts of auxiliaries drawn from places as far apart as Spain and Thrace, Syria and the Rhine. But though the purple moorlands must have seemed strange to them, their immediate surroundings would be familiar, for a Roman fort was a Roman fort all the world over, on the Danube or the Rhine as on the Forth or the Clyde. Always in the centre you had the stone-built *principia*, or headquarters building, and not far away another stone building, the commanding officer's house. The *principia* stood at the intersection of two broad streets which divided the camp into four equal parts. The great majority of the buildings in these four blocks were wooden huts, 150 feet long and 30 feet broad, which served as quarters for the soldiers; the granaries, however, were always built solidly of stone. One or two of the forts in Scotland had ramparts of masonry; in most, an embankment of turf raised on a stone foundation had to suffice. But the plan was the same—the great square of the rampart with its enclosing ditch, the two straight streets, the four blocks of barrack-buildings. And the garrison had ample opportunity of becoming accustomed to what had once been unfamiliar to them, for there was no system of reliefs in the Roman army, no chance of a spell of home service; a fortress might be garrisoned by the same unit, not simply for years, but for centuries. So it is little wonder that a veteran, discharged on account of age, often retired, not to his distant and half-forgotten home, but to the little settlement outside the fort where the women and children lived. In this enclosure, too, stood the big stone bath-house, where the soldiers spent much of their leisure.

But the Antonine Wall was no place for women and children. In the year 155, when a rebellion was raging farther south, the Britons broke through and forced the Romans to abandon the line of the Forth and Clyde altogether. The rebellion was suppressed; the Romans came back, repaired the damaged forts, and waited. Again the Britons broke through; again some of the forts were lost and recovered.

Soon after 180 the end came. In the confusion of another rebellion the wall was abandoned, but not till the barracks had been set on fire and the boundary slabs, set up proudly by the legionaries forty years before, removed from their places and laid face downwards upon the ground. The same thing happened at Newstead and the other southern forts; altars were buried to save them from desecration, and everything that would burn was set on fire. Soon the last soldier disappeared over the slopes of the Cheviots, leaving behind him as memorials of the ineffectual might of Rome the smoking ruins of the forts and the long empty road.

The Romans did return to Scotland, however. About thirty years later the stout-hearted old Emperor, Septimius Severus, sailed into the Forth at the head of a fleet, seized on the deserted harbour of Cramond, and used it as a base whence he launched an attack on Fife and north-eastern Scotland. He did succeed in forcing a way through the marshes and forests of this unexplored country, but it was at a terrible cost to his own army. He returned south to make plans for the conquest of what he knew was a still unconquered country, but after his death in 211 all these plans were abandoned. For the remainder of the period of the Roman Occupation—almost two centuries—Hadrian's Wall again marked the northern limit of the province of Britain.

CHAPTER III

THE OTHER SIDE OF THE WALL: A.D. 80–410

Grey recumbent tombs of the dead in desert places,
    Standing stones on the vacant wine-red moor,
Hills of sheep, and the homes of the silent vanished races,
    And winds, austere and pure.

R. L. STEVENSON.

WHAT was happening on the other side of the frontier
during all these years can be only dimly conjectured.
Even of the Romans we know little enough, for the historians
who lived in those days did not concern themselves much with
what was happening in a remote corner of the Empire, and
the scanty scraps of information they have left us have to be
eked out with other scraps gained from a careful examination
of their forts and settlements. The inscribed slabs fixed at
intervals along the Antonine Wall, for example, let us know
that it was built by men of the Second, Sixth, and Twentieth
Legions, and altars found within the forts give us the names of
the cohorts that garrisoned the Wall after it was completed.

But the natives have left neither histories nor inscriptions
to help us. Still, one or two things are certain; they were not
savages, nor were they for ever fighting with the Romans. It
seems, in fact, that Septimius Severus had builded better than
he knew; for almost a century and a half after his famous
northward march there was no serious fighting on the frontier.
Nor were the Britons entirely uninfluenced by the civilization
of Rome: the remains of one of their towns, recently discovered
on a hill-top in East Lothian, tell another story.

For fifteen centuries Traprain Law has been untenanted
save by the rabbit and plover. But it was not always so: the
Stone Age hunter wandered over it and left his axe-head in
the grass; the men of the Bronze Age dwelt here; here they

buried urns containing the ashes of their dead; and towards the end of the first century a town was planted upon it—a town of bee-hive huts of wattle and daub, raised upon circular stone foundations. It seems a strange site to choose, for the east winds blow chill on this unsheltered hill-top, but the men who chose it had to consider security as well as comfort.

They got water from a stone tank near the summit of the hill; their food they cooked in earthenware pots over fires kindled on stone hearths outside the huts. A paved road led through the great rampart of piled stones that surrounded the settlement to the plain below; when it was unearthed a year or two ago the ruts made by the cart-wheels and the hollow in the middle worn by the feet of the horses or oxen could still be plainly seen. There was much coming and going between the hill and the plain; down on the plain lay meadows where sheep and oxen grazed, and waving fields of wheat and barley. For the people of Traprain Law, though they killed the red deer occasionally, were farmers and herdsmen rather than hunters. Nor were they badly equipped for their work: their ploughs had iron ploughshares, at harvest-time they used iron sickles and shears, and they prodded the reluctant oxen with iron-pointed ox-goads. The harness of the draught animals glittered with studs of bronze, sometimes decorated with bright enamels.

For some men stayed on the hill-top while others worked in the plains—stayed to watch the crucibles of molten bronze, to snatch them from the fire with iron pincers, and run the molten metal into moulds of stone or clay. They liked to work with bronze; they could do things with it that they could not do with iron—make the most beautiful rings and brooches and buttons and fibulae, safety-pins we should call them now, ornamented with enamel or with little touches of silver. They worked for people who liked bright colours, who insisted on decking themselves with beads and bracelets of coloured glass.

Probably, like the Gauls, they wore tunics and breeches of brightly coloured cloth, but not a shred of these garments is left, though many spindle-whorls—perforated stones which they used when they spun the thread—and loom-weights of clay have been picked up. Some of these spindle-whorls are not stone at all, but pieces of glazed red pottery—Samian ware it was called—from the Roman potteries in Gaul. Hundreds of other fragments, both of Samian ware and of other kinds of Roman pottery, have been picked up on the hill. Nor is this all: Roman coins, some of them dating from the end of the fourth century, have been found among the foundations of this British hill-town.

What is the explanation? Simply that the dwellers on Traprain Law preferred the beautiful glass and earthenware vessels that the Romans made to the clumsy products of their own potteries, and bought them from Roman traders, and further, that this trade went on for two centuries after the Antonine Wall had been abandoned. From these traders the natives learned the use of coins as a medium of exchange, and so Roman coins found their way into the remotest corners of Scotland, into regions that neither Agricola nor Severus had ever seen.

As with the coins, so with the fragments of Samian ware; we find them in dwellings that no Roman ever built, in the crannogs for example, in the 'weems' or earth-houses, and in the brochs that dot the shores of northern Scotland and rise beside the voes and flows of Orkney and Shetland.

A weem was meant to be inconspicuous; it was a long narrow tunnel, anything from fifty to a hundred and ninety feet long, made by digging a trench, about six feet deep, and roofing it over either with branches or with large stone slabs, on the top of which earth was piled. In some earth-houses the tunnel was approached by a flight of well-hewn stone steps, and it usually bulged out after a certain distance to form a fairly commodious chamber. It is hard to believe that men with skill enough to construct these damp and airless dwellings would not have sense enough to keep out of them once they were built. They did not stay there from choice; they preferred to live in their bee-hive huts of wattle and daub or of piled stones, but when danger threatened they disappeared

GROUP OF SAMIAN POTTERY

into these burrows. Even should an enemy track them down they had little to fear, for a too bold pursuer would probably trip over the slab set on end across the tunnel and be dispatched before he could rise; if he escaped that danger he might be stabbed as he tried to squeeze past the stone pillar set in the middle of the passage, or take the wrong turning in the darkness, and meet the dagger of his foe as he blundered back.

Far more imposing structures were the brochs—massive round towers sixty feet high and sixty feet in diameter. Their enormously thick walls, built of unmortared stone, rose unbroken on the outside by any window opening. The circular space enclosed by the wall was covered with a roof of stone slabs or of timber, little more than six feet high, with an opening in the centre. Above this the interior of the tower was open to the air: to build a series of rooms one on top of the other was beyond the skill of a builder who worked without mortar. But some of the occupants of the broch stowed themselves away, not in the central chamber, but inside the wall. For it was hollow: it contained a series of narrow galleries, lighted by windows opening on the interior of the broch and connected with one another by stone stairs.

An enemy would find the broch as difficult to tackle as the earth-house. There were no windows on the outside through which he could send an arrow; he could gain the interior of the broch only by squeezing himself through a low and narrow doorway, and crouching almost double in a long, low passage. He would be lucky if he got to the end of the passage, for over the passage was a guard-room with a hole in the floor, through which a sword or a spear could easily be thrust into a stooping back.

The occupants of the crannogs were equally shy of strangers; they crossed to the mainland by causeways of stone or wood an inch or two below the surface of the water. But uninvited guests, if they were wise, crossed in boats, for the causeway had gaps and surprising bends in it, and the stranger who did not walk warily would find himself drowning in ten feet of water.

Crannog, broch, earth-house, hill-town, all tell the same story, all reveal the same secret—Fear. But fear of what? Not of the Romans. In the third and fourth centuries the Romans had more reason to fear the peoples beyond the Wall than they had to fear the Romans. It came in part, we may guess, from the old feud between the mountain and the plain; the feud that continued to distract Scotland down to the time of the last Jacobite rebellion. In times of dearth the hunters and herdsmen would sweep down from their hills into the cornlands below to carry off everything that could be carried, and to burn everything that had to be left behind. We may guess, too, that, as in later centuries, the raiders came sometimes, not for food, but to avenge an injury or extend the territory of an ambitious chief. There may have been the fear, too, of raiders from overseas, for in the closing years of the third century Saxon pirates began to plunder the eastern coasts of Roman Britain.

In the fourth century something happened beyond the Wall, something that we cannot understand: tribes that had remained quiet for generations were seized with a strange restlessness. It may be that the long years of peace had allowed their numbers to increase but had not brought a corresponding increase in the supply of food. It may be that the people of the brochs were pressing southward and spreading confusion among the more civilized Britons immediately to the north of the Wall; and that the confusion was increased by the Scots from the north of Ireland, who in the fourth century began to harry the west coast of Britain. It may be that the withdrawal of some of the troops from the Wall to the new forts on the east coast tempted them to plunder the villas and rich cities of the south.

In 367 it seemed as if the province of Britain were to be lost to the Empire: the invaders swept right through the Midlands and got within a few miles of the walls of London; bands of them even appeared in Kent. But the inevitable collapse was delayed for another half-century; in 368 the Roman general Theodosius crossed to Britain at the head of a large army, swept the invaders back over the Wall, recaptured the forts that they had taken, and repaired their broken ramparts. But when Theodosius departed, back they came—Pict,[1] Scot,

---

[1] The natives of central and north-eastern Scotland were called 'Britons' by Agricola's biographer, Tacitus, and 'Caledonians' by the historians of the campaigns of Severus. But the Romans of the fourth century looked on all the peoples north of the Wall as painted savages, and gave them the common name of 'Picts'.

and Saxon. If the Roman regular troops had stood by them, if the Roman commanders had been faithful to their trust, the Romanized Britons of the south might have beaten off these painted kinsfolk of theirs that they had come to regard as barbarians. But the Roman commanders were thinking of other things than the broken Wall, or the forts with their ghastly garrisons of corpses on the pirate-haunted coasts; their eyes were turned southward to Rome, where an emperor's purple might be the lot of any soldier bold enough, or un-scrupulous enough, to seize it. Lured by this ambition, the Spaniard Magnus Maximus in 383 proclaimed himself emperor, and squandered part of the precious garrison of Britain in an attempt to make himself master of Rome. Duped by the same vain dream, the private soldier Constantine in 407 copied the mad adventure of Maximus and shared his fate.

The attenuated garrisons of the Province had been re-inforced after the death of Maximus, but after the departure of Constantine no more troops were sent to the island from Rome. Rome herself was under the hammer now, and could not spare them. If the town-dwelling Latin-speaking Britons of the south could keep within the Empire by their own exertions, well and good; if they could not——.

If they could not? The alternative was too dreadful to think about, but, like some other things too dreadful to think about, it came to pass. Farther and yet farther did the raiders penetrate into the country, away into peaceful regions of meadows and cornlands, of stone-built villas rising white among blossoming orchards, regions where there were no fortresses, where troops had not been seen for hundreds of years. Places like these were a tempting and easy prey; soon the whole of central England became a wilderness, soon the forest began to invade the cornland, soon the wolf prowled unmolested through the market-place of the little town.

Of Scotland in these dark years we know next to nothing.

One thing, however, we do know: in the early years of the fifth century Traprain Law was abandoned, but whether it was the lust for plunder or the fear of plunderers that drove its inhabitants forth no man can tell.

And so the curtain descends, black, impenetrable. Let us be thankful that we cannot see the grim tragedy enacted behind it.

A ROMAN CENTURION
From a statue found at Colchester

CHAPTER IV

NINIAN AND COLUMBA: 397–717

'That man is little to be envied, whose patriotism would not gain force upon the plains of Marathon, or whose piety would not grow warmer among the ruins of Iona.'—DR. JOHNSON.

THOUGH Christianity reached southern Britain during the Roman occupation, we look in vain for any sign of church or altar in the Roman forts north of Hadrian's Wall. Altars have been found in plenty, but they are dedicated to Mars, to Mercury, to Fortune, to the Emperor, to the strange gods of the Britons, or to the gods whom the soldiers believed to watch over their own distant homes.

Some sculptured stones found in a remote corner of southern Scotland tell another story. Three of them come from the old churchyard of Kirkmadrine, in Wigtownshire. On each appears the same design—an equal-armed cross, one arm of which forms the Greek letter P, surrounded by a circle.[1] All three crosses bear Latin inscriptions, one of which may be translated as 'Here lie the holy and renowned priests Viventius and Maiorius'. A fourth slab, with the same symbol upon it, was found at Whithorn, a few miles farther east.

What is the meaning of these Roman names and this Christian symbol—a symbol that began to be used on the Continent about the end of the fourth century? Something hard to believe, that at the very time when Roman Britain was distracted by the onslaughts of Picts, Saxons, and Scots, a Romanized Briton settled in the unknown country to the north of the Wall, and tried to convert the Picts to Christianity.

[1] The equal-armed cross stood not only for the Cross on which the Saviour was crucified, but for the Greek letter X, representing the ch sound. So, along with the P, representing the sound r, it gave the beginning of the word Χριστός or Christ.

His name was Ninian, he had lived in Rome itself, the un-
spoiled Rome of the Caesars, and he had talked with the great

THE KIRKMADRINE CROSSES

The inscription on the cross on the right means 'Alpha and Omega. Here
lie the holy and renowned priests that is Viventius and Maiorius'. The
inscription is continued on the other slab '. . . s and Florentius. The beginning and the end.' For many years these stones were used as gate-posts in
the churchyard wall at Kirkmadrine

St. Martin of Tours face to face; in fact, he brought with him
from St. Martin's monastic settlement at Tours men skilled
in the building of churches. With these followers—perhaps
with 'the holy and renowned priests Viventius and Maiorius'—

he passed Hadrian's Wall, now stripped of its garrisons, and
held westward till he reached the secluded peninsula of Whithorn. Here, on the shore of Wigtown Bay, he began in 397 to
build Candida Casa—'the little white church'—the first Christian church to be built in Scotland. Before it was finished he
heard that St. Martin had died; he resolved therefore to
dedicate the new church to him.

Ninian was not content, as people once believed, with the
evangelization of one little corner of Scotland; he went on
missionary journeys that took him farther and farther afield,
till at last he reached the shores of the Moray Firth. His
followers continued his work, and so at the end of the fifth
century a chain of little churches, each with its colony of
clerics, stretched across the country from the extreme south-
west almost to the extreme north-east. But pagan beliefs and
rites were hard to kill; almost two hundred years after Ninian
planted his church at Whithorn heathen priests were to be
found in the capital of the Pictish king.

Meantime much was happening in other parts of the island.
Early in the fifth century the Saxon pirates began to make
permanent settlements on the southern shores of the province,
which they had plundered and rendered desolate. Adventurers
of a kindred race, the Angles, planted themselves on the east
coast, and about the middle of the sixth century began to raid
Lothian, the name given in early times to the whole of the
region between the Forth and the Tweed, and in the seventh
century the Northumbrian king, Oswald, added it to his
realm.

This barbarian conquest of Britain proceeded slowly, and
with many long pauses, for the Britons resisted stubbornly,
but at length they had to fall back into the barren and moun-
tainous west, leaving the fertile plains of the midlands and
south to the invader. Some of them took refuge in western
Gaul, where their descendants, the Bretons, to this day speak

a language not unlike Welsh; others made their way across the ruined and deserted Wall into south-western Scotland. It was on these rolling moorlands that the British hero, Arthur, fought some of his battles against the encroaching heathen, and, according to the old Border tradition, it is not in 'the island-valley of Avilion' but in a great cavern under the Eildons that he lies entranced, with all his knights about him.

This stream of refugees from the south separated the Picts of Galloway from the Picts of eastern Scotland. The sea-rovers from the north of Ireland, too, had begun to make settlements in Kintyre and by the shores of the sea-lochs in Argyll; in 501 Fergus, son of Erc, a Scot from Ireland, became the first king of this new Scottish kingdom of Dalriata. The Scots spoke a Celtic language, which, however, differed so much from the speech of the Picts and Britons as to be all but unintelligible to them. It is from this language that modern Irish and modern Scottish Gaelic are descended.

The Scots had some tincture of religion: before the middle of the fifth century Patrick, a Briton, had brought the Gospel to Ireland, and so, when the churches in the devastated province of Britain lay empty and silent, the sound of the bell calling to prayer could be heard from many a green Irish valley. But the Christianized Scots were every bit as restless and pugnacious as their heathen ancestors had been: they strove to 'birze yont' like the Campbells who inhabited Argyll at a later day—to push eastward into the country of the Picts.

So in the middle of the sixth century Scotland was only a name. In fact, it was not even that: not till the tenth century was the name 'Scotland' applied to the country north of the Cheviots. It seemed hopeless to expect that out of this medley of races a single nation, subject to one king, obeying one code of laws, could ever be evolved. There was one king in Dalriata and another in Pictavia, the land of the Picts.

How could these two hostile kingdoms ever be united? And even if they were united, what of these lands south of the Forth? There seemed no possibility of Lothian escaping the clutches of the Northumbrian kings; on the other hand it seemed highly probable that the Angles, after possessing themselves of Lothian, would add Fife and Angus to their other conquests. So with the country between the Clyde and the Solway: it formed part of a great British kingdom, which, even after the victory of the Angles at Chester in 613, stretched south as far as the Cheshire Dee.

Meantime it fared ill with the Scots: in the year 559 they were defeated in battle by the Pictish king, Brude mac Maelchon. It seemed as if they must come under the yoke of the Picts, but four years later a strange ally appeared.

There is many a town-dwelling Scotsman who has never set eyes on the strange, lonely region that lies to the west of Scotland, a region of mountains, and long sea-lochs, and rocky islands, where the whistle of the locomotive is never heard, where you may sail for half a day and see no vessel but a solitary, brown-sailed fishing-boat, no sign of human habitation but a gleaming white lighthouse, or, on one or two of the larger islands, a little cluster of stone-built cottages. But if you hold westward, under the frowning red cliffs and dark mountains of Mull, till you feel the slow surge of the Atlantic rocking your boat under you, you will notice a little to the north a low, grassy island with beaches of glittering white sand. It seems a cheerful place by contrast with the lonely seas and dark, empty mountains. So you think; so, almost fourteen hundred years ago, thought the conscience-stricken fugitive who came to this same island of Iona.

They called him Columba, 'the dove', but it would have been hard to see anything dove-like in this loud-voiced, aggressive Irish ecclesiastic. Enraged by the refusal of the Irish king Diarmit to give up a book which he claimed as his own

IONA CATHEDRAL

The church was not founded till the thirteenth century, and very little of it is older than the fifteenth century. It is no longer a ruin; a few years ago it was restored and re-roofed. On the right is St. Oran's Chapel, supposed to have been built by order of Queen Margaret, while in the centre foreground can be seen the cross of St. Martin property, Columba stirred up his friends, and in 560 they defeated Diarmit at the bloody battle of Cuildremne. But his triumph turned to bitterness; people shrank from the turbulent priest whose obstinacy had cost the lives of so many men. According to an old story, he was ordered to go into exile, and forbidden to return to Ireland, or even to come within sight of it, until the number of souls he saved equalled the number of those that he had caused to perish in battle. Be that as it may, he had made Ireland, for the time, too hot to hold him. He landed on Iona in 563, with twelve companions, and proceeded to build a little monastery, after the pattern of the ecclesiastical settlements that were familiar to him in Ireland.

For all the Irish clergy were monks: they did not mingle with ordinary people, but lived apart in self-contained communities. The rath, a four-square rampart of turf, shut the monks off from the outer world. Within the enclosure the most important building was the church, a building so small that priest and worshippers often stayed outside while the psalms were being sung and the gospel read. At first the church was only a hut of clay and wattles, but after a time logs of pine and oak were floated over from the mainland, and a more substantial building erected. At a little distance from the church stood the huts of the monks, for, unlike the monks of the later Middle Ages, they did not share the same dormitory, but each had his beehive-shaped hut of wattle and daub, or of unmortared stones. There were other buildings; a guest-house, a granary, cattle-sheds, and stables. Two huts were set apart for Columba: one, which was floored with planks of wood, was his study and contained the library of the monastery; in the other, where there was no floor but the bare earth, he lay at night, with his head resting upon a pillow of stone.

Though Columba became gentler, more considerate of others, his fierce, unsleeping spirit would not let him rest. He would study and write all day, and stay awake half the night chanting the psalms in the black darkness of the little church or under the stars on the seashore. But there were times when this seemed inglorious ease, when he would order a boat to be manned and set out with one or two companions on a long and perilous journey. The first and most famous of the journeys, made soon after he settled in Iona, took him to the stronghold of the Pictish king, on the banks of the River Ness. For Columba was a statesman as well as a missionary; before he left Ireland he knew that his kinsmen the Scots were in danger of being overwhelmed altogether by the Picts, and he seems to have resolved to plead their cause before the victorious King Brude.

When he came to the King's stronghold he found that the gates had been barred against him. He touched the ponderous timbers with the cross that he carried, whereupon the bolts clattered back and the doors swung open. It seemed to his simple-minded followers that the saint had worked a miracle, and their belief was confirmed when the King himself stepped forward to greet the saint.

The King promised to stay his hand against the Scots and to refrain from hindering Columba in his missionary work. But the priests of the old religion who haunted Brude's palace looked on the stranger with no friendly eye; a few days later they came up to Columba and his companions as they were singing psalms outside the green ramparts of Brude's stronghold and tried to interrupt the service by shouting some heathen chant of their own. But lo! another miracle. The saint sang the forty-fifth psalm so lustily that the wizards could not make themselves heard, and shrank away defeated. So when the missionaries were delayed by contrary winds on their homeward journey down Loch Ness, they were convinced that the revengeful wizards had raised a magic gale, and when the saint uttered a prayer and the wind died away, they believed that he had wrought still another miracle.

We may smile at these 'miracles'; we must not smile at the courage and devotion that made Columba brave not only the imaginary dangers from wizards and demons and water-kelpies, but the very real dangers from treacherous seas, flooded rivers, and barbarous men. For Columba was not content with founding Iona; he planted similar monasteries up and down the west coast of Scotland, and on many a Hebridean island, and manned them with the clerics who flocked over to him from Ireland.

They marvelled at his gentleness and humility. It seemed strange to them that a man who was master of a great ecclesiastical organization should wash the feet of the brethren, or carry sacks of corn to the mill. They told how, when a robber who had, time and again, killed seals belonging to the monastery was brought before him, Columba simply inquired why he had not asked for food instead of stealing it, and told him that he would get all that he required in future. But there were times when the Old Adam was too strong for the saint, when he hurled the most terrible curses at the heads of people who had thwarted him, or prophesied horrible deaths for his enemies. Once, when he was in Ardnamurchan, he met a robber laden with plunder. Columba reminded him that this was the third time that he had plundered the same man, and told him to restore the booty. The robber refused, got on his ship, and made Columba furious by laughing and gibing at him as he sailed away. The saint dashed into the waves after him, and with outstretched hands prayed that the robber might get his reward. As he gazed after the vessel he noticed the sky darken and the sea grow white with foam, and a moment later he had the satisfaction of watching the pirate craft stagger and sink before the sudden squall.

But children and dumb animals had no fear of him; when, a few days before his death, the white horse that drew the monastery milk-cart came up to him and nuzzled into his bosom, he forbade his servant to drive it away, and gave the affectionate beast his blessing. And his last utterance to his monks was a prayer that they would live together in unfeigned charity and peace.

Columba died in 597, but his influence grew and spread far beyond the bounds of Dalriata. A few days before his death he had climbed to the little hill that overlooks the monastery and, looking down on it, had blessed it. 'Upon this place,' he declared, 'small and mean though it be, not only kings of the Scots and their peoples, but even rulers over strange and barbarous nations, with the peoples subject to them, will bestow great and especial honour.'

In the half-century following his death his prophecy came near to fulfilment. But there were other workers in the field. The dwellers in the Clyde valley, for example, heard the Gospel first, not from Columba or any of his followers, but from Kentigern the Briton, whose empty shrine can still be seen in the crypt of Glasgow Cathedral. Then neither the Pictish kings nor the Pictish clergy seemed to be very fond of the new-comers, and so the monks from Iona made very few settlements east of Drumalban, the great mountain ridge that divide the streams flowing to the North Sea from the streams flowing to the Atlantic, and formed a barrier between Dalriata and the land of the Picts. In 597, too, St. Augustine and his Roman monks landed in Kent, and began their work of re-converting England to the Christian faith.

For a time, however, it seemed as if the churches in the north of England were to be ruled, not from Canterbury or Rome, but from Iona. In 634 a sudden twist of Fortune's wheel placed upon the throne of Northumbria the exiled prince Oswald, who had spent his youth in the monastery of Iona. No sooner did he become king than he sent a request to the community at Iona for some one to preach the new faith to his people. One of the monks was accordingly dispatched to Northumbria, but he returned in a short time to confess that his preaching had been a failure because the Northumbrians were 'intractable men, and of a hard and barbarous disposition'. One monk, Aidan by name, hinted very gently that the hardness and obstinacy might not have been confined to the hearers. The shot went home; the assembly promptly decided that Aidan must go south in place of his crabbed comrade. He succeeded; noble and peasant alike came under the spell of one who was completely free from all self-seeking, all priestly arrogance. They felt that there must be something in the religion of one who might have been rich and yet chose to remain poor, who gave away the costliest gifts as soon as the donor's back was turned, whose episcopal palace was only a rickety lean-to propped against the buttress of a church, and who, in spite of his austere manner of life, did not become soured or self-righteous, but remained courteous and cheerful.

On the island of Lindisfarne he erected his cathedral, a structure with oaken walls and a thatched roof. All over Northumbria similar churches sprang up, ministered to by Celtic clerics from Iona.

But the stories of Aidan and of Cuthbert, the border shepherd-boy in whose honour the great cathedral of Durham was erected, belong to English rather than to Scottish history. For Iona was not destined to become the ecclesiastical capital of northern England. The Celtic churches in Ireland and Scotland had been founded at a time when Rome had ceased to exercise any control over her distant province; the result was that for two and a half centuries they had existed and developed in complete isolation from the rest of Christendom. But now, at the court of the Northumbrian king, Romish priests from Canterbury or York met Celtic priests from Iona. Though their religious beliefs were the same, the southern priest recoiled in horror from the Scottish monk, for he noticed that the front of his head had been shaven bare. A priest must shave his head, he believed, but why should he refuse to shave it at the proper place, which was the crown? He was confirmed in his belief that his Scottish rival was an impious heretic when he learned that the Celtic method of computing the date of Easter differed from the Roman one, so that Easter might fall in March at Canterbury, and in April at Lindisfarne and Iona.

The controversy about these differences was allowed to sleep while Aidan was alive, but after his death in 651 it raged fiercely, till in 664 King Oswiu of Northumbria grew alarmed, and summoned the Romish and the Celtic champions to meet in his presence at Whitby. Colman, the Celtic bishop of Lindisfarne, buttressed his arguments with the authority of St. Columba; the arrogant Wilfred of York boldly claimed that he had on his side St. Peter, the keeper of the keys of Heaven. 'Has a similar power been conferred on your Columba?' the King asked Colman anxiously. The bishop admitted that he could not honestly make such a claim. 'Then', said the King, 'this is the doorkeeper whom I am loath to contradict, lest haply when I arrive at the doors of the Kingdom there shall be none to open them unto me.'

So the decision went against Colman, and he and the other Celtic monks who refused to conform to the Roman usage returned sorrowfully whence they had come.

The controversy spread to Scotland. In 710 King Nechtan became seriously concerned about the two questions, and wrote to Ceolfrith, the Abbot of Jarrow, to ask for a supply of useful arguments and for architects who would show him how to erect a church of stone. Ceolfrith responded to the appeal, and in a short time Nechtan succeeded in persuading or compelling all the clergy in his realm to shave their crowns and to observe Easter at the orthodox time. Six years later Iona and the churches under its jurisdiction conformed to the Roman usage.

But the Scottish churches still kept apart from the church

in England. Though Whithorn became the seat of an English bishop, and though the surrounding district became part of the ecclesiastical province of York, the rest of Scotland owed no allegiance to either York or Canterbury. And though Columban and Pictish clergy now shaved their heads in the same way, they still regarded each other with unfriendly eyes, especially after 717, when King Nechtan sent the monks of Iona who had settled in his realm back to their native Dalriata.

'But what of St. Andrew?' you ask. 'Why have the Scots chosen him, rather than Ninian or Columba, as their patron saint?' It is true that St. Andrew never set foot on Scottish soil, but in the reign of Aengus, King Nechtan's successor, a stranger appeared bearing with him some bones which he said were the veritable bones of the Apostle. The King believed his story, and allowed him to build a church to enshrine the relics at Kilrymont on the Fifeshire coast. Later a great cathedral, the finest in Scotland, took the place of the older church, and people came from far and near to St. Andrews, as Kilrymont was now called, to gaze on the shrine of the Apostle. So the patron saint of the greatest church in Scotland came, in the course of time, to be regarded as the patron saint of Scotland itself. In the later Middle Ages the banner of St. Andrew, the white cross placed diagonally on a blue ground, became the national flag of Scotland; it was retained at the Reformation, the Covenanters fought under it, and to this day it can be seen, combined with the red and white banner of St. George, in the Union Jack.

CHAPTER V

THE BUILDING UP OF SCOTLAND: 597–1005

'Yet, as he said, one cannot build a house all of straight sticks.'—KIPLING.

AFTER the death of St. Columba more than four centuries had to elapse before Scotland was united under the rule of a single king. The obstacles to unification were many. He who aspired to rule the whole of Scotland must break three rival kings in battle, or march into their kingdoms when they were attacked by other enemies, or take advantage of a disputed succession to snatch the coveted crown. Even if he succeeded in breaking his rivals, he had no guarantee that his new-made kingdom would not crumble to pieces in his hands. How can you hold the stones of a house together without mortar? How could you build up a nation when the very idea of nationality did not exist, when no inhabitant of Scotland thought of himself as a Scotsman, when the Pict regarded the Scot as an alien, speaking a barbarous jargon, ruling his life by laws and customs that seemed ridiculous just because they were unfamiliar? And, as we have seen, the Christian missionaries had failed to bridge the gulf that separated Pict from Scot and Scot from Angle; if anything, they had made it wider than it was before.

To these invisible barriers of race, language, and custom must be added certain visible, tangible barriers—the great marshes that stretched where now one sees only fertile corn-land, the virgin forests that still clothed many of the valleys in central and southern Scotland, the trackless moorlands, and the unbridged rivers. To add to the difficulties of the traveller, the Roman roads in the south had been allowed to fall into hopeless disrepair, there were no inns, and few would care to spend a night in a wolf-haunted forest. There could be little

trade, little peaceful intercourse of any kind between one part
of Scotland and another, and so unfamiliarity bred suspicion
and fear.

Moreover, these natural barriers made effective government
almost impossible. How was the King to make his authority
felt in every part of his kingdom? More than once, for
example, there were two rival kings in Pictavia, one ruling
over Moray in the north, and the other Fortriu in the south.
Often he had to let well alone, and letting well alone was, of
course, no solution of the problem.

For a time it seemed as if the whole of Scotland would be
merged in the English kingdom of Northumbria. Soon after
his accession in 634 King Oswald made himself master of
Lothian; his successor, Oswiu, forced the rulers of Pictavia and
Strathclyde to acknowledge him as their overlord. But when
Oswiu died in 671 the Picts drove his vassal Drust from their
country, and put the more vigorous Brude in his place.
Brude's attempts to carry the war into the enemy's country
met with no success; in 685 he found that he had to deal with
an invading army led by Ecgfrith of Northumbria himself.
The crafty old Pict lured his enemy on, beyond the Forth,
beyond the Tay, till at Nechtansmere, among the lonely
marshes and moors north of the Sidlaws, he turned upon the
invader. The English army was cut to pieces; King Ecgfrith
was among the slain.

The Picts, freed from the Northumbrian menace, began to
wage a vigorous warfare against the kings of Dalriata, and
before the middle of the eighth century, in the reign of King
Aengus, Dalriata had become, to all intents and purposes, a
Pictish province. But at the same time the conquered were
invading the territory of the conquerors: bands of Scots, tired
of the hopeless fight for a livelihood in the rain-washed, rocky
west, drifted eastward into the more fertile Strathmore, and
hacked great clearings in the virgin forest. So Gaelic began to

be spoken in places where hitherto only the ancient Pictish speech had been heard, and so some of the Picts began to use the language of their new neighbours.

It seemed, then, that Picts and Scots were to be united under the rule of a Pictish king. But in 794 a story spread through the Western Isles that seemed to rob the spring of its brightness—the 'Gentiles' had come.

The 'Gentiles' were Norsemen, the Scots discovered afterwards, from the south-west corner of Norway, and they had come partly because the spring brought a strange restlessness into their blood that drove them out to discover new lands, partly because they had heard from other voyagers of a land not far to the west where all sorts of things could be had for the mere trouble of taking them. They came in vessels of a new fashion: long, narrow boats of wood, with a single mast and a single square sail. Along the bulwarks were hung the shields of the forty warriors who crowded the vessel, and on either side half a dozen oars flashed in the water. Swifter ships had not been seen in Scottish waters since the Roman galleys departed; they could overtake any vessel, and show a clean pair of heels to any pursuer. But few cared to pursue them.

The Celtic monasteries, planted as they often were on lonely islands or by the shores of some secluded inlet, were peculiarly exposed to the attentions of these visitants. But what could robbers find worthy of notice in these insignificant little stone churches, no bigger and no more imposing than the cottage of a present-day ploughman, and the still more insignificant huts clustered about them? Bread that they had not baked, and ale that they had not brewed—and much more.

These Celtic monks, though they could not rear beautiful buildings, were lovers and makers of beautiful things. If one of them set himself to copy a manuscript of the Gospels, he filled the margin of his parchment with a maze of intricate

designs, and made the initial letter of each chapter gorgeous
with colour. If only he had put in pictures we should know
much more than we do about the appearance of the people of
these far-off times; but the Celtic artist preferred patterns to
pictures; if he had to bring in an animal he chose the serpent
because he could twist and stretch its body into so many
interesting shapes. But the heathen Norsemen were more
interested in the cover than in the book, for many of these
beautiful manuscripts were enclosed in cases that were even
more beautiful—caskets of silver and gold, covered with the
same intricate patterns and studded with precious stones.
Similar caskets of gold or silver were made to contain the little
hand-bells used by the saints of an earlier day, and the plain
oaken staff of the founder of the monastery was usually transformed by the monkish artist into a glittering silver crosier,
twinkling with gems. Even on brooches and other trifles these
old craftsmen lavished the same fastidious workmanship.

So there was enough plunder even in the barren Hebrides to
lure the Norsemen back again and again. And they soon discovered that the Hebrides formed only the fringe of Scotland;
they descended on the mainland and showed the luckless
natives that no ruler—Scot, Pict, Briton, or Angle—was
strong enough to keep them out if they chose to come. Nor,
if they plundered a place once, did it follow that they would
leave it alone ever after. In 795, for example, they sacked
Iona, in 802 they burned the monastery, in 806 they killed all
the monks. Then they left it alone for almost twenty years,
and a new monastery rose on the ruins of the old.

Hither in 825 came Blathmac, an Irish monk who had once
been a soldier, and who had now deliberately elected to court
death at the hands of the Norsemen. He himself, as his monkish
biographer says, had 'stripped his mind of empty dread', but he
knew that not all the brethren could be trusted to stand firm in
the hour of trial. Accordingly, when a rumour reached the island

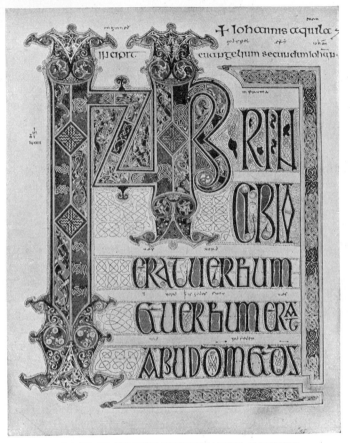

A PAGE FROM THE LINDISFARNE GOSPELS

First page of St. John's Gospel written (in Latin) about A.D. 700, or earlier. Though it was written in England, it may be taken as an example of the illuminated books found in the Scottish monasteries, for the English scribe has copied the lettering and ornamentation used by the Celtic monks that the pirates were coming, he asked them to consider carefully whether they would have sufficient courage to stay with him and wait for certain death. Those who did not feel sure of themselves he urged to get away while there was yet time.

Some decided to go, and without a word of reproach Blathmac watched them depart. Knowing that the pirates would try to carry off the jewelled shrine containing the bones of St. Columba, he ordered it to be removed and hidden in some place unknown to him. He had not long to wait. One summer morning, when he stood at the altar celebrating mass, he heard a wild shouting which told him that the pirates had come. The Norsemen broke into the church, slew the kneeling brethren, and hunted everywhere for the missing shrine. For a time they seemed to be daunted by the calm dignity of Blathmac, who disdained either to kneel or to make any effort to defend himself, but when they could not find the shrine, they seized him and threatened to kill him if he did not tell them where it was. 'I know nothing at all of the gold you seek,' he answered proudly, 'and if I did know, never would my lips speak it. Barbarian, draw thy sword and slay.'

So the heroic Blathmac died, and so the shrine of St. Columba remained inviolate. But as no one knew when the monastery might not be raided again, twenty-five years later the relics of the saint were divided, and removed, some of them to Kells in Ireland, and the remainder to Dunkeld. With the bones of Columba the mother church at Iona lost the supremacy which it had enjoyed over the churches of Ireland and Dalriata; for half a century Dunkeld remained the ecclesiastical capital of Scotland, till, at the beginning of the tenth century, it was overshadowed by the new cathedral of St. Andrews. But, though St. Andrews had now become the Canterbury of Scotland, a special sanctity attached to Iona: hither for another two hundred years the bodies of the Scottish kings were brought for their burial.

AN EXAMPLE OF CELTIC ORNAMENTATION:
THE ABERLEMNO CROSS-SLAB

This slab, which still stands in the churchyard of Aberlemno, Forfarshire,
may have been carved as late as the tenth or early eleventh centuries. A comparison with the page from the Lindisfarne Gospels, however, will show that
the carver has worked out in stone patterns which the Celtic scribes had
designed centuries earlier

It was not only Iona and the other Western Isles that attracted these Scandinavian pirates; some held on past Kintyre till they reached Ireland, others—from Denmark apparently—sailed straight across the North Sea and descended on the unprotected English coasts; others again sailed right up the Seine and threatened Paris itself. Wherever they went it was the same story, first plundering raids on the coast that were over in a few weeks, then prolonged campaigns carried out by larger forces, then a permanent occupation of the country. For long they seemed invincible: their shields of linden wood and shirts of mail could stop any ordinary blow, their ships could out-distance anything else that sailed, and when they left their ships behind they seized the first horses they came across, and changed from sailors into swift-moving, hard-fighting cavalry. Then we must remember that, for all their ferocity and barbarian ignorance, they were men who knew how to 'live dangerously'. 'Fate rules life,' said one mother to her warrior son, 'but not where a man is come; better it is to die with honour than to live with shame.'

When England, France, and Ireland were assailed, Scotland could not hope to escape. Again and again the Picts strove to beat back their invaders, but they were hampered by a rebellion of the Scots under Alpin, a descendant of the old kings of Dalriata. In 839 disaster overwhelmed the Picts; their king with a great multitude of his followers was slain by the Norsemen, and though the rebel Alpin was slain soon after, his son Kenneth possessed himself of the stronghold of the Pictish kings at Forteviot and became king of both Picts and Scots.

How he did it no one knows. There are dark stories of treachery, of the Pictish lords being invited to a banquet and there foully slaughtered.

Whether Kenneth had built his house all of straight sticks or not, his accession marks the end of the first stage in the unification of Scotland. But he would have been bold indeed who would have prophesied that this new kingdom of Alba, built up by treachery and violence, would not crumble as quickly as it had been built. The Norsemen had unwittingly

THE BELL OF ST. FILLAN

It is quadrangular in shape, and made of sheet-iron, although originally it had been coated with bronze. In height it measures 11 inches, exclusive of the handle

helped Kenneth to his kingdom, and the Norsemen were no more friendly to the supplanters of the Pictish kings than they had been to the Picts themselves.

In fact, the Norsemen were becoming more dangerous: about 872 Harald Harfagr made himself master of the whole of Norway, and so Scotland was now harassed both by rebel chieftains who settled there to be safe from Harald, and by loyal chieftains whom he sent there to act as his lieutenants. In 874, for example, Harald reduced the Orkneys and handed them over to Earl Sigurd; a little later he dispatched Ketil Flatnose to the Hebrides to enforce his authority there; towards the end of the century Sigurd, along with Thorstein, the grandson of Ketil, crossed to the mainland of Scotland and conquered Caithness, Sutherland, Ross, and Moray.

Farther south, as the Britons of Strathclyde knew to their cost, they had made their power felt. In 870 they captured Dumbarton, the fortress which guarded the northern frontier of the British kingdom, and overran the valley of the Clyde. The frontier was pushed back to the neighbourhood of the Solway, and Carlisle replaced Dumbarton as the capital of the shrunken kingdom of Cumbria.

The Norsemen allowed Kenneth and his brother Donald, who succeeded him in 858, to die in peace. Few of their successors shared their fortune; of the princes who reigned between the death of Donald I in 862 and the accession of Edgar in 1097, the great majority died in battle or by the hand of the assassin. Three perished fighting against the Norsemen —Constantine I in 877, Donald II in 900, and Indulf in 962.

About the end of the ninth century the Danes and Norsemen seemed to become less dangerous. Alfred of England set a definite limit to their advance, and in the first half of the tenth century Alfred's vigorous successors freed northern England from their control. But this English advance brought a new anxiety to the kings of Alba.

When the Norsemen loosed their hold on Strathclyde, the Britons who had fled southward before them did not return. They could not, for English settlers from Northumbria had slipped into the lands that they had once occupied. Was there not a danger that the English advance into Strathclyde might be followed by an English advance into Alba? Might not some southern monarch, fired by Ecgfrith's ambition, avoid Ecgfrith's doom?

Such questions as these agitated the mind of Constantine II, the shrewd and ambitious prince who became King of Alba

SCOTTISH WARRIORS
From the reverse of the Aberlemno Cross-slab

in 900. In the early part of his reign the Norsemen penetrated almost to the heart of his realm and plundered Dunkeld, but Constantine soon began to look on the Norsemen as less dangerous neighbours than the all-conquering English. In 921, along with the Danish rulers of Northumbria, he did homage to Edward of England. Five years later Sigtrygg, the Danish Earl of Northumbria, died, whereupon Athelstan, the new King of England, drove out his two sons Olaf and Godfrey. Constantine befriended the exiles: he welcomed Godfrey to his court and married his daughter to Olaf, who had crossed to Ireland and become a leader of the Norsemen there. Athelstan retaliated by harrying Constantine's kingdom, and so drove the wavering Scot into the arms of the Norsemen. In 937 Athelstan learned that Constantine and his son-in-law Olaf, at the head of a great host of Scots, Norsemen, and Britons of Strathclyde, were hovering on the northern borders of his realm. It seemed for a time as if the newly fashioned kingdom of England would be shattered to pieces, but Athelstan did not shrink from the trial; he advanced over the Cheviots with his army and came upon the Norse and Scottish hosts encamped about the lofty, flat-topped hill of Birrenswark, some ten miles north of the Solway. Here eight and a half centuries earlier the garrison of a British hill-fort had stood at bay, and here, among the crumbling ramparts and choked trenches built by Agricola's legionaries, another grim battle was fought. It began at dawn; all day long it raged; but when evening came the enemies of Athelstan had had their fill of fighting. They fled under cover of darkness; the Scots northward to the hills beyond Forth, the Norsemen to their ships.

> Many a carcass they left to the carrion,
> Many a livid one, many a sallow-skin—
> Left for the white-tailed eagle to tear it, and
> Left for the horny-ribb'd raven to rend it, and
> Gave to the garbaging war-hawk to gorge it, and
> That gray beast, the wolf of the weald.

So sang an English bard. In his exultation he gibed at the vanquished king:

> Slender warrant had
> *He* to be proud of
> The welcome of war-knives—
> He that was reft of his
> Folk and his friends that had
> Fallen in conflict,
> Leaving his son too
> Lost in the carnage,
> Mangled to morsels,
> A youngster in war.[1]

There was no other way for it: Constantine had to humble himself before Athelstan, and become his vassal once more.

A year or two later he gave up the unequal struggle, resigned his crown to his kinsman Malcolm, and sought peace in a monastery at St. Andrews. But even in this remote and lonely place, where the moan of the sea mingled with the chant of the monks, memories of his past defeats troubled the old king. According to one legend, he persuaded his successor to give him back his kingdom for a week, mounted his horse, headed a foray into England, and returned to his monastery at the end of his seven days' reign, well content.

Before this, however, King Malcolm, Constantine's successor, had received an unexpected gift of territory. Edmund of England discovered that he could never hold Northumbria as long as the Norsemen settled in Ireland could sail over unchecked to the Cumbrian coast and wander at will across the British kingdom of Strathclyde. To drive the Norsemen out of Cumbria was easy enough—Edmund succeeded in doing it in 945—to keep them out was a different matter. Edmund got over the difficulty by presenting Strathclyde to Malcolm of Scotland on condition that Malcolm promised to be his helper and to defend his new province. Malcolm, like many of his successors, saw no objection to becoming a vassal of the

[1] From Tennyson's translation of the *Battle of Brunanburh*.

King of England if something substantial was to be gained by the transaction, and so Cumbria was added to the territory controlled by the Kings of Alba.

Malcolm discovered, too, that Norse pirates and English kings were not his most dangerous enemies. His stronghold at Forteviot and his newer palace at Scone commanded the fertile and populous plains of Strathmore, Strathearn, and Gowrie, but the Grampians formed a barrier between the central part of his realm and the northern province of Moray. Further, while the Kings of Alba believed Moray to be part of their kingdom, their belief was not shared by the rulers and people of Moray. Malcolm was not the last King of Scotland to be slain by the men of Moray, nor was Macbeth the first 'mormaer' of Moray to claim to be King of Scotland.

To Malcolm in 954 succeeded Indulf, and again the frontiers of Alba moved farther south. Before Indulf perished by the swords of the Norsemen in 962 Lothian north of the Pentlands and Lammermoors, and with it Strathclyde, had passed into the hands of the Scots.

In addition to this ever-present danger from the men of Moray—they slew King Dub in 966—Alba was distracted at the end of the tenth century by a dispute about the succession. Before the time of Kenneth II, who reigned from 971 to 995, a king was succeeded not by his eldest son but by the eldest of his near male relatives. Furthermore, by this old Scottish law of succession, the Law of Tanistry, the heir or tanist was chosen in the King's lifetime. The same rule applied to lesser dignitaries; the mormaer or ruler over a province was succeeded by his brother, cousin, or uncle, not by his son. King Kenneth, however, decided to set aside the claims of the other branches of the royal family and make his son Malcolm heir to the kingdom. Kenneth himself died suddenly and mysteriously—his disaffected kinsmen had a hand in the matter—and the claim of Malcolm was brushed aside. First Constantine the Bald and then Giric seized the crown. But the reigns of these disaffected kinsmen were short and troubled; each of them, Constantine in 997 and Giric in 1005, was slain by the son of the man whose death he had compassed, and in 1005 Malcolm II became King of Alba.

Kings of Alba

Kenneth I, son of Alpin	843–858
Donald I, son of Alpin	858–862
Constantine I, son of Kenneth I	862–877
Aed, son of Kenneth I	877–878
Eochaid, son of Run	878–889
Donald II, son of Constantine I	889–900
Constantine II, son of Aed	900–943
Malcolm I, son of Donald II	943–954
Indulf, son of Constantine	954–962
Dub, son of Malcolm I	962–966
Culen, son of Indulf	966–971
Kenneth II, son of Malcolm I	971–995
Constantine III (the Bald), son of Culen	995–997
Giric, grandson of Dub	997–1005
Malcolm II, son of Kenneth II	1005–1034

CHAPTER VI

QUEEN AND SAINT: 1005–1097

Kings of Scotland					*Kings of England*				
Malcolm II	.	.	.	1005–1034	Cnut	.	.	.	.	1016–1035
Duncan I	.	.	.	1034–1040	Harald	.	.	.	1037–1040
Macbeth	.	.	.	1040–1057	Harthacnut	.	.	.	1040–1042
Lulach	.	.	.	.	1057–1058	Edward the Confessor	1042–1066
Malcolm III	.	.	.	1058–1093	Harold	.	.	.	1066
Donald Bane	.	.	.	1093–1094	William I	.	.	.	1066–1087
Duncan II	.	.	.	1094	William II (Rufus)	.	1087–1100
Donald Bane	.	.	.	1094–1097					

MALCOLM II, like all the kings who preceded him, is little more than a name to us. We know that he became king in 1005, that he died in 1034, and that he was succeeded by his grandson Duncan, but we do not know the man himself. No portrait of him has survived, no fragment of his conversation, no tell-tale anecdote. Yet we would gladly know more about him, for he was victorious in a battle that meant as much to Scotland as Bannockburn itself.

Though in the early part of his reign he dealt out sharp punishment to any marauding Norseman who dared to invade his kingdom, he succeeded in winning the friendship of Sigurd, the Norse Earl of Orkney, who, as we saw, had become the master of a great part of northern Scotland. For one thing, Sigurd had become a Christian; for another, he did not relish the manner of his conversion: his over-lord, King Olaf of Norway, had threatened to kill him and harry his lands if he remained a heathen. So when Olaf departed for Norway, Sigurd transferred his allegiance to King Malcolm, and married his daughter, and when in 1014 Sigurd set off on an expedition to Ireland, he left his young son Thorfinn not with his elder brothers in Orkney, but with the King of Scots.

Sigurd never returned from Ireland; his dead body was

found on the fatal field of Clontarf, wrapped in the enchanted raven banner that was supposed to bring victory to the soldiers who marched behind it. When the news of his death reached Scotland, King Malcolm bestowed Caithness and Sutherland upon the young Thorfinn on condition that Thorfinn should hold these lands as his vassal. Moray reverted to Findlaech, the representative of the old mormaers of Moray, but four centuries and a half had to pass before the Orkneys were united to Scotland.

Malcolm's attempt to push his frontiers southward at first met with no success: though in 1006 he advanced far into England, he was driven back from the walls of Durham by Utred, the son of the aged Earl of Northumbria, and fled to Scotland with only a remnant of his army. As a reward for his valour King Ethelred of England bestowed his father's earldom upon the victor.

Utred had soon to reckon with a more formidable adversary than Malcolm. Though the hold of the Norsemen on Scotland had relaxed, the Danes had come back to England; in 1013 their random plundering raids developed into a war of conquest, and in 1016 Cnut, the Danish king, seized the crown of England. Utred, after fighting against him for a time, surrendered, only to be treacherously murdered, and his brother, Eadulf Cudel, succeeded to his earldom. But the new earl was a timorous soul: fearing that Malcolm might try to avenge his ten-years-old defeat, he bought him off by surrendering to him the whole of Lothian. Thus, without a battle, the frontiers of Scotland were advanced to the Cheviots and the Tweed.

But Cnut had no share in this transaction, nor did he mean to let Lothian slip out of his grasp; in 1018 he sent an army northwards to do battle with the Scots. It was not for nothing, the superstitious said, that a comet had flamed for thirty nights in the heavens: at Carham, on the Tweed, his army was cut to pieces by the Scots and the Britons of Cumbria. Cnut next tried negotiations, but though he got some sort of submission from the Scot, he had to leave Malcolm in possession of Lothian.

In the same year the bond that united Cumbria or Strathclyde to Malcolm's other possessions was tightened. Up to this time Cumbria had had its own line of kings, rulers of Scottish descent, who acknowledged the King of Scots as their overlord. When in 1018 Owen the Bald, the last of his line, died, he was succeeded by Duncan, the son of King Malcolm and the heir to the Scottish crown.

So in the year 1018 the boundaries of Scotland became pretty much what they are at the present day. There were two important differences: the southern boundary line dipped much farther down than it does now, for Strathclyde included not only the basin of the Clyde, but Cumberland, Westmorland, and part of Lancashire, and the western boundary line kept close to the mainland, for though the Norsemen in the Hebrides seldom obeyed the King of Norway, they never obeyed the King of Scots.

But though Malcolm had gathered the stones, he had not built the house. Six years after his death the fires that had smouldered in the north burst into flame; in 1040 Macbeth, the Mormaer of Moray, slew King Duncan, the grandson of Malcolm II, and ruled in his stead.

Here at last we seem to encounter a king of Scotland who is something more than an empty name. Shakespeare has made us familiar with the great soldier who is led astray by his ambition and murders his royal guest. We see him tortured by remorse, haunted by the ghost of the 'blood-boltered Banquo', hemmed in by Duncan's avengers, yet meeting them with a courage in which hope has no part. Yet as we gaze back through the centuries at the figure of Macbeth, his features dislimn; he becomes as colourless and shadowy as the Kenneths and Malcolms whose crown he had usurped. Shakespeare's Macbeth was not the real Macbeth; of this we are sure, but what the real Macbeth was like we do not know. We do know, however, that the slaying of Duncan was not quite so black a business as Shakespeare made it out to be: Duncan was not a frail old man, but a monarch in the prime of life; both Macbeth and his wife were of royal descent, and Macbeth probably considered that he had as good a right to the throne as Duncan himself. But some compunction about the manner of Duncan's death seems to have disturbed him; a few years after his accession he did what no Scottish king had ever done before: he went as a pilgrim to Rome and there 'scattered money among the poor like seed'.

His pilgrimage availed him nothing. Duncan's two sons had escaped at the time of their father's murder, the elder, Malcolm Canmore—'Big-headed Malcolm'—to England, and the younger, Donald Bane, to the west of Scotland. Edward the Confessor supported the cause of the exiled prince, and in 1054 sent Siward, Earl of Northumbria, into Scotland with an army. Macbeth was defeated, and Malcolm became ruler of southern Scotland. But this did not content Malcolm; he carried on the war after his English allies had departed, drove Macbeth far away from Birnam Wood and Dunsinane Hill, and in 1057 slew him in battle somewhere in Aberdeenshire. Even then the men of Moray would not yield to Malcolm; they took Macbeth's stepson, Lulach, as their king. Only after Lulach had been slain in 1058 did Malcolm III sit securely upon the throne of Scotland.

Eight years later something happened which changed the whole course of Scottish history: William, Duke of Normandy, made himself master of England. We are apt to look on the Norman Conquest as something that affected England alone; as a matter of fact, it wrought almost as big a change on Scotland. But the change came more slowly, for Scotland was never actually subjugated by the Normans: the Norman Conquest of Scotland was carried out by the Scottish kings themselves.

The first sign of the coming change was a curious one: Scots began to be spoken in Scotland. The Scottish kings were Gaelic speakers; Gaelic had ousted the ancient Pictish tongue in the east and was ousting Norse among the Scandinavian settlers in the Hebrides. In the south, a language akin to Welsh was spoken, in Lothian as well as in Strathclyde, for though the people of Lothian had been subject to whatever king ruled over Northumbria, few, if any, English-speaking settlers had made their homes north of the Tweed. But the first effect of the Conquest was to send crowds of fugitives from north-eastern England into south-eastern Scotland. These refugees spoke English, but an English that differed in many respects from the English of London and the Midlands, which is the ancestor of modern English speech, and this Northern or Northumbrian English became in the course of time the speech of the whole Scottish lowlands. So modern Scots is really an importation from the north of England; in fact, all through the Middle Ages the Lowland Scot called his speech not 'Scots' but 'English'; 'Scots' to him always meant Gaelic.

Among these refugees came, in 1070, a prince and princess of the house of Alfred, Edgar Atheling, the rightful heir to the English throne, and his sister Margaret. They had been making for Hungary, the land of their birth,[1] but they had been driven into the Firth of Forth by contrary winds. They anchored their ship in a bay, which is still called St. Margaret's Hope,[2] about three miles to the south of Dunfermline, where King Malcolm had built a palace.

The messengers from the King who had been sent to interview the strangers returned with such a glowing account of the beauty of one of the ladies that Malcolm himself set out

[1] Their father was the English prince Edward, who, after the death of his father, Edmund Ironside, had been banished by Cnut to Hungary. In 1057 he returned to England with his children, but died soon after landing.

[2] That is, St. Margaret's Haven. It is now part of Rosyth Naval Base.

to welcome his uninvited guests. No sooner had he set eyes on Margaret than he determined to marry her. At first the lady refused; she wanted to be a nun, not a queen, she said, but she yielded at length to the prayers of Malcolm and her brother.

Her longing for the quiet of the convent was not a weak shrinking from the turmoil of the everyday world. With all her tenderness and sweetness, Margaret possessed an indomitable will, a restless conscience, and clear-cut and definite ideas of what was right and wrong. Even the King was moved by this passionate piety, which he did not quite understand: the grim warrior who had slain Macbeth and who tried to defy the Conqueror himself, would kneel beside the Queen to wash the grimy feet of some old beggar-man, or help her to distribute food to the three hundred poor folks who were her guests at Advent and in Lent. Sometimes, as Margaret's English chaplain tells us, he would take up one of the Queen's books of devotion, gaze at the unintelligible Latin, and then put his lips to the parchment; sometimes he would remove it altogether, and return it a few days later in a cover of gold and precious stones. Some of the King's gifts, however, were involuntary; he would find that a costly ornament, or a handful of gold coins had disappeared, and would learn later that the Queen had bestowed his property upon some 'gangrel body' whose tale of woe she had been unable to resist. Her generosity must have often embarrassed her attendants: a foppish young thane might be suddenly invited to hand over his silver brooch or brightly coloured cloak to some old crone, and might not be quite consoled by the Queen's promise to pay him in full for the loss of his gay plumage.

Margaret would see nothing ridiculous, or even unusual, in an action like this. She had no sense of humour—her chaplain tells us that she never laughed—and no sense of proportion. To her everything was as serious as everything else.

This was plainly revealed in her dealings with the Scottish

clergy. There was much in the state of the churches in Scotland to perplex and worry her. Though as far back as the beginning of the eighth century the breach between the Scottish churches and continental Christendom had been closed, the reconciliation was not complete, certain differences still remained. The Scottish clergy now observed Easter on the same day as the rest of western Christendom, but they refrained from celebrating mass on that day, and they shortened Lent, the fast that precedes Easter, by almost a week.

To us these do not seem the most serious differences. In the eleventh century a new religious zeal had begun to burn in the churches on the Continent. This enthusiasm showed itself in all sorts of ways : in the building of larger and more beautiful churches, in the founding of new monasteries, and in a general tightening up of church organization and discipline. Even the secular priest, who lived in his own house, and dressed like an ordinary merchant, found that certain things permitted to his predecessors were forbidden to him. He was not allowed to marry, for example. He found, too, that his bishop visited the parish more frequently and asked some very searching questions about the spiritual welfare of his parishioners. And there was many a man who felt that the secular priest was too much exposed to temptation, who did not feel safe till he had entered a monastery to spend the remainder of his life with men of the same mind as himself. He was left with nothing of his own, for he surrendered all his belongings to the monastery when he put on the plain black or white robes of a monk ; he had not even a room of his own ; he slept in the common dormitory and had his meals in the common refectory or dining-room. Even his will he surrendered : he had taken the vow of obedience, and must now regulate his life by the 'rule' of the monastery to which he belonged.

Of all this stir of life on the Continent the Scottish clergy knew little. There had been bishops at St. Andrews ever since the beginning of the tenth century, but at St. Andrews they seemed content to remain. Even if he would, however, the Bishop of St. Andrews could not have supervised the work of the lesser clergy all over Scotland. And though the Scottish clergy were all monks living in monasteries, they were somewhat different from the monks that Queen Margaret had seen in England and on the Continent. They did not take the vow of poverty, and each had his own little house within the monastery grounds. Many of the monks, too, were married; in fact, in most of the monasteries the office of abbot had become hereditary. As for their work, the average monk seems to have given more thought to the ploughing and sowing in his portion of the monastery fields than to the infrequent services in the little church of stone beside which he dwelt. In effect, the monasteries had become exclusive communities of hereditary landowners, who had often ceased to be clerics even in name.

In all this there was much that required to be changed, and much that Queen Margaret wanted to change. Some things, however, the Queen did not attempt to meddle with: she could not, or would not, diminish the number of lay proprietors of church lands; in fact, she allowed one of her sons to be a lay abbot. Nor did she try to reform the organization of the church, and though her own chaplain was an Englishman, she made no attempt to replace the easy-going Celtic clerics by the more enthusiastic and austere English and Normans. But the example of her life of alms-giving and prayer had its effect on both clerics and ordinary people. She visited monasteries, too, and talked to their occupants; from some she came away, not censorious but full of humility. For not all monasteries were like those we have described; in some, occupied by men called Culdees, the life was as hard, the fire of religious enthusiasm as pure and keen, as in any of the new monasteries on the Continent. But even in these Culdee communities she saw something to grieve her. Why did the Scottish clergy begin Lent a week after the proper time ? Why did they make Easter more like a fast than a feast ? Why, on the other hand,

THE EXTERIOR OF ST. MARGARET'S CHAPEL

The cannon on the left is 'Mons Meg'. It is believed that it was fired at Mons in 1466, and used at the siege of Norham Castle (see p. 186), 1497. It was sent to the Tower of London, 1754, but returned to Scotland by George IV, 1829

did they allow people to work on Sunday just as if it were an ordinary day ? Why had certain strange ceremonies become interwoven with the orthodox ritual of the Mass ?

In the end she summoned an assembly of the clergy and tried to argue them out of their old customs, and into conformity with the practice of the rest of Christendom. There was much excited Gaelic speech, but the clerics at last admitted that they were beaten, and agreed to abandon the practices to which she objected. Perhaps they were moved less by the arguments of Margaret than by the frowns of the grim warrior her husband, for Malcolm, who knew both English and Gaelic, had been compelled by Margaret to attend as her interpreter.

Saint though she was, Margaret did not despise pomp and display. Not only did she wear beautiful and costly raiment

THE INTERIOR OF ST. MARGARET'S CHAPEL

herself, she ordered her subjects to do the same. Rich hangings now brightened the bare walls of the King's palace, gold and silver plate glittered on his table; his meat was seasoned with spices brought from the ends of the earth; the liquor that sparkled in his cup was not home-brewed ale, but wine from France. So the little communities of fishers and farmers along the east coast—hardly deserving as yet the name of towns—became familiar with the Flemish and Frisian merchants who imported these new and strange wares, and some of the merchants in their turn found it profitable to act on the Queen's advice, and make their homes among the people with whom they traded. It was at the Queen's wish, too, that the King never stirred abroad without an imposing escort of well-disciplined troops, for she knew that people are impressed by the outward shows of kingly power.

But though Margaret brought English fashions and customs into Scotland, though she encouraged English refugees to settle there, her coming involved King Malcolm in a quarrel with the Norman King of England. It was only natural that Malcolm should take up the quarrel of Margaret's kinsfolk and invade England on their behalf, but he burned his fingers badly in the process: in 1072 William penetrated into the heart of Scotland, and forced Malcolm to do homage to him at Abernethy.

Worse followed in the reign of the Conqueror's successor: in 1092 William Rufus occupied Carlisle; the whole of Cumbria south of the Solway was at this one blow lost to Scotland. A year later Malcolm invaded England, but he was slain in battle near Alnwick. His son Edgar went back to Edinburgh, heavy at heart, to break the news to the Queen. He found his mother lying stricken with a mortal sickness, with just enough strength to ask him how her husband fared. 'He is well,' the prince answered, but she would not let herself be deceived. 'I know, my son, I know,' she sighed; 'but tell me what you know to be the truth.' He stammered out the miserable story. Not a word of complaint did she utter, only a prayer of thanksgiving that this grief should have been sent her at the very end of her life to purify her soul from the last stains of sin.

'So we enshrouded her body honourably, as befitted a queen,' said her chaplain, and so the tall candles burned around it, and the penitential psalms were chanted by the priests in the little church that she had caused to be built in the castle of Edinburgh—the church that is still called St. Margaret's Chapel. But outside confusion reigned. Donald Bane, the brother of the dead king, put himself at the head of those who disliked English innovations and half English princes, and besieged the castle. Not till a thick mist descended were the Queen's attendants able to steal out with the body and ferry it over the Forth, to lay it in the new church that she had built at Dunfermline.

It seemed for the moment as if her work had been undone. Donald Bane made good his claim to the crown, and though in 1094 he was deposed by Duncan, the son of Malcolm III and his first wife Ingibiorg, the murder of Duncan a few months later put him again in possession. But William Rufus, who had helped Duncan to his temporary success, was equally ready, and for the same reason, to support the sons of Margaret. He suggested to Edgar Atheling, who had now become his very dutiful subject, that he should lead an army into Scotland and put his nephew Edgar on the throne. For once Edgar Atheling acted with promptitude; Donald Bane's army retired before his force of English and Norman adventurers; the usurper himself was captured, and so, in 1097, Edgar, the eldest surviving son of Malcolm and Margaret, became King of Scotland.

CHAPTER VII

BARON AND PRIEST : 1097–1153

Grey sky, brown waters, as a bird that flies,
　　My heart flits forth from these
Back to the winter rose of northern skies,
　　Back to the northern seas.
And lo, the long waves of the ocean beat
　　Below the minster grey,
Caverns and chapels worn of saintly feet,
　　And knees of them that pray.

ANDREW LANG.

Kings of Scotland						Kings of England				
Edgar	.	.	.	.	1097–1107	William II	.	.	.	1087–1100
Alexander I	.	.	.	1107–1124		Henry I	.	.	.	1100–1135
David I	.	.	.	.	1124–1153	Stephen	.	.	.	1135–1154

THE time was to come when in Scotland the phrase 'the Auld Enemy' would have only one meaning—England; when men, looking back on two hundred years of open war or of brief truces, made only to be broken, would find it impossible to imagine that England and Scotland could ever be other than mortal foes. But the two and a half centuries of open warfare were preceded by two centuries of almost unbroken peace, during which Scotland—lowland Scotland, at any rate—was fashioned into the likeness of the southern kingdom. The merchant who went from Newcastle to Dundee in the twelfth century found himself in a town governed exactly as Newcastle was governed, among merchants who dressed exactly as he did, and who spoke the same dialect of the same language. The English lady who became the wife of a Scottish baron found that her new home was built on the same plan as the Norman castle she had left, and that though her husband could speak a few words of Gaelic, he preferred to talk in Norman-French. The large and beautiful monasteries that arose in the twelfth and thirteenth centuries were little more than copies of the larger and more beautiful monasteries of England and northern France, and their inmates, to begin with at least, were usually Englishmen or Normans. So the Lowland Scots—and among them we count the dwellers on the east coast as far north as the Moray Firth—were not simply abstaining from war with their English neighbours; they were, more or less willingly, copying English speech and learning English ways.

Why did they do it? Partly because England was their nearest neighbour, and, as Henry VII sagely remarked, 'the greater will always draw the less'; partly because the Scottish kings deliberately set themselves to make Scotland another England. This is not to be wondered at: they were as much English as Scots, and they were closely connected with the royal house of England. In 1100, for example, Henry I married Edgar's sister, Matilda. Edgar's youngest brother, David, spent much of his time at the English court, and by marrying the Countess of Huntingdon he became an English baron, lord of the two counties of Huntingdon and Northampton, full ten years before he became King of Scotland.

The anglicization of the Lowlands was helped on, too, by the fact that the English kings showed no desire to unite Scotland by force to their own realm. They were wise enough to let well alone, to be content with the homage of the King of Scots without asking what precisely it was that he rendered homage for, and though the long period of peace was thrice interrupted by war, it was the ambition of the King of Scots, not the ambition of the King of England, that caused the breach.

In fact, danger threatened the Scottish kingdom not from the south, but from the north and the west. The Western Isles were still under the rule of Norse or half Norse chieftains, who, however, showed little more deference to the King of Norway than they did to the King of Scots. In 1098 Magnus Bareleg, King of Norway, harried the Hebrides far and wide, and forced a reluctant acknowledgement of his supremacy from their inhabitants. Not content with this, he threatened to invade Scotland itself, and forced Edgar to buy him off. It was arranged that Magnus was to have all the Western Isles: however near the island might be to the mainland it was to be his, provided that he could go between it and the mainland in a boat with rudder in position. But Magnus succeeded in getting the peninsula of Kintyre as well; when he approached Tarbert he ordered his men to beach the boat, without unshipping the rudder, and drag it across the isthmus. Still Edgar had simply given up what neither he nor Magnus could control; though the Hebrides nominally belonged to the King of Norway, from the middle of the twelfth century their real rulers were the half Celtic, half Norse Kings of the Isles.

But the Hebrides were far away; if you could not get at the Islesmen, neither could they get at you, whereas a rebellion of the men of Moray, under a descendant of Lulach, for example, might be fatal to the dynasty.

When Edgar died in 1107 he was succeeded by his brother Alexander, who, however, entrusted to Prince David the rule over southern Scotland. Neither of these princes trusted their Celtic subjects overmuch, and when David became King of Scotland in 1124 he began what we may call a peaceful Norman Conquest of Scotland. Knights whom he had met at the court of Henry I he invited to settle beyond the Cheviots, and so many an ambitious younger son who had despaired of ever becoming a great baron in England found himself enrolled among the Scottish nobility. Such was Walter, the third son of the Breton Alan Fitz-Flaad, whom David made Steward of Scotland; such, too, was Robert de Brus, an English baron whose father had come from Normandy with the Conqueror, upon whom David bestowed great estates in Annandale. The son of the Breton became the founder of the royal house of Stewart; from the Norman adventurer the patriot king, Robert the Bruce, was descended.

Sometimes the new-comers were given lands that had been forfeited by their Celtic lords; sometimes they gained their new estates by marrying Celtic heiresses, but though they held the same territories, the relation in which they stood to the land and its inhabitants was different. The Celtic mormaer, like the old Scottish king, succeeded according to the Law of Tanistry: he was looked on not so much as a landowner but as the ruler, judge, and leader of the people inhabiting a certain area. His privileges and duties were determined, too, not by any written agreement between him and the King, but by immemorial custom; just as his people paid him 'cain'—gave him a pig or a few hens or a bushel or two of oats—because their grand-fathers had rendered the same tribute to his grandfather.

But the new Norman lord usually held his land by virtue of a written charter granted him by the King, specifying the exact extent of his estate, the privileges which he enjoyed as lord of that estate, and the conditions on which he held it. The most important condition was usually military service: the land-owner was expected to follow the King to war with a specified number of knights for a period of forty days. Nor was there any Law of Tanistry now: if a baron died he was succeeded by his eldest son, or by his eldest daughter if he had no son. Even if the son or daughter was an infant, the claims of the defunct baron's brothers or cousins were set aside, and the King became guardian both of the child and of the estates. Should the child be a girl, he might reward some faithful follower by bestowing her upon him as a bride. Even when the child was a boy, the King drew the revenues of his estates till he came of age, and even then the heir could not enter into possession of his estates till he had paid into the royal treasury a sum equal to the yearly revenue which he would derive from them.

So in a sense the baron was only joint owner of the land with the King: on the other hand the dwellers on the land were the baron's men rather than the King's. Only in exceptional cases did the King's justiciars and sheriffs interfere with the administration of justice within the lands of a baron, and there was no penalty which the baron could not inflict. Ordinary offenders he would thrust into his own private 'pit' or prison; criminals who had committed really serious offences, such as stealing more than one sheep, would be strung up on his private gallows.

Just as the King would deal out land to one of these Norman adventurers on certain conditions, so his new tenant, after reserving a portion of the land as his demesne or private estate, would divide the remainder among his followers on similar conditions. Just as the baron followed the King, so they had to follow their lord to battle; just as he had to attend the King's Council along with the other great barons, so they had to be present whenever he dealt out rough justice to the trembling malefactors. Some of the original Celtic occupants of the land remained free tenants, paying their 'cain and conveth'[1] to a Norman as they had done aforetime to a Celtic lord; others became serfs, compelled to work on their lord's demesne without money payment, forbidden to leave the place where they had been born, forbidden even to allow their daughters to marry without their lord's consent.

These Norman knights and men-at-arms were evidently meant to be a garrison, a bulwark against invasion from the north. Mounted on horseback, protected by a conical steel helmet and coat of mail, equipped with shield and lance, they were more than a match in hand-to-hand fighting for the Celtic warrior, who despised armour, and rushed into battle protected only by a helmet and a light shield of leather.

Besides, as soon as the Norman baron entered his new territories, he set about building a castle. He chose, if he could, a hillock near a river; if a loop of the river almost enclosed the site of his castle, so much the better. Where a natural hillock

---

[1] Contributions of food-stuffs.

was not available, he got his men to raise a great mound of earth, surrounded by a deep trench; the top of the mound, or mote, as it was called, he encircled with a stout palisade; the trench he flooded with water from the river. Within the palisade he erected a stout tower of timber, daubed with clay. There was usually an exterior set of defences as well: in most castles the mote was set at one corner of a large rectangular or oval

NORMAN CAVALRY, ATTACKING SAXON FOOTMEN

enclosure, a little above the level of the surrounding ground, from which it was separated by a palisade and a ditch. Within the bailey, as this enclosure was called, were other wooden buildings, stables, workshops, and stores. Most of the occupants of the castle, however, took their meals and slept, not in any of these outhouses, but in the great hall on the ground floor of the tower, which they approached by a drawbridge spanning the inner ditch. Here the lord of the castle dined at a trestle-table, that was piled up against the wall when the meal was over; here he sat in the dark nights of winter, before the fire that burned in the middle of the earthen floor, cursing the wind that blew through the chinks in the timber and sent the smoke eddying round the room, or listening to some old story of Arthur or Gawain. For a carpet underfoot he had rushes, for pictures a yard or two of tapestry stretched on the wall behind him; there was no room to which he could withdraw with his friends, for in addition to the great hall, the tower contained only one or two tiny bedrooms.

One would expect him to be dissatisfied with such quarters, but if he objected to them at all, it was not because they were uncomfortable—he did not know that they were uncomfortable —but because they were not absolutely secure. A stone castle, like those which were being raised in England, could not be set on fire by the enemy; still, a castle of earth and timber could be rushed up in a week or two at very little expense, and would defy any force not provided with siege engines. So these palisades and wooden towers were the rule in twelfth and thirteenth century Scotland, and even in the fourteenth century they continued to be built.

But Alexander I and David encouraged an invader of another type: along with the Norman noble came the Norman bishop and the Norman abbot. Alexander put English or Norman bishops into the old Celtic cathedrals at St. Andrews and Dunkeld, and founded the new bishopric of Moray; David went further, he revived old, or founded new, bishoprics in Glasgow, Brechin, Dunblane, Aberdeen, Ross, and Caithness.

There had been bishops in the ancient Celtic church, but while every one believed that there were certain ceremonies, such as ordaining a priest, which only a bishop could perform, no one could be certain what authority, if any, the bishop should exercise over that priest once he was ordained. Under David this confusion came to an end. Each bishop had his own special bishopric or diocese allotted to him; the district controlled by the Bishop of St. Andrews, for example, stretched from the Dee to the Tweed, and the diocese of Glasgow ex-

tended from the head of Loch Lomond to the Solway. And just
as the whole country was divided into dioceses, so each diocese
was subdivided into parishes, in
each of which one found a parish
church and the adjoining parson-
age, where the parish priest dwelt.
In districts where an old Celtic
church already existed, the new
Norman lord waited till a suitable
opportunity arose. When the old
Gaelic-speaking priest died, he put
an Englishman or a Norman in his
place; when the little old church
fell into disrepair, he pulled it down
and substituted a larger and more
beautiful building, with massive
walls, small, round-headed windows filled with stained glass, and
doorways framed by two twin clus-
ters of pillars, supporting a round
stone arch. The church was maintained and the parish priest supported by the offerings of the
parishioners, who were required
to pay him every year a tenth or
tithe of the produce of their fields.

ST. RULE'S TOWER, ST. ANDREWS
(used as the Cathedral till the middle
of the twelfth century)

This division of the large dioceses into parishes was not com-
pleted all at once: long after the end of David's reign many
districts, even in the populous diocese of St. Andrews, remained
without a parish church. Still, a beginning had been made.

The parish priest was not a law to himself. At intervals his
bishop would descend upon him and ask him a multitude of
inconvenient questions. Did he hold divine service regularly?

Did his parishioners attend regularly, and how did they behave when they were persuaded to come to church? Did they gossip or laugh at the most solemn parts of the service, as was the habit in some churches? If they did, whose fault was it? Had they been sufficiently instructed by their priest? Did he make them confess their sins to him regularly, and were the penances that he laid upon them sufficiently severe? And if the bishop did not come in person, he sent his deputy, the archdeacon, whose frown was only a little less terrible.

In the intervals of rest from his travels among the country clergy, the bishop lived in his castle or palace in the cathedral town. For in every bishopric there was one church, conspicuous by its size and beauty, which was regarded as the principal church of the diocese. Here, not far from the high altar, stood the 'cathedra', or bishop's throne, which gave its name to the building. Here the newly consecrated bishop was installed, here he officiated in person at the high festivals of the church, and here, under the flagstones of the choir, his bones were laid when in his turn he had to make way for a new bishop.

Not only were the services more frequent in the cathedral than in the parish church—seven times in the twenty-four hours the white-robed priests filed into the choir and took their places in their elaborately carved stalls—but they were also more elaborate, special attention being paid to the beauty of the singing. So in addition to the higher ecclesiastical dignitaries like the dean, whose business it was to see that everything worked smoothly within the cathedral, and the archdeacon, there had to be a fairly large body of canons or cathedral clergy. In most Scottish cathedrals the canons were secular priests, living in separate houses in the cathedral close or chanonry; in St. Andrews, however, they were canons regular, living together in the priory, a group of buildings that differed in no important respect from the great monasteries that were springing up in southern Scotland.

DUNFERMLINE ABBEY, THE NAVE

The Abbey was founded by Malcolm III, and refounded in 1150 by
David I, in whose reign the nave was built

For King David was a builder of monasteries as well as of cathedrals, monasteries which he manned with English or French-speaking monks of the new, strictly disciplined orders. It was he who founded Holyrood, where he enshrined a piece of wood that Queen Margaret had believed to be a fragment of the true Cross or 'holy rood'; it was he who reared the 'antique pillars massy-proof' that loom through the darkness of the nave in Dunfermline Abbey; it was he who brought the white-robed Cistercians to Melrose, where the loveliest abbey in all Scotland—lovely still in its ruin—rises by the placid waters of the Tweed.

A few miles below Melrose the River Tweed in its winding course almost encircles the ruins of Dryburgh Abbey, another monastery founded in David's reign, though not by David himself. Very little is left of the church, but to the other monastic buildings Time and the spoiler have been unusually merciful; as we stand on the smooth turf of the cloister garth and look around, it is comparatively easy for us to imagine what the monastery was like seven hundred years ago, when the great church stood entire and complete.

The chief purpose for which a monastery existed was the daily performance of the services of the church. Every morning, at mass, the officiating priest must consecrate the bread and wine and so transform them, it was believed, into the veritable body and blood of Christ; seven times daily, as in the great cathedral churches, the appointed prayers had to be said, and the appointed psalms and hymns sung. For this solemn and beautiful ceremonial a solemn and beautiful background had to be provided—a great church, cross-shaped in plan, the lofty roof of which was supported by a double row of stone pillars. The head of the cross always pointed to the east, the shaft to the west. The western half of the church was called the nave: here ordinary folk might come and go freely, but the rood-screen, a decorated partition of wood or stone, surmounted by a great cross, shut them off from the choir in the eastern half, which only the monks could enter. Here stood the high altar, and here a light burned night and day before the sacrament-house, the little recess containing the consecrated wafer which was believed to be the very body of the Saviour. The other

THE RUINS OF MELROSE ABBEY
(South Transept and part of Choir)
The Abbey, founded by David I, was destroyed by Edward II in 1322. It was rebuilt in the reign of David II, but was again destroyed, this time by Richard II. The South Transept, on the right, was rebuilt in the late fourteenth century, the Choir in the fifteenth century

buildings of the monastery were usually erected to the south of the church; they were always arranged in the form of a square, the northern side of which was formed by the south wall of the nave. On the eastern side came the south transept, or arm, of the church, and then a long building, containing, first, the sacristy, where the costly vestments and other articles of value were kept, then the chapter-house, where the monks met in

council, and where the abbot dealt out admonitions and penances to careless brethren, and, adjoining the chapter-house,
the parlour, where the monks could gossip in winter over one
of the few fires in the monastery. Above these rooms was the
dormitory, where the monks slept in the coarse white robes
that they had worn all day. It was with good reason that they
went to bed fully dressed, for soon after midnight the great
bell of the church would begin to ring, and they had to rise,
shuffle along a draughty corridor, past the room of the wakeful
abbot, and down a flight of chilly stone stairs into the cold
blackness of the great church.

The southern side of the square was occupied by the refectory or dining-hall, a more stately apartment than the hall in
the king's palace. Little of it is left at Dryburgh, but we can
still see the remains of the kitchens, wine-cellars, and store
rooms that filled up the basement below. On the west side of
the square stood buildings that were probably occupied by the
lay-brethren, these servants of the monastery who were not
actually monks.

Round the four sides of this quadrangle ran a covered walk
or cloister, where the monks spent most of their leisure in milder
weather, some of them sitting near the big stone bookcase that
we can still see, reading some legend of the saints full of the
most incredible miracles and adventures—the nearest thing to
a novel that the monastery possessed.

But some of the monks had duties that took them away from
the church and the cloister. One of the brethren had to distribute food to the crowds of poor people who pressed round the
monastery gate every morning; others had to see that the uninvited guests of the monastery were properly lodged. For the
monks looked upon hospitality as one of their chief duties;
every monastery contained a hostel or guest-house, where
travellers were accommodated according to their rank. We
must remember that in those days inns were few and bad, and

that to the wandering packman or minstrel, journeying through
the Forest of Ettrick, and listening to the howl of the wolves

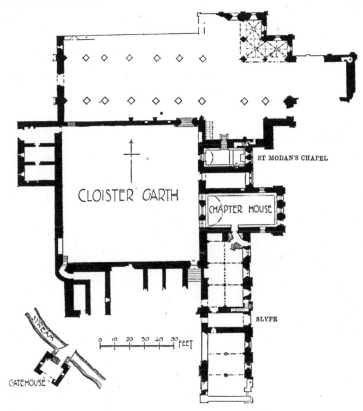

PLAN OF DRYBURGH ABBEY

Notice, on the north of the cloister garth, the cross-shaped church; on
the east, the sacristy (St. Modan's Chapel), the chapter-house, and the
parlour; on the south, the basement of the refectory; and on the west, the
cellars of the lay brethren's quarters

reverberating from the sides of the Eildons, the sound of the bell
of Melrose or Dryburgh must have come with a peculiar sweet-

ness. But kings and barons did not disdain to become guests of the monastery; after all, bare and chilly as they seem to us, the rooms in the monastery were far more comfortable than those in the king's castle.

Similarly, the monks set an example to the ordinary farmer: the cold stone buildings of the monastery were soon embowered in orchards and gardens; in spring one might see a white-robed brother guiding the clumsy wooden plough with its team of eight straining oxen; in autumn one might see him again, watching the lay-brethren as they led in the heavy ox-wains under the great gateway.

But the monks did not depend for a livelihood on the produce of the fields and orchards round about the monastery; they had estates in every part of Scotland, occupied by their tenants or vassals, who made to them, just as they would have done to an ordinary landlord, regular payments in money or, more usually, in food-stuffs. In addition, every monastery had certain parish churches which belonged to it, from which it collected the bulk of the tithes, leaving only a pittance for the parish priest. So the monk whose business it was to collect these revenues would have very little time for the seven daily services in the monastery church; would be in danger, to tell the truth, of forgetting that he was a monk, and of looking on himself as a business man, one, too, who handled far larger sums of money than the ordinary merchant. The time was to come, in fact, when men would ask if David's zeal for the church had been altogether wise, if the great monasteries which he had endowed did not take far more from the community than they gave back to it. But in the twelfth century that time was far away.

CHAPTER VIII

SCOTLAND, ENGLAND, AND NORWAY: 1107–1286

Where the Norwayan banners flout the sky.—SHAKESPEARE.

Kings of Scotland				*Kings of England*			
Alexander I	.	.	.	1107–1124	Henry I	1100–1135
David I	.	.	.	1124–1153	Stephen	1135–1154
Malcolm IV	.	.	.	1153–1165	Henry II	1154–1189
William	.	.	.	1165–1214	Richard I	1189–1199
Alexander II	.	.	.	1214–1249	John	1199–1216
Alexander III	.	.	.	1249–1286	Henry III . . .	1216–1272
					Edward I	1272–1307

THERE were limits to the English enthusiasms of these half English Kings of Scotland: none of them, for example, wanted the remodelled Scottish Church to be brought into subjection to the English Church. Though Alexander I brought an English monk, Eadmer, from Canterbury to be Bishop of St. Andrews, Eadmer found, when he proposed to be consecrated by the Archbishop of Canterbury, that the King was justly named Alexander the Fierce, and both Alexander and his brother David turned a deaf ear to the remonstrances of the Pope himself, when he tried to insist on the consecration of the Bishop of Glasgow by the Archbishop of York.

The dispute smouldered on for half a century, to flare up again in the reign of David's grandson, William the Lion. This time, however, more was at stake than the independence of the

Scottish Church: the cathedral clergy of St. Andrews had appointed a certain John Scot to be their bishop, as they were entitled to do; the King declared the election void, which he was not entitled to do, and tried to force the canons to accept his own chaplain instead. This high-handed action brought him into conflict with the Pope, who excommunicated him and laid his land under an interdict. But the trouble blew over: in 1188 the King's candidate, Hugh, died; John declared himself willing to accept the inferior bishopric of Dunkeld rather than brave the King's wrath; the canons, summoned to Perth to choose a bishop in the presence of the King and his barons, accepted William's suggestion that they should choose his cousin, Roger de Beaumont, Chancellor of Scotland; and, finally, in 1192 Pope Celestine III announced that he had taken the Scottish Church under his special protection. Any dispute which the Scottish prelates could not settle themselves was now to be taken not to York or Canterbury but straight to Rome.

The King's defeat was more apparent than real: though in theory the chapter—the cathedral clergy—appointed a new bishop, in practice they could not proceed to an election without the King's permission, and they seldom dared to vote against a candidate whom the King favoured. The election had to be confirmed by the Pope, it is true, but if the King anticipated opposition, he sent ambassadors to Rome armed with copious explanations and ample sums of money, and the Pope's objections almost always disappeared.

It was not mere caprice that made the King interfere with his cathedral chapters; he required judges, ambassadors, auditors, and other officials, but as few of his barons and knights had more than a smattering of letters, he had to recruit his civil servants from the ranks of the clergy, and as he could not pay them out of his own pocket, he secured handsome incomes for the most efficient of them by making them bishops. And the bishops repaid their debt; they stuck to the King through thick

and thin and opposed any attempt to increase the political influence of the English King in Scotland, for they feared that if
the Scottish King became the vassal of the King of England,
they would become the humble servants of the Archbishops of
York and Canterbury.

Such fears would have seemed foolish in David's reign. In
1135 the death of Henry I plunged England into anarchy: one
set of barons bestowed the crown on Stephen of Blois; another
set supported the claim of Henry's daughter, Matilda. David,
who was Earl of Huntingdon as well as King of Scotland, had
vowed to Henry that he would support his daughter's cause, so
no one was surprised when, in 1136, he crossed the border at
the head of an army, seized Carlisle and Newcastle, and marched
on Durham. But his action was not quite as chivalrous as it
seemed: he was more anxious to gain territory in England than
to help his niece to the crown; when Stephen hurried north with
his barons he found that David was willing to refrain from
further fighting if the three northern counties of England were
bestowed upon his son Henry. Stephen let Prince Henry have
Carlisle and the surrounding district, and with this David
appeared to be satisfied. Two years later, however, he invaded
England at the head of a great army, drawn from every part of
his realm. He advanced to the borders of Yorkshire without
meeting any serious opposition, nor did he expect any, for he
knew that Stephen was fully occupied elsewhere. But David
reckoned without the stout-hearted Thurstan, Archbishop of
York, who summoned noble and peasant alike to meet the invader. His appeal was answered; from every village the country
folk came tramping in to the rendezvous, with their parish priest
at their head, bearing aloft a sacred banner. They knew their
own minds, they were Englishmen, and their plain duty was
to fight against the barbarian Scots. But some of the great
northern nobles were not in such a happy position. What of
Robert de Brus, Lord of Annandale in Scotland, and master of

ninety-four separate lordships in Yorkshire? Was he an Englishman or a Scot? He did not know. One thing he did know,
however: if he sided with the English and the Scots were
victorious, he would lose his Scottish estates; if he sided with
the Scots and the English were victorious, he would lose his
English estates. In vain he pointed out to the King of Scots
that he himself was really more a Norman than a Scot; David
refused to be turned from his course. De Brus thereupon renounced his fealty and went over to the English; he left one of
his sons, however, in the Scottish camp, and made over his
Scottish estates to him before he went away. He was now
fortified against every risk, even against bodily hurt in the
battle, for it had been arranged that if success seemed to incline
to the Scots, the son should make the father a prisoner, while
if the day went in favour of the English, the father was to
capture the son.

The prudence of de Brus was justified when the two armies
met at Northallerton. David found it difficult to maintain discipline in his motley host; the wild Picts from Galloway got out
of hand altogether on the southward march, and they now insisted that they, and not the mail-clad cavalry, should lead the
attack upon the English position. When it was pointed out to
them that their only protection was a light shield of leather,
they answered proudly, 'We surely have iron sides, a breast of
bronze, a mind void of fear, and our feet have never known
flight, nor our backs a wound'. The King let them have their
way, and with wild yells of 'Albany! Albany!' they rushed at
the English position.

The English were ready for them: alternating groups of
archers and of spearmen and dismounted knights had been
arranged in a compact body round a great ship-mast, from
which floated the sacred banners of St. Peter, St. Paul, and
St. Wilfrid of York. Few of the Galwegians crossed spears with
their opponents, for as soon as they got within range the pitiless

hail of arrows descended. 'Like a hedgehog with quills,' says an old writer, 'so would you see a Galwegian bristling all round with arrows, and none the less brandishing his sword, and in blind madness rushing forward now smite a foe, now lash the air with useless strokes.' Those who did reach the English ranks had the shafts of their spears broken in two, and were slain while they fumbled with their swords.

The gallant Prince Henry, seeing the Galwegians waver, called up his mail-clad cavalry, hurled himself at another part of the English line, broke it ' like a spider's web', and fell upon the guards who had been left with the horses of the dismounted knights. For a moment it seemed as if the English were to be seized with panic, but they rallied when some one held up a dead man's head, and shouted that the King of Scots had been slain. The Galwegians fell back in confusion, their exultation of a few minutes before changed to terror; a chance shot killed the leader of the men of Lothian and created a panic among them, a panic which spread to the Highlanders and Islanders in the reserve division, commanded by the King. Even when David saw the remnants of his army streaming past him in wild disorder, he refused to budge, 'thinking that he was bound by his promise to conquer or die'. His knights, however, compelled him to mount his horse, and, forming a close body about his dragon standard, they escorted him from the field.

Many a time we shall see the same story repeated, see the mad rush of the Scottish spearmen checked when the English archers loose their arrows; once or twice we shall see the spear beat the bow. But Northallerton was not Flodden, the Scottish army, though defeated, was not destroyed, and in 1139 Stephen, moved by the prayers of his Queen, who was a niece of King David, granted the earldom of Northumberland to Prince Henry. This transaction did not hinder David from taking up arms again for Matilda when she landed in England, but Stephen could not take back his gift by force of arms, and David remained master of the three northern counties of England. When in 1149 young Henry of Anjou, Matilda's son, came to England, it was David who knighted him in Carlisle, which for the time had become a Scottish town. Henry promised in return that when he became King of England he would confirm the King of Scots in his possession of the northern counties and of Huntingdon. How he kept his promise will soon appear.

In 1152 Prince Henry of Scotland died, and in 1153 King David followed him to the grave. He was succeeded by his grandson Malcolm, a boy of twelve. In 1157 Henry of Anjou, who since 1154 had been King of England, invited the youngster to Chester, made him do homage, though for what he did not specify, and wheedled him out of the three northern counties. He was generous enough, however, to take Huntingdon from Malcolm's younger brother William and bestow it upon Malcolm.

Malcolm did not re-open the question, but after his death in 1165 his more ambitious and energetic brother William followed King Henry to France and asked that the three counties should be restored. Henry was a dangerous man to cross; when an English knight tried to say a word in William's favour, he flung his cap, belt, and mantle into the corners of the room, tore the silken cover from the couch on which he was sitting, and began to chew the straw stuffing. William went away ill content, but he was afraid to risk a war with Henry as long as Henry had the united strength of England behind him. In 1173, however, it seemed that William's chance had come. Henry's sons had risen in rebellion against their father, and England and Normandy were distracted by civil war. William promptly sided with the rebel princes, on the understanding that he was to have Northumberland for his pains, and led his army over the border, not under the dragon banner of his ancestors, but under a golden-yellow flag blazoned with a crimson lion. He was forced to retreat, but in the summer of 1174 William the Lion, as he was called from his lion standard, returned with a larger army.

Northern England lay at his feet, for Henry was far away, at Canterbury, kneeling in an agony of remorse and wounded pride before the shrine of the Saint to whose murder his own rash words had led. But William's over-confidence was his ruin: he allowed the bulk of his army to scatter far and wide in search of plunder, while he remained near the castle of Alnwick with a bodyguard of sixty knights. A mist rolled over the level ground on which he was encamped, but even when he caught sight of the vague, gigantic figures of horses and their riders looming through the fog he was unperturbed. They were some of his own cavalry, he was sure, returning from a foray. Only when they were a few yards away did he see that they were English. 'Now will it appear who knows how to be a knight,' he shouted, as he drove the spurs into his horse and charged. He did not go far; his horse was slain and he himself made prisoner.

He travelled in no dignified fashion through England—on horseback, with his feet tied together—while in every town and village through which he passed the church bells rang merrily. Henry could not afford to be generous; he shipped his captive overseas to his castle of Falaise in Normandy, and refused to release him till he had become his vassal.

Other Scottish kings had done homage to Henry's predecessors, just as Henry's predecessors had done homage to the kings of France for their duchy of Normandy. But in the second half of the twelfth century no one knew what precisely the kings of Scotland did homage for. It might be for their estates in England; it might be for Lothian, or for Lothian and Strathclyde together; the one thing of which they were certain was that they did not do homage for the whole of Scotland. Besides, the English kings did not dream of treating the kings of Scots as they treated their English vassals; they did not, for example, listen to complaints by Scottish barons about the quality of the justice dealt out to them in the Scottish courts. But there was to be no ambiguity about the position now: William had to do homage to Henry for the whole of his possessions; his barons had to follow his example and take the oath of fealty to the English King, while the castles of Edinburgh and Stirling and three border fortresses were to open their gates to receive English garrisons.

William made no attempt to free himself from the yoke of his vassalage during Henry's lifetime. But with the accession of Richard Cœur de Lion in 1189 deliverance came: Richard was so eager to go on a crusade to the Holy Land that he allowed William to buy back for ten thousand marks all that Henry had taken from him.

In 1215 the wheel had come full circle: William the Lion, grown cautious, and even timid with old age, had died in 1214, and an ambitious young monarch, his son Alexander II, now sat on the throne of Scotland. Civil war had again broken out in England, this time between King John and his barons; again the King of Scots joined the rebels that he might gain possession of the northern counties, and invaded England. But, like his father, Alexander burned his fingers badly: when King John died in 1216 he joined the English barons who supported the French Prince Louis against the young Henry III, and so drew down a Papal interdict upon his country. The reconciliation of Henry and Louis, in 1217, left him with no choice but to abandon his conquests in the north of England and do homage to Henry for his English earldom of Huntingdon.

Twenty years later the question that had caused so much heart-burning and bloodshed was finally settled: Alexander agreed to drop his claim to the three northern counties in return for certain small estates in the north of England, worth only £200 a year altogether.

THE SOUTH TRANSEPT OF ARBROATH ABBEY

Founded by William the Lion in 1178 and dedicated to St. Thomas
of Canterbury

These 'alarums and excursions' in 1138, 1174, and 1216 must not blind us to the fact that during the greater part of the period between the death of Malcolm III in 1093 and the death of Alexander III in 1286 the two countries were at peace. Strange as it may seem, the kings of Scotland waged war against their own subjects far more often than against the kings of England, and on one or two occasions they actually got troops from England to help them to subdue the northern rebels. In 1130, for example, while King David was at the English court, a rebellion, headed by Angus, the grandson of Lulach, broke out in Moray. Troops were hurried north from England by one of David's English cousins, the rebels were completely defeated, and Angus their king was slain.

Trouble threatened in the west as well: when in 1153 David was succeeded by Malcolm IV, Somerled, the half Norse ruler of Argyll, threw off his lightly-worn allegiance to the King of Scots, and began to plunder the rich and peaceful country in the neighbourhood of Glasgow. For eleven years the reign of terror continued, till Glasgow had become a desert, and bishop and canons alike had abandoned the cathedral. But Somerled raided Glasgow once too often; when he came in 1164 he found himself opposed by a determined little army, 'very bold, like dragons or lions', headed by the old bishop himself. The bishop's troops advanced without waiting to be attacked; when they got within range they hurled their spears into the ranks of the enemy, and, drawing their swords, charged home. One of the spears laid Somerled low before the battle had well begun. Bereft of their leader, the invaders surged back in confusion towards their ships, but the bishop's troops followed them and drove them headlong into the Firth. Never again do we hear of the men of the west menacing Glasgow.

The men of Moray were not so easily daunted. Although the last descendant of Lulach had perished, they had found another prince of the blood royal to lead them to battle, Donald

Ban MacWilliam, the grandson of Duncan, the eldest son of Malcolm Canmore. In 1179 and again in 1187 William the Lion had to lead an army into Moray against the rebels. Though on the second occasion the rebel army was defeated and its leader slain, other three rebellions followed within little more than forty years. But the merciless suppression of the rebellion of 1230, and the brutal execution of the last descendant of Donald Ban MacWilliam, a little girl who was hardly more than an infant, brought peace in the north at last.

For people could be cruel in those days. Only eight years before, Adam, Bishop of Caithness, had had a dispute with the people of his diocese about the payment of tithes. They refused to pay, and when he still insisted they attacked him in his own episcopal palace, wounded him with a battle-axe, dragged him into his kitchen, stoned him till he dropped exhausted, then set fire to the building and let him burn to death. A swift vengeance overtook the murderers; the King hurried north, arrested ninety suspects, and ordered their hands and feet to be cut off.

No sooner was the north pacified than trouble began in the south-west. Galloway had been subjugated by Malcolm IV in 1160, after three hard-fought campaigns, and the Celtic lords of Galloway had lived in amity with their half Norman kings. But Alan, Lord of Galloway, died, leaving three daughters and one illegitimate son, Thomas. Alexander II divided the province into three parts, and gave one third to each daughter. The Galwegians, suspecting that the King's next step would be to marry each of the three heiresses to a Norman baron, declared for Thomas, and, in 1234, rose in rebellion. In the following summer the King's forces appeared in Galloway, and, driving the apparently timorous foe before them, marched into the heart of that wild country and camped on a beautiful green plain in the recesses of the mountains. They had walked into a trap, the green meadow was really a marsh, and when the Galwegians saw the mail-clad troops floundering in the mud, they swept down from the heights and fell upon them. The King's troops would not have escaped had not the Celtic Earl of Ross, coming up soon after the battle had begun, hurled his men at the rear of the Galwegians. As soon as the rebels saw that it was they who were in the trap, they broke and fled to the hills.

A few weeks later the rebel Thomas gave himself up to the King. The land was apportioned as the King had desired, and each of the three heiresses in time married the inevitable Norman baron. Dervorgilla, the eldest, married Sir John de Balliol, a name with which we shall soon be more familiar.

Alexander might well have rested content. The men of Moray had now no descendant of Lulach or Duncan for whom to fight, and the Norman baron had at last got a footing in the most Celtic part of southern Scotland. But the King's eyes were turned westwards, to the islands which had once been part of the heritage of the Kings of Scots. For a century and a half they had belonged to the King of Norway, but as Norway was far away they had come under the control of the descendants of Somerled, who were known as the Kings of the Isles.

Alexander first tried what money could do: in 1243 he sent two bishops to the court of King Hakon to offer to buy back the lands. 'I am aware of no such urgent need of money that I need to sell the lands,' answered the Norse King dryly. Other ambassadors received no more polite a reply, and in 1249 Alexander resolved to attempt the conquest of the Hebrides. At the head of a fleet he sailed down the Firth of Clyde, round the Mull of Kintyre, and northwards into the unfamiliar Firth of Lorne. But while his ship lay in Kerrera Sound he was stricken with a fever and died.

It seemed that with the death of Alexander II more than the Hebrides would be lost to Scotland. His successor was a boy of eight, and, as was to happen so often in Scottish history, two hostile factions, one of them suspected of being in English pay, strove to gain complete control over the King, and so rule

the country in his name.   But the defeat and banishment of
one faction, and the sudden death of the leader of the other,
left Alexander III, at the age of seventeen, master in his own
house.

In the year 1263 a fear that had been dead for centuries
suddenly came to life again: news arrived that King Hakon,
with the greatest fleet that had ever left the shores of Norway,
was making for the west coast of Scotland. The old King,
fearing that the Hebrides were slipping out of his grasp, had
come to frighten the Islesmen back to their allegiance. Southward through the Hebrides the great fleet sailed, round the Mull
of Kintyre and up the Firth of Clyde till it anchored off the
island of Arran.

King Alexander kept his head in this time of danger; he
knew that the summer was waning, and that if Hakon lingered
much longer he ran a serious risk of being overwhelmed by the
equinoctial gales. So he sent ambassadors to the fleet, apparently to negotiate a treaty of peace, but really to waste
Hakon's time.

At the end of September Alexander broke off the negotiations, whereupon Hakon led his great fleet farther up the Firth,
and made it anchor under the shelter of the Cumbraes. He
then sent a request to Alexander either to fight or to make
peace. Alexander would do neither; he continued to watch
the sky.

Sure enough, at the beginning of October, a great storm
rolled up from the west, so furious that the Norsemen thought
it must have been raised by magic. Eight anchors could not
keep the King's flagship from drifting, and the other ships
fared worse; ten of them, including a merchant ship stuffed with
provisions, were driven ashore at Largs. Nor was that all; as
the crews of the stranded vessels tried to push off and get into
deep water again, they heard arrows whistle past their ears,
and saw that the Scots were assembling on the beach, ready at

last to do battle with them. But Hakon, taking advantage of a lull in the tempest, sent ashore a strong landing-party, which succeeded in driving back the Scots.

On the following day Hakon himself landed to supervise the salving of the goods on the wrecked merchant ship. Seven hundred men were on the beach with him, another two hundred had occupied a mound some little distance away. But now they had to deal with more dangerous foes than the Scottish archers, for King Alexander had brought up his mail-clad cavalry, five hundred horsemen in all. The old King's followers, as they watched the dense masses of the Scots moving towards them, urged him to make his escape while he could; very reluctantly he allowed himself to be put into a boat and rowed out to the fleet.

The Scots began the battle by launching an attack upon the mound. It was successful; the Norsemen abandoned it and fell back in confusion towards the beach. The Scots followed them up, but the Norsemen, with a treacherous sea behind them, fought on with grim determination. All through the afternoon the battle went on, till the archers had exhausted their stocks of arrows, and were reduced to throwing stones at their enemies. The plight of the Norsemen seemed absolutely hopeless now: if they abandoned their position on the beach and waded out to their boats, they would be pursued and cut down by the Scots; even as it was, some of the more timorous had been drowned while attempting to row back to the fleet. They succeeded in holding on till evening, when the Scots withdrew to the mound; then they suddenly delivered a counterattack, drove the Scots down, and ere they could recover, returned to the beach and pushed off.

Thus ended the famous battle of Largs, an indecisive skirmish that brought little glory to either side. When Alexander watched the sails of Hakon's fleet sink below the horizon, he must have asked himself anxiously when it would return, for though a few ships had been lost, it was still a mighty armada. He did not know that it would never return, that it had the pestilence on board even then, and that a few months later his brave old adversary would be lying on his death-bed in Kirkwall, fortifying himself for the coming ordeal by reading, not books of devotion, but tales of the old Norse kings and heroes.

When he did learn of the death of Hakon, Alexander opened negotiations with the new King of Norway, Magnus; again the offer of money was made, and this time it was accepted. In 1266 Magnus agreed to surrender Man and the Hebrides for 4,000 marks down, and an annual payment of 100 marks.

So Kintyre and the Hebrides at last formed part of the kingdom of Scotland. It made very little difference to the Islesmen: hitherto they had disobeyed the King of Norway; now they disobeyed the King of Scots. In the Hebrides the Lord of the Isles, as the King of the Isles now began to be called, was for long a much more powerful potentate than his overlord, the King of Scots.

CHAPTER IX

SCOTLAND IN THE TIME OF ALEXANDER III

When Alexander our King was dead
That Scotland led in love and le,[1]
Away was sons[2] of ale and bread,
Of wine and wax, of gamen and glee:
Our gold was changed into lead,
Christ, born into Virginity,
Succour Scotland and remede[3]
That stad[4] is in perplexity.

SO sang a forgotten Scottish poet. For the quarter century between the battle of Largs and the death of King Alexander was indeed a golden age. Nevermore would Scotland be disturbed by the fear of a Norse invasion, for had not Eric, the young King of Norway, taken the Princess Margaret, the daughter of the King of Scots, to be his bride? As for a war with England, that had become, to all appearance, quite impossible. Had not the King married a sister of Edward I of England? After the death of his wife, was it not to his brother-in-law that Alexander turned for comfort, in that black hour when he saw his son, the Prince of Scotland, follow his daughter to the grave? Then there had been no serious rebellion either in the north or in the south-west, for many years, partly because the remoter regions were now very effectively bridled with castles of timber or of stone, partly because Galwegian and Highlander alike no longer regarded the King and his barons as aliens and intruders.

For in the thirteenth century a curious change came over Scotland : the Norman baron, the bishop who knew more Latin and French than English, the English-speaking traders and farmers of Fife and Lothian, the Gaelic-speaking herdsman from the hills, all began to look on themselves as Scotsmen, as

----

[1] loyalty.   [2] abundance.   [3] remedy.   [4] placed.

BOTHWELL CASTLE FROM THE SOUTH

Showing three of the four flanking towers. The largest, on the left, is the Valence Tower; next comes the small Prison Tower; then, on the right, the Douglas Tower

people bound together by some mysterious tie, like, but not quite the same as, the tie of kinship. In other words, they were no longer a collection of odds and ends drawn from different races; they had become a nation. But this sense of national solidarity, this belief in the mystic kinship of all who lived between the Cheviots and the Pentland Firth, was still very vague ; it was something that seemed as if it might be lost far more easily than it had been won. For it could not be denied that the Scottish baron had really more in common with the English baron than with the Scottish peasant at his castle gate, and that the douce burgess of Edinburgh or Berwick would feel more at ease in the company of a merchant or master-mariner from Newcastle than in that of a wild, shock-headed Highlander, gabbling a language that to him was incomprehensible.

Though the Scotland of Alexander's time was in after years regarded as an earthly paradise, to us it would seem bleak and comfortless enough. It is true that the King and some of his great barons had begun to make extensive alterations to their older castles of timber and earth. Sometimes they replaced the wooden palisades by walls of stone, which were seldom less than ten feet thick and twenty-five feet high; sometimes, in addition, they placed a massive stone tower or donjon on the site of the old wooden tower. But even in the newest castles many of the interior buildings were still made of wood, or of wood and clay, and always the main consideration was not comfort, but security.

This will be apparent if we look at the most splendid of these thirteenth-century structures, Bothwell Castle on the River Clyde. Its very position shows how anxious its builder had been to make it secure: on the south and west it was protected by the river; on the north and east by a great ditch. The bailey or courtyard was enclosed by a lofty and massive stone wall or 'curtain'. Along the top of this ran a walk protected by a

battlemented parapet, from the cover of which the archers
could take leisurely aim at the besiegers below. At four of the
five angles of the curtain stood a great flanking tower, from the
loop-holes of which arrows could be directed against any of
the besiegers who attempted to undermine the curtain with
pick and crowbar. At the fifth angle stood the gatehouse,

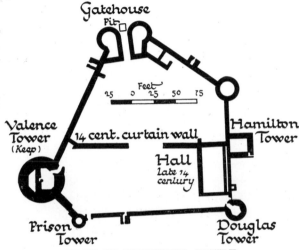

PLAN OF BOTHWELL CASTLE

This castle, built soon after the middle of the thirteenth century, was
demolished after Bannockburn. The southern half was rebuilt by
Edward III in 1336, and before the end of the century Archibald
the Grim, 3rd Earl of Douglas, added the hall

where the great gateway of the castle was almost lost to view
between two projecting towers. It was approached by a drawbridge, very tempting to a bold besieger. But he would be
well advised to give it a wide berth, for if he set foot on it one
end would sink beneath him, and deposit him in a deep pit,
while the other would tilt up, and block the gateway completely. Should he be lucky enough to get over the drawbridge before the bolts holding it in position had been removed,

he would probably be crushed beneath the portcullis, a heavy wooden gate shod with iron spikes, which slid down from a chamber above the gateway; if he slipped past he had still to grope along a long, dark passage, and batter in a massive wooden door. Even when the besiegers reached the courtyard they could not call themselves masters of the castle, for each of the four towers was really a miniature fortress, capable of being defended for days by a few resolute men.

The change from wood to stone made no difference to the comfort of the castle: the gales of winter still blew through the unglazed windows, the acrid wood smoke still eddied round the room, and the dogs still fought for bones and scraps of meat among the rushes that carpeted the floor. But it was luxurious in comparison with the huts that clustered not far from its gates, huts walled and roofed with turf, without windows, without chimneys, with no door but a curtain of hide. Here the peasant—serf, or free tenant—slept under the same roof as his cattle, as people do in some parts of the Hebrides to this day.

Though the Scottish village changed little in five hundred years—when the poet Gray visited Forfarshire in 1765 he noticed 'just above ground, the huts . . . built of and covered with turf'—in the Scottish burgh changes came more rapidly. We can only guess how the older Scottish burghs came into existence at all. No single explanation will fit all of them; some, like St. Andrews and Glasgow, obviously grew up round a great religious establishment; others, like Edinburgh and Stirling, plainly owe their origin to the presence of a fortress. They were almost always situated beside some good natural harbour; even Stirling and Perth, which we now look on as inland towns, could be reached by a medieval ship of ordinary size, and were regarded as seaports. Their position attracted foreign traders, who brought into port goods far in excess of what the inhabitants required for their own use. The wealthier inhabitants deliberately bought more than they required, and sold the surplus at a profit after the traders had departed.   In this way a merchant class came into existence.   Nor were these merchants all Scottish: Queen Margaret and her successors encouraged foreign traders to settle in Scotland; in Berwick, for example, there was a large colony of Flemings.   On the other hand, all the goods that were sold in a Scottish burgh were not imported from over-seas; some were made by the local craftsmen. They too made more than their fellow-towns-men required, in the hope that, sooner or later, the surplus would be bought by people from the rural districts near the burgh.

So a burgh was more than a collection of houses, it was a trading community.   But all trading communities were not necessarily burghs; they be-came burghs in the full sense of the word only when they enjoyed certain definite rights

SEAL OF THE BURGH OF ABERDEEN IN USE PRIOR TO 1440

The cast was taken from the Burgh seal affixed to a Bond of Ransom for David II, 1359 (see p. 149), and pre-served in the Public Record Office, London

or 'liberties', granted to them by the King or by some great lord, and embodied in a written 'charter'.   The members of such a privileged community were allowed to manage their own affairs, or rather to elect officials who would direct the policy of the burgh, make special laws, settle disputes between one burgess and another, and punish evil-doers.   In addition, the burgh was given a monopoly of the trade of the district in which it was situated; for example, every foreign ship that entered the Firth of Tay was expected to put in first of all at the port of Dundee.   Only after the wares that it carried had been displayed in the market-place, only after the Dundee merchants had chosen what they wanted, was it allowed to proceed up-stream to the rival burgh of Perth. Nor was that all: within the sheriffdom of Forfar no one who was not a burgess of Dundee was allowed to buy wool and hides, the only Scottish commodities, with the exception of salt fish, that the foreign merchants were eager to take home with them. So the foreign merchant could buy wool only from a burgess. Further, the weekly market and annual fair were taken under the King's protection: to assault or rob any one coming from or going to a fair or market was looked on as an offence against the King himself, to be dealt with, not by the burgh officials, but by the sheriff or some other representative of the sovereign.

The burgesses had to give something in return; for the land which he held within the burgh, every burgess had to pay an annual rent of seven pence to the King's Chamberlain. It seems a paltry sum, but the thirteenth-century master crafts- man never dreamt of paying more to his journeyman for a week's work.

The burgh, as we have seen, was self-governing. The King or his Chamberlain may have appointed the mayor or chief magistrate to begin with, but in the thirteenth century the mayor, the four bailies, and the treasurer were appointed by the burgh council, which in its turn was elected by the whole body of the burgesses. Such a burgh could not be browbeaten by any baron, however powerful he might be, for the burgesses, like the great barons themselves, owed allegiance to the King, and to the King alone. Not all the Scottish burghs, however, were royal burghs; in some, like St. Andrews and Glasgow, the burgesses were vassals of the bishop; in a few, of some great earl or baron.

Though none of the burgesses was very rich, and none very poor, a thirteenth-century trading community was not exactly a band of brothers. They might present a united front to out- siders, but they were divided themselves: the merchants were in general more wealthy than the craftsmen; they knew that without trade the prosperity of the burgh would disappear, and so they began to look on themselves as more important than they really were. They strengthened their position by organizing themselves into a Merchant Gild, from which all craftsmen, however wealthy, were excluded. The gild con-

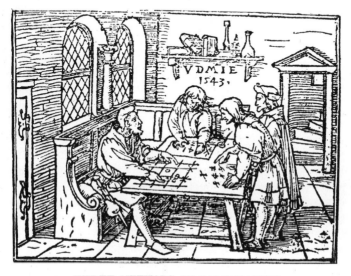

THREE METHODS OF CALCULATING
With casting-counters, ciphering on paper with pen and ink,
and reckoning with chalk

trolled the wholesale and the external trade of the burgh; if a strange merchant came to town, he had to display his wares first of all to the members of the gild, and similarly no burgess who was not a member of the gild could put his goods on a ship bound for a foreign port. And just because the gild included the majority of the wealthiest and most influential burgesses, it came in many places to control the government of the burgh; the members of the burgh council were most of them gild brethren, and the gild hall was used indifferently for meetings of the council and of the gild.

We have seen what a twelfth-century monastery and a thirteenth-century castle looked like; can we form any very clear idea of the appearance of a thirteenth-century burgh? It will be all but impossible, for though the castle and the church have sometimes survived, the dwellings of the thirteenth-century merchants and craftsmen have long since disappeared; our most ancient town houses are not much more than four hundred years old. But suppose we make the attempt; suppose we take a modern industrial town, Dundee, for example, and try to see it as it was in the year before the death of Alexander III.

We look, and in a moment the wilderness of stone and mortar—tall, gaunt tenements, villas, factories, towering chimneys, warehouses, wharves—seven miles from end to end, shrinks into a little cluster of houses, strung along the two sides of a single broad street. Behind the lines of houses long, narrow gardens stretch north and south, for every town then was a garden city. Beyond the gardens on the landward side is a broad stretch of cornland, and beyond that again rough pasture covered with whin and broom, for the burgesses are not all merchants or craftsmen, some are farmers, grazing their sheep and cattle on the common pasture, growing wheat and oats in their holdings in the burgh fields, and taking their corn to be ground in the burgh mill. Town wall there was none, though the east and west ends of the solitary street are protected by a substantial gate-house. But you will not linger outside these ports, as they are called, else you will be beset by creatures whose faces have been eaten away by some strange disease, who stretch out wooden bowls to you, and, in hoarse, unhuman voices demand an alms. They are lepers, who have been thrust out of the town, and who will be killed if they dare to enter again.

You hurry through the East Port, and find yourself in the one main street, the Mercat Gait, or Market Street, as it is called. You notice few houses of any size; even the mayor is content with a squat little wooden structure, roofed with thatch. There are one or two more imposing buildings, however; the east end of the burgh is dominated by the castle, perched on an eminence that rises sheer from the water's edge; at the west end rises the parish church. About half-way between them another of the rare stone buildings catches the eye; the pillar on the stone pedestal in front of it tells you what it is: it is the gild hall, and the pillar is the market cross. The market cross, you may say, is the very heart of the burgh. It is here that strange merchants have to display their goods to the burgesses; it is at the tron, a great balance a yard or two away, that their goods have to be weighed; it is from the steps of the pedestal that the town-crier announces any new regulation made by the rulers of the burgh; it is from the same steps that the royal herald or pursuivant, all glorious in his tabard of scarlet and gold, announces the forthcoming visit of the King, or of his representative, the Justiciar of Scotland. Another group of stone buildings stands beyond the gardens to the north of the town. We would call it a monastery, but the inmates are not monks. They are friars, Franciscan or Grey Friars, to be exact; members of one of the new religious orders that came to Scotland about the middle of the thirteenth century. Like their rivals, the Dominicans, or Black Friars, they considered that their duty was not to shut themselves up away from the world, but to go out into the world and do the work that the parish priest often left half done. They knew how to preach, but though their audiences were thrilled by their eloquence, they were moved even more by their devotion to a life of poverty and good works.

As you move along the street you see nothing that you can recognize as a shop. Shops there are indeed, but they have no windows by which you can identify them, and they are few in number. For the average household is practically self-supporting; the housewife and her daughters bake bread, brew ale—there is no coffee or tea—spin and weave, and make the cloth into garments. People's wants are few: a furniture shop would not thrive in a town where the best room in the mayor's house is furnished with a trestle table, one solitary chair, and a few stools and benches. There can be no china shops when no one knows how to make china, no confectioners' shops when sugar is unknown.

Most of such buying and selling as there is takes place at the weekly market, when people come in from the neighbouring districts to buy what their own villages cannot produce. Then you will see stalls set up in the middle of the street and surrounded by a motley throng, in which the herdsman from the Sidlaws, as shaggy and towsled as his own cattle, rubs shoulders with the merchant, very stately in his long robe, with the hood flung over his shoulder, or the merchant's wife, whom you would mistake for a nun, if you judged her by the cut, and not by the gay colour, of her raiment.

On the fifteenth of August the stalls are more numerous and the crowd about them far larger; it is the first day of the Lady Mary Fair, the great annual fair which lasts for a week. The people of Dundee, like the people of other Scottish burghs, have found that their community cannot be absolutely self-contained and self-supporting. The bailie's wife would fain rustle in silks, but only coarse homespun can be obtained in Dundee; she wants pungent spices to disguise the taste of the salt meat that must be her diet for almost six months of the year, but cinnamon, ginger, cloves, and nutmeg do not grow in Scotland; she has seen a panel of tapestry in the mayor's house, and is determined to have one like it, but no Dundee webster would attempt to weave these gay, pictured cloths. The bailie would like something better than home-brewed ale to set before the mayor or the dean of the gild; his business has prospered and he wants to invest his money in jewellery for his wife, and in two or three pieces of silver plate, but wine and wine-cups must alike be brought from over the sea. In the fair week, however, silks and spices, wines and silver plate, may be obtained by all who can pay for them, for merchants from England, France, and Flanders have set up stalls in the Mercat Gait on which these costly wares are displayed.

Hovering on the verge of the crowd you may notice a mail-clad knight with a party of spearmen. He is the Constable or Keeper of the Castle, the King's special representative in these parts. Usually he does not interfere if any disorder breaks out in the town—that is the bailies' business, not his—but in the fair week it is different: a breach of the peace is a breach of the King's peace, and the offender must be haled off to the castle, to hear his sentence from the mouth of the constable.

For though the burgh, like the baron's estate, was almost a kingdom within a kingdom, the burgh was not absolutely independent and self-contained, nor was the baron's will always law, even on his own estate. Certain crimes, like murder, were deemed too serious to be dealt with by an ordinary court; persons suspected of these crimes had to be handed over to the sheriff of the county, who either pronounced sentence himself, or waited till the royal Justiciar or the King appeared to relieve him of the responsibility. The King had two justiciars: one, the Justiciar of Scotland, toured through the northern half of the kingdom at regular intervals; the other, the Justiciar of Lothian, perambulated the country south of the Forth. A conscientious king like Alexander III was not content with this; he knew that a justiciar might become slack, or a sheriff allow himself to be browbeaten by a powerful baron, so with his great officers of state he travelled from one county town to another, pronouncing sentence at each on such criminals as the sheriff brought before him, or dealing with complaints from people to whom the sheriff had failed to do justice.

Most people preferred King's justice to baron's justice, but both were equally rough and ready. If a man accused of a felony could produce twenty-four people willing to swear that he had not committed it he got off. If he failed to produce the required number, or if his accuser arrived with another twenty-four, various things might happen, but no one would dream of cross-questioning the twenty-four 'witnesses', and asking them if they really knew anything about the crime. The accused might be required to fight his accuser, or to grasp a bar of red-hot iron. 'God will not allow the innocent to be hurt,' argued the pious but indolent judge. Or he might be flung into a pool of water; it made little difference what happened then, for only if he sank was he pronounced to be innocent. Imprisonment was not a popular penalty with the judge; how liberally he dealt out the sentence of death we can estimate from the humane statute which recommended that no man should be hanged for theft unless he had stolen at least two sheep. Sometimes, however, the penalty fitted the crime; if a man drew a knife and threatened to strike, that same knife was driven through his own hand; if he struck and drew blood, his hand was cut off.

But wild justice, as the people of Scotland were soon to learn, was better than no justice at all. In 1285 some vague premonition of coming evil disturbed their minds; all over the country ran the frightened whisper that the Day of Judgement would come at the end of the year. A terrific storm of snow and lightning at Christmas confirmed their fears; still, nothing untoward happened till the 19th of March, 1286,[1] when a

---

[1] Until 1600 in Scotland, and until 1752 in England, the 24th of March was looked on as the end of the Old Year. What we call 19th March, 1286, was therefore, to the people of that time, 19th March, 1285. So, though March had come, the Old Year had not yet gone.

tempest of wind and rain swept over Scotland. But though it buffeted the towers and walls of Edinburgh Castle it did not perturb the King as he sat within, discussing affairs of state with his Chancellor and the two dozen prelates and great barons who made up his council. He even joked about the prophecy; when the discussion was over and dinner had been brought in he ordered a dish of eels to be set before one of his barons, and told him, with a laugh, to eat heartily, as this was the Day of Judgement.

Afternoon was darkening into evening when the King horrified his lords by announcing that he intended to cross the Forth that very night and ride to Kinghorn, where Queen Yolande, was living.[1] They tried to dissuade him, for the wind was howling more loudly than ever, but the King would listen to no entreaties; with three followers he rode off through the driving rain to South Queensferry. There the master of the ferry-boat urged him to go back. 'Are you afraid to die with me?' asked the King. 'Far be it from me, sire,' answered the man; 'it well befits me to meet my fate in company with your father's son.'

He reached Inverkeithing in safety, and, after obtaining two guides, set off on the last stage of his journey. But the tempest raged more furiously than ever, and in the pitch-black night the King became separated from his companions. They shouted, but no answer came except the wild, melancholy shriek of the wind; he had vanished into the darkness.

Next morning the mystery was solved; the King's dead body was found on the beach, bruised and broken as if by a fall from his horse.

The Day of Judgement had come.

[1] Alexander's first wife, Margaret, daughter of Henry III of England, died in 1275. In 1285 he married Yolande, daughter of the French Count of Dreux.

COIN OF JOHN BALLIOL

CHAPTER X

THE SCOTTISH WAR OF INDEPENDENCE
FIRST STAGE: 1286–1306

Long afterward did Scotland know
Fell Edward as her deadliest foe.

SCOTLAND was indeed 'stad in perplexity'; troubled by the foreboding of an approaching calamity, but ignorant of the quarter from which the danger was to come. Though Alexander III was not an old man, he had outlived all his children; his sole living descendant was a little girl of three, the only child of his daughter Margaret, who had married King Eric of Norway. But how could this little 'Maid of Norway' control an 'old and haughty nation, proud in arms'? Might not some proud and ambitious baron, some distant relation of the King, grasp the crown before the girl-queen had crossed the seas? There was the old Lord of Annandale, Robert de Brus, who had been acknowledged heir to the throne almost half a century before, at a time when Alexander II thought that he was destined to die childless. He was convinced that he ought to be King. What if he defied those who thought differently, and plunged the country into civil war? But for a time nothing very dreadful happened; a few weeks after the King's death the Scottish nobles and prelates appointed six Guardians to rule the country in the name of the young Queen.

Meanwhile one very shrewd and ambitious person had been

watching the turn that affairs were taking in Scotland. In the hour of his most bitter affliction King Alexander seemed to feel that the one thing sure in a world of uncertainties was the friendship of his brother-in-law, Edward of England. 'Death only can dissolve our league of amity,' the bereaved King had protested. Little did Alexander dream that when death came to Edward the sculptors would inscribe on his tomb 'Here lies King Edward, the Hammer of the Scots'. Alexander did not judge Edward's character amiss. He was a staunch friend, a gallant and fearless enemy, a man with a very clear sense of what was right and wrong, of what was reasonable and what absurd, a man who prided himself on keeping his word whatever the cost might be.

It seemed absurd to him that the island of Britain should be divided into three separate countries, each with its own ruler and its own separate laws. A few years before he had succeeded in making himself master of Wales; he would not see anything wrong in making himself master of Scotland if the opportunity should occur. The Scots would be no worse off under him, and, besides, their kings had often done homage to English kings in the past. If an eleventh-century King of Scots had acknowledged that he was the King's 'man', then the thirteenth-century King of England must be the lawful master of the realm of Scotland.

Edward was right up to a certain point: an enduring friendship between the two countries could bring nothing but gain to both. And up to a certain point his conduct was wise and tactful; he secured the consent of the Scottish nobles to the marriage of their young Queen to his son, Edward of Carnarvon, afterwards the luckless Edward II. But the death of the Maid in 1290 brought his scheme to naught. The game was lost, it seemed; he must stand aside and watch old Robert de Brus make himself King of Scotland.

But the Scots themselves would not let Edward stand aside.

The old Lord of Annandale, with a formidable company, had come to Perth; it was plain that, in spite of the opposition of the Guardians, he meant to be crowned King of Scotland; it was plain, too, that if he did succeed in his attempt, he would be attacked at once by one of the eleven other great nobles who asserted that their claim to the crown was better than his. But they were in no stronger position than De Brus; not one of them could be sure of the undivided support of his countrymen. Civil war was inevitable, unless the Scots could find some one in whose wisdom and impartiality they had absolute confidence, whom they could ask to decide the dispute about the succession.

Such a disinterested judge they seemed to have in the person of Edward I. An invitation was issued to Edward to act as arbiter; he accepted, and in 1291 he met the nobles and prelates of Scotland at Norham on the Tweed. The opportunity had presented itself at last, and he yielded to the temptation; it was announced that no candidate would be considered who did not acknowledge Edward as his overlord, and promise to do homage to him for the whole of Scotland, should he be lucky enough to be awarded the crown. The Scottish nobles yielded to the temptation too; if the price of a crown was dependence on Edward, they were quite willing to pay the price. After all, they probably argued, the oath of fealty was little more than a form; the Scottish borders were two weeks' march from Westminster, and the King could not, even if he would, meddle with purely Scottish affairs. They did not know Edward.

It was soon discovered by the auditors to whom Edward remitted the case that the claims of only two of the competitors required to be seriously discussed. One was the old Lord of Annandale, the son of the second daughter of David, Earl of Huntingdon, the younger brother of William the Lion; the other was John de Balliol, a grandson of the eldest daughter of Earl David. The auditors were hopelessly perplexed; if Scotland had been a private estate they might have divided it into three, and assigned the parts to Brus, Balliol, and John de Hastings, the grandson of Earl David's third daughter. But Scotland was not an ordinary estate, and the ordinary rules of succession might not hold. Towards the end of 1292 they referred the matter back to Edward, who decided in favour of Balliol, and at Christmas the new King went to Newcastle and did homage to Edward for his kingdom.

Edward's conscience was absolutely clear. He had kept to the letter of the law; he had given the crown of Scotland to the man who had the best claim to it. And he intended to keep to the letter of the law in future; he would let Balliol see that his homage was not an empty form, that by accepting a king of England as his lord he had reduced himself to the level of an ordinary English baron, and his kingdom to the level of an ordinary English county. He would impose one or two tests, then, if Balliol proved docile, Edward would know that he had conquered Scotland without striking a blow; if Balliol resented his overlord's interference, Edward would treat him as any contumacious vassal ought to be treated and deprive him of his kingdom. So Edward let no chance slip of reminding Balliol that he was not master in his own house; he displayed a remarkable degree of sympathy with any one who complained that he had not obtained justice in the Scottish courts. When one of Edward's Gascon subjects complained that he had dunned Balliol in vain for the sum of £2,000 in payment of wine consumed by his predecessor Alexander, Edward summoned the King of Scots to appear at Westminster and explain why he had not paid his wine merchant's bill. Complaints from King John's own subjects received the same over-scrupulous attention, till at length the docile and long-suffering Balliol began to understand why his people called him 'the Toom Tabard'. He was an 'empty-coat', a 'king of shreds and patches'; the real King of Scotland was not John de Balliol, but Edward Plantagenet.

There seemed to be only one way out of this intolerable position. Balliol knew that Edward had quarrelled with the King of France and was meditating an invasion of his country, so when he received orders to follow Edward across the Channel he flatly refused, and in the autumn of 1295 he entered into an alliance with Philip of France.

Edward was furious when he learned that the worm had turned at last. 'Ah! this foolish scoundrel,' he exclaimed, 'what folly he has committed! If he won't come to us, we will go to him.'

He kept his promise. In the spring of 1296 he crossed the Tweed at Coldstream and suddenly appeared outside Berwick, which, like most Scottish towns, was unwalled, with no defences except a shallow ditch and a hastily constructed palisade. But the burgesses were full of confidence; as the English squadrons approached they chanted a derisive song:

> What! weens King Edward with long shanks
> To have won Berwick all our unthanks?
> Go pike him.
> And when he hath it
> Go dike him.[1]

Suddenly the trumpets blared; the English soldiers rushed across the ditch, swarmed over the palisade 'as if it were a thing of naught', and fell upon the burgesses, who were so stupefied with astonishment and fear that they stood like men in a trance, not offering to raise a sword or bend a bow. In a few minutes the town was in Edward's hands. Only at two points was any resistance offered—at the Red Hall, the hostel occupied by the Flemish merchants who traded in the burgh, and at the castle. The castle surrendered before nightfall; the thirty gallant Flemings, however, defended their hall even after it had been set on fire, and to a man perished in the flames.

[1] What! does long-legged King Edward think that he can win Berwick in spite of us? Let him build a fence, and then, when he has it, let him build a ditch.

Edward determined to teach a lesson to Berwick and to the whole of Scotland; for three days he let his soldiers roam through the streets at will, killing and plundering. Only when the King saw an infant crying and clinging to its dead mother did he turn away in horror from what after all was his own handiwork, and cry 'Laissez! laissez!'

While Edward stayed behind in Berwick superintending the building of stouter fortifications, his lieutenant, the Earl de Warenne, hurried forward to besiege the powerful castle of Dunbar. But the defenders sent an appeal for help to Balliol, and went almost mad with delight when a powerful relieving army appeared. They waved flags from the battlements and shouted insults to the besiegers, calling them long-tailed curs, and threatening to kill them and cut off their tails. For the more ignorant Scots believed then, and long afterwards, that the English did actually have tails. But Berwick had taught the besiegers how much the insults of the Scots were worth. Leaving a small force to watch the castle, they advanced in good order to meet the relieving army, but fell into some confusion as they crossed a ravine that separated them from the Scots. Again the shout of exultation arose, mingled this time with the blast of horns 'terrible enough to reach to the uttermost depths of hell'. But the shouting died away when the English ranks closed, and the phalanx of mail-clad men-at-arms loomed up only a few yards away. The miserable story of Berwick was repeated; a sudden panic seized these warriors who had never before gazed upon the stern face of War, and they took to their heels. The English walked into the castle of Dunbar unopposed.

The news of these two disasters paralysed nobles and people alike. They seemed to look on Edward as invincible. The defenders of the powerful border castle of Roxburgh surrendered the moment they were asked to do so; Edinburgh Castle held out for eight days; the garrison of Stirling prudently cleared out as soon as word was brought of Edward's approach. Finally, when Edward reached Perth, three months after he had first crossed the Tweed, he received a letter from Balliol praying for peace 'not according to his own deserts, but according to the King's loving kindness'. A fortnight later, in the hall of Brechin Castle, Balliol, who had already repudiated his alliance with France, formally surrendered his kingdom to Edward.

The remainder of Edward's first Scottish campaign was simply a triumphal procession; he marched northward unopposed as far as Elgin, halted at the Abbey of Scone on his way south to remove the Stone of Destiny on which the Kings of Scots from time immemorial had been crowned, and returned to Berwick, to hold a Parliament at which practically every man of note in Scotland did homage to him.

So in the autumn of 1296 King Edward crossed the Tweed well content; it had taken him ten years to subdue the little country of Wales; he had conquered Scotland in half as many months.

But the campaign of 1296 had not been a fight to a finish, and the Scots, after they had gained some experience of the ways of English officials and English garrisons, began to wish that they had fought a little harder. But where were they to find a leader? Balliol had proved himself to be a 'toom tabard' after all; old de Brus was dead and his son had supported Edward in the vain hope that Edward would hand over the kingdom to him after he had defeated Balliol. His grandson, the young Earl of Carrick, had ambition and ability, but he could not be trusted to run straight; he did not want to see Edward King of Scotland, but still less did he want to see the feckless Balliol back again, and least of all did he want to do anything that would set Balliol's kinsman John Comyn, Lord of Badenoch on the throne. So he pursued a zigzag course, appearing now as a Scottish patriot, now as Edward's ally.

Salvation came, not from any of the noble or semi-royal families of Scotland, but from a 'kinless loon', knighted no one knew when or by whom. In the early summer of 1297 William Wallace slew the English Sheriff of Lanark; then with a band of determined men which grew in numbers daily he advanced into the north of Scotland, and set about capturing the castles that had been manned by English troops. Castle after castle fell into his hands, but while he was besieging the castle of Dundee, news was brought to him that the Guardian of Scotland, old Earl de Warenne, had shaken off his lethargy and was advancing on Stirling. Wallace hurried southward and posted his army at the northern end of the narrow wooden bridge that spanned the Forth.

To Wallace it must have seemed a desperate gamble. He was outnumbered; he had no heavy cavalry—and in those days battles were decided by the heavy cavalry—and his position was not so strong as it looked. Though the bridge was so narrow that horsemen had to cross it two abreast, there was a ford not far away where sixty horsemen could cross at once. But the English leadership at Stirling was as bad as the Scottish leadership had been at Dunbar. The commander was old and sleepy, and his second in command, Hugh de Cressingham, the Treasurer of Scotland, was a fat and conceited churchman who had turned amateur soldier. So it came about that a large body of English troops actually crossed the river before the Scots were ready for them, and after waiting in vain for orders from their slumbering commander, retreated to their own side of the stream. So it came about that, after precious hours had been wasted, De Warenne refused to let the troops cross by the ford, and Cressingham bullied them into crossing by the bridge. No one molested them, the King's standard-bearer, the handsome and insolent Treasurer, the long line of knights in their glittering mail, the dark, squat bowmen from Wales, all passed undisturbed.

But Wallace knew what he was about; his men, lying almost invisible on the hill-side, only waited the word to charge. When barely half the hostile army had crossed the word was given; the Scots rushed pell-mell down the slope, and while one party made straight for the bridge, cutting the English army in two, the remainder hurled themselves upon the distracted vanguard. On the bridge itself confusion reigned; of the mob of armed men that surged to and fro many were swept off and drowned. Meanwhile De Warenne could do nothing but gaze helplessly at his vanguard being cut to pieces; then after ordering the bridge to be broken down and burned, he returned to Berwick with more alacrity than one would have expected from one of his years. Cressingham's dead body remained on the field of battle.

The victory of Stirling Bridge made Wallace master of southern Scotland. Nor was he content to remain on the defensive; before the end of the year he had raided the northern counties of England.

But though by his prowess in the field Wallace had won the title of Guardian of Scotland, his position in 1298 was really a precarious one. An unknown knight could not command the allegiance of the great Scottish nobles; gallant soldier as he was he could not hope to be a match for one of the most skilful generals in Europe, for it was with Edward himself that he had now to deal. So when on a summer morning he stood on a moor beside Falkirk and compared the proud squadrons of mail-clad knights with his own little army—some cavalry whom he did not trust, four circles or 'schiltroms' of spearmen joined up by lines of archers in loose formation—he can have had little doubt of the result. Yet for a time it seemed as if the day might go in his favour. The foremost division of English cavalry charged straight down on the enemy, and plunged into a marsh which guarded the front of the Scottish line. The second division, headed by the warlike Bishop of Durham, made a detour to the east, and arrived without mis-

hap on the left flank of the Scots. The bishop signalled to
them to halt till the third line came up, but in vain. 'Leave
soldiering alone, Bishop, and get on with your mass,' shouted
the young knights as they galloped down upon the Scots. The
Scottish cavalry fled almost without striking a blow; but
though the English horsemen easily overwhelmed the lightly

WESTMINSTER HALL

armed archers they recoiled baffled from the impenetrable
hedge of spears. Again and again they charged, but if a front
rank man fell a rear rank man stepped into his place; the circle
remained unbroken.

The end was not far off. The English archers picked their
way forward to the edge of the marsh, and drawing the cords
of their great long bows back to their shoulders, they loosed
flight after flight of arrows into the serried ranks of the spearmen. It was more than flesh and blood could stand; one after
another the circles were broken, and as the gaps appeared the

English cavalry swept forward and completed what the archers had begun.

If Edward thought that his triumph at Falkirk would reconcile the Scots to his rule, he was mistaken. They never seemed to know when they were beaten; they would be hopelessly smashed in the autumn, mope all winter, and then rebel again in the following spring. Twice did Edward spend Christmas in Scotland and, contrary to the medieval practice, carry on war all through the winter. At last, in 1304, he began to see something definite result from his labours. One after another, the more obstinate patriots surrendered to him; in February his most dangerous opponent next to Wallace, John Comyn, Lord of Badenoch, went over to his side; in July Stirling Castle, the last Scottish fortress to hold out against him, was battered to pieces by his great new engine, the 'War Wolf'.

Only Wallace remained at large, and Wallace was now a hunted outlaw, powerless for good or ill. Then in 1305 Wallace himself was captured, and brought to Westminster Hall to stand his trial for treason. He proudly declared that he was no traitor, that he had never taken the oath of allegiance to an alien monarch, and so could never have broken it. This defence availed nothing; he was found guilty and dragged to the gallows at Tyburn, there to die the unspeakably horrible death that in those days was reserved for traitors.

At last Edward had got his heart's desire.

COIN OF ROBERT BRUCE

CHAPTER XI

THE SCOTTISH WAR OF INDEPENDENCE
SECOND STAGE: 1306–1329

Young Mortimer (*to Edward*): When wert thou in the field with banner
        spread,
    But once? and then thy soldiers marched like players,
    With garish robes, not armour; and thyself,
    Bedaubed with gold, rode laughing at the rest,
    Nodding and shaking of thy spangled crest,
    Where women's favours hung like labels down.

Lancaster: And therefore came it, that the fleering Scots,
    To England's high disgrace, have made this jig:
    'Maids of England, sore may you mourn,—
    For your lemans[1] you have lost at Bannockburn.'

MARLOWE.

King of Scotland		*Kings of England*			
Robert I (The Bruce) .	1306–1329	Edward I	.	.	1272–1307
		Edward II	.	.	1307–1327
		Edward III	.	.	1327–1377

AMONG his Scottish supporters there were few whom
Edward trusted more than the younger Robert de Brus,
Earl of Carrick. It is true that he had taken up arms against
Edward in 1297, but he had laid them down again before the
battle of Stirling Bridge. It is true that after the eclipse of
Wallace at Falkirk he figured for a short time as Guardian of
Scotland, but he went over to Edward's side in 1302, taking all

[1] lovers.

his own vassals with him, followed him to Scotland in his last campaign, served as commander of the English garrison at Ayr, and supplied him with engines for the siege of Stirling Castle. Edward did not suspect that Bruce might have sided with him partly out of regard for the safety of his cautious, time-serving father, and partly through jealousy of his rival, John Comyn; he did not guess the effect that the surrender of Comyn and the death of the elder Bruce in 1304 would have on a mind as keen and ambitious as his own, nor did he know that at the very time when Bruce did homage to him for his father's English estates, he was actually negotiating with the Bishop of St. Andrews for his support in an attempt on the Scottish crown.

Bruce gained Bishop Lamberton's support easily enough— the Scottish clergy feared that the rule of an English archbishop would be the necessary consequence of the rule of an English king—but he found it more difficult to get the support of the powerful Lord of Badenoch. Early in 1306 Bruce invited Comyn to come to the Church of the Greyfriars in Dumfries and there discuss the business, but though Comyn came, he flatly refused to co-operate with Bruce. A blind fury overcame Bruce; he drew his dagger and plunged it into Comyn's body. The friars bore the wounded man from the cloister to the church, and laid him before the high altar, but they were interrupted by Bruce's followers, who rushed in and killed him before the eyes of the terrified clerics.

It was a black and horrible story, and it lost nothing in the telling. Everybody in England believed that Bruce had lured the 'Red Comyn' to Dumfries and deliberately picked a quarrel with him so that he might remove his only possible rival from his path. The best that can be said of it is that it was a ghastly blunder. It drew down on Bruce's head the undying hatred of Comyn's kinsmen and friends, men like the Earl of Buchan, Alexander of Argyll and his son, John of Lorne, and the Mac-

Dowalls of Galloway. So he had to fight with England and half Scotland as well. Worst of all, he had to face the wrath of the Church; as soon as the Pope was informed that Bruce had slain Comyn in a consecrated building, he pronounced on him the dread sentence of excommunication.

When a few weeks later the slayer of Comyn was crowned at Scone with maimed rites, his wife said to him, 'It seems to me that we are but a summer King and Queen, whom the children crown with flowers in their sports'. There was no need for King Edward to come north; Aymer de Valence, his lieutenant, came upon Bruce's army at Methven all unprepared, with no outposts or sentinels, surprised and scattered it, and almost succeeded in capturing Bruce himself.

At the head of a few hundred followers Bruce retreated westward, to the seeming security of the hills and moorlands, only to suffer another crushing defeat at the hands of Alexander of Argyll. The game was played out; in the late autumn of 1306, after dispatching his Queen and his young brother Nigel to the strong castle of Kildrummie, he left Scotland altogether, and took refuge in the island of Rathlin, off the north coast of Ireland.

A weakling would have been broken altogether by these trials, but adversity developed qualities in Bruce that hitherto he had not seemed to possess. He learned to school his temper, to be cheerful and good-humoured whether things went well or ill, to be courteous to friend and foe alike. Best of all, the self-seeking adventurer who would not fight for Scotland if Scotland was not to be his, learned that a great leader, a man who is a king in the fullest sense, must be willing to spend himself in the service of his followers, must do work which is too hard for them, and encounter dangers which they dare not face. Long afterwards did those who had been fugitives from that disastrous battle in the west tell how the King deliberately placed himself in the rear of the retreating army, and how he did not flinch when three Highlanders rushed at him, but waited for them and slew them single-handed.

With the return of spring the King's hopes revived and, accompanied by his brother Edward and his lieutenant Sir James of Douglas, he crossed the sea to his own country of Carrick. News of disaster met him: Kildrummie Castle had been taken, his brother Nigel had died on the scaffold, and the Queen and her ladies were prisoners in the hands of the English. For the high-spirited Countess of Buchan, who had placed the crown on the King's head, Edward reserved a peculiar punishment; he shut her up in a wooden cage within the castle of Berwick.

The King's own prospects were black enough. Fear of the English garrisons kept his Ayrshire vassals from joining him; the armies of John of Lorne and Aymer de Valence were closing in on him from the north and the east; though the hills of Galloway seemed to promise safety, he knew that there lurked the armed forces of the MacDowalls. With his small, badly equipped force he could not risk a battle; if an enemy came in sight he could only order his men to scatter and vanish. Then, separated from his companions, with at most one attendant, he was dependent for his safety on his quick wit and his skill as a swordsman.

Once, for example, John of Lorne almost succeeded in rounding up his little army. The King discovered his danger in time and ordered his men to scatter. His brother Edward went off with one small party, Douglas with another, and he himself with a third. To his astonishment the pursuers did not hesitate, but made straight for the party which he commanded. Again Bruce gave the order; again some strange instinct seemed to tell the Highlanders which knot of fugitives he was with. Even when his following was reduced to one man the whole of John of Lorne's army kept steadily on his track.

The explanation was a simple one: John of Lorne had with

him an innocent traitor, a hunting dog that had belonged to the King, and was now eager to rejoin his master. At a word from John of Lorne five fleet-footed Highlanders now sped after the two fugitives; they overtook Bruce and his companion, but in the wild struggle that followed all five perished, four by the terrible sword of Bruce. The two weary men made their way through a wood to the side of a stream and sank down exhausted, but they had not thrown off their pursuers; a minute or two later the baying of a dog echoed through the trees. For a moment Bruce thought of giving up the struggle, then, followed by his companion, he stepped into the water and, after wading down the stream for some distance, scrambled ashore on the other side. He listened; the disappointed yelping of the dog soon told him that his plan had succeeded.

One would think that he had had more than his fair share of danger and adventure for one day; but no, a few hours later he fell in with three men, one of whom carried a sheep. They approached him and told him that they were looking for Robert the Bruce. 'Come with me and you will find him,' said the King simply. But he was careful to make them walk in front, and though they offered him a share of their sheep when they halted for the night at a ruined house, he insisted on cooking and eating his portion of the meat at a separate fire. Even when he saw the three close their eyes he remained on his guard, but he began to nod over the fire and, after warning his companion to stay on the alert, he fell fast asleep. His companion could not keep awake, and when a chance noise aroused the King a little later he opened his eyes to find the three strangers with their swords drawn ready to close with him. He sprang up and drew his sword, giving his companion a push with his foot as he did so; but before the luckless wretch knew what was amiss he was stricken down by a mortal blow. Then began the struggle of the one wearied man against three, but fatigue did not weaken the arm of Bruce, or fury make him

3437.1   K

forget his skill; one by one the would-be slayers were them-selves slain.

Gradually more men came to his standard; he defeated various small hostile forces, and in the early summer of 1307 he felt strong enough to accept Aymer de Valence's challenge to do battle with him in the open. The two armies met at Loudoun Hill. Every one except Bruce thought that de Valence's squadrons of heavy cavalry would make short work of the scanty band of spearmen opposed to them. But the hidden trenches that Bruce had dug in front of his position flung the dense masses of horsemen into hopeless confusion, and the impetuous charge of the Scottish infantry drove them headlong from the field.

All through the winter of 1306–7 King Edward had been lying in the grip of a mortal sickness at the Priory of Lanercost, near Carlisle. The news of the defeat at Loudoun Hill fanned his dwindling energy into a flame. Again he put himself at the head of his army, though he had to be carried in a litter, but, before he had gone more than a few miles towards Scotland, the flame flickered down, and he knew that his end had come. Even in that awful hour his conscience seems to have been untroubled; his only regret was that he would not live to com-plete the conquest of Scotland. He resolved that if he could not lead the victorious army living he would lead it after he was dead; he gave orders that after his death the north-ward march was to be resumed, and that his bones were to be carried in a leathern sack at the head of the invading army.

His successor paid no heed to his request. For Edward II was a king of a different stamp, brave enough when danger was to be faced, but not over-anxious to seek it out if it could be avoided; fonder of enjoying himself than of organizing foreign conquests or attending to the routine business of govern-ment. As long as the English generals and garrison commanders in Scotland managed to hang on somehow or other, he did not worry over their complaints, or see that they were supplied with the reinforcements and provisions that they demanded.

And they did hang on for some time, for Bruce first gave all his attention to those Scots who were hostile to his cause. At the beginning of 1308 he devastated the district of Buchan, one of the strongholds of the Comyns, and in the summer of the same year he penetrated into Argyll and drove both John of Lorne and his father, Alexander of Argyll, from the kingdom.

The turn of the castles came at last. The walled town of Perth was the first to go. In 1312 some Scottish troops appeared before it, only to recoil in seeming dismay from the broad and deep moat by which it was surrounded. But Bruce had ordered soundings to be taken, and a fortnight later he returned at dead of night, led his men across the moat at the one place where it could be forded, over the walls, and into the sleeping town. The castles of Dundee and Dumfries soon followed; then in the early summer of 1313, Bruce dispatched his brother Edward to besiege the castle of Stirling, which, looking down as it did on Stirling Bridge, commanded the easiest route between northern and southern Scotland.

Edward Bruce had already distinguished himself by capturing thirteen castles in Galloway within a single year, but most of them were 'peels', the old-fashioned timber block-houses and palisades. The capture of the big stone castles, many of which had been rebuilt or strengthened by Edward's skilled engineers, was a much more difficult matter, especially to a besieging general unprovided with siege artillery and with only a handful of troops. He could do one of two things: he could capture the fortress by a trick, as the King had done at Perth, or he could cut off its supplies and starve it out, as he himself had done at Dundee. But the second method demanded patience, and excess of patience was not one of Edward Bruce's faults. As he looked at the frowning crags, topped by the massive walls of the fortress, he remembered that in 1304 King Edward's mangonels and trebuchets and 'war wolves' had battered at it for three months before the garrison had seen fit to surrender. So when Sir Philip de Mou-bray, the Governor, offered to surrender the castle without any fighting if it was not relieved by the English King within a twelvemonth, Edward Bruce gladly consented.

The King did not share his delight with the bargain. He had taken risks in his time—no man more—but he fought for victory, not for fun, and if victory could be got without actual fighting, he preferred not to fight. In 1310, for example, he had baffled an attempt at invasion by laying waste the country through which the English army had to advance, and then retreating before them till they were exhausted by hunger and fatigue. But this agreement pinned him down to fighting on a definite spot at a definite time, against an army far superior to his own in numbers and equipment. For there was no doubt that King Edward would accept the challenge; the successful Scottish counter-raids of 1312 and 1313, following on his own unsuccessful invasion of 1310, made his northern subjects complain bitterly of his lethargy, and he knew that if he let Stirling Castle go without a fight, there was more than a chance that he would have to deal with a rebellion in his own kingdom.

Meantime the capture of the castles continued. Roxburgh fell on a night in the year 1314, when the hall of the castle was crowded with Shrovetide revellers. The sentinels had noticed what in the gathering dark seemed to be a herd of cattle grazing in the meadows, but naturally did not challenge them even when they came to the foot of the castle wall. It would have been well for them if they had given the alarm, for the horned beasts were none other than Douglas and his men. Edinburgh went a few weeks later. One dark night, while the main part of the besieging force thundered at the gatehouse of the castle, Thomas Randolph, the King's nephew, led a band of thirty men up the face of the castle rock, scrambled over the unguarded wall, and gained possession of the castle before the garrison knew what had happened.

But these exploits could not delay the inevitable approach of the English army. On the 23rd of June, 1314, from his position two miles to the south of Stirling, Bruce looked with feelings akin to those of Wallace before Falkirk at the squadrons of cavalry with dancing plumes and banners, and the companies of archers, which advanced in seemingly endless procession. He had an army of only six or seven thousand men —spearmen, with a handful of light cavalry—to oppose to a force three times as large. Still, he had tried to make the best of a bad bargain. He had chosen his position carefully: westward, on his right flank, loomed the dense forest of the Torwood; along his front flowed the Bannock Burn; a little to his left stretched almost impassable marshes, through which the Bannock Burn meandered till it joined the Forth about three miles east of Stirling. He had strengthened his position, too, by constructing a multitude of concealed pits in the firm ground immediately to the north of the stream.

But things did not fall out exactly as the King had planned. A large body of English cavalry under Sir Robert de Clifford made a detour and succeeded in crossing the Bannock Burn unopposed and in getting almost half-way to Stirling unobserved by Randolph, who had been told to look out for such a movement. The King's eyes were quicker than those of his lieutenant; he rode up to Randolph and said, 'Sir Thomas, a rose has fallen from your chaplet'. Randolph took the hint, and at the head of his division of infantry set off in pursuit of the English horsemen. It seemed to be an utterly mad attempt, but it succeeded; the young knights in De Clifford's division, instead of holding on their course and setting the castle free, turned about and charged the marching infantry. At a word

from Randolph the ranks closed, and an unbroken line of
bristling spears confronted the English horsemen. They
charged again and again, but they could not bend or break the
ring of steel, and when they saw another body of Scots
approaching they turned tail and rode off to the main army.

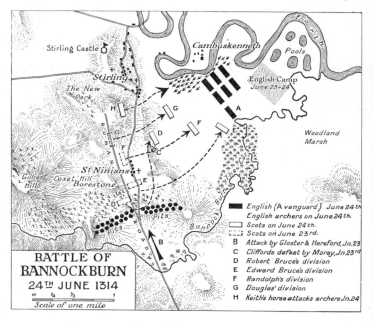

Stirling Castle

Cambuskenneth   Pools

Stirling

The New
Park

English Camp
June 23–24

H   G

Woodland
Marsh

D

C

F

A

St Ninians

Coxet Hill
Borestone

Gilles
Hill

Pits

Bannock Burn

■■ English (A vanguard) June 24th
✦ English archers on June 24th.
☐ Scots on June 24th.
⌐⌐ Scots on June 23rd.
B   Attack by Gloster & Hereford, Jn.23
C   Cliffords defeat by Moray, Jn. 23rd
D   Robert Bruce's division
E   Edward Bruce's division
F   Randolph's division
G   Douglas' division
H   Keith's horse attacks archers Jn.24

**BATTLE OF
BANNOCKBURN
24TH JUNE 1314**

0   ¼   ½   1
Scale of one mile

Meantime the Bannock Burn had been crossed nearer the
Scottish position by another body of cavalry under the Earl
of Gloucester. One of the English knights, Sir Humphrey de
Bohun, who rode a little in advance of his comrades, attracted
the attention of a horseman who had been riding slowly along
the Scottish ranks. This horseman, though he bore no lance
and was mounted on a light palfrey, turned and deliberately
approached the venturesome knight. De Bohun clapped spurs
to his steed, levelled his lance, and galloped down on the Scot,

who waited calmly, then swerved quickly aside to avoid his
impetuous rush, and, as he passed, cleft his skull with one
mighty blow of his battle-axe.

As the victor rode back the English horsemen noticed that
his leathern helmet was encircled by a slender band of gold;
they knew then that their comrade had been killed by the
King of Scots himself. They charged, but half-heartedly, and
they were easily repulsed.

Two attempts to cross the Bannock Burn and to break
through to Stirling had now been made and had failed, but
late at night the English army swept round to the east,
plashed through the Bannock Burn not far from the point
where it falls into the Forth, and, weary and disheartened,
bivouacked among the pools and marshes in the Carse of
Stirling. This movement caused dismay among the Scottish
leaders; their flank had been turned; the English were in communication with Stirling Castle and were threatening their
rear. To slip out of this too tight corner seemed the only
sensible course, and the King had actually decided to retreat,
when a stranger was ushered into his presence. He was Sir
Alexander de Setoun, a Scottish knight in the English service
who had repented at the eleventh hour. He had come to tell
the King that the English were depressed out of measure by
their two reverses, and that if the Scots chose to attack they
would almost certainly have the victory. There was a chance,
Bruce saw, and the prize was enormous; he decided to attack
when morning came.

When at sunrise on the twenty-fourth of June Edward
looked westward and saw four bodies of Scottish spearmen
advancing in good order towards him he could think of only
one explanation. His surmise seemed to be confirmed when
the Scots halted and dropped on their knees. 'Ha!' he said
to a veteran knight who rode at his elbow, 'they kneel
to ask for mercy.' 'They do indeed ask for mercy,' replied

De Umfraville grimly, 'but not of you. I tell you, these men will not flee for any fear of death.'

There was method in Bruce's madness: he had no mind to stand on the defensive and see his closely packed schiltroms first riddled with arrows, and then ridden down by the English knights; he intended to launch his men on the English while they were still crowded together in the narrow wedge of land between the Forth and the Bannock Burn, and so make their superior numbers of no avail. It all worked out as he had planned; the four clumps of spearmen advanced unmolested by the English archers, who had been pushed aside and ridden down by their own over-eager cavalry, and crashed one after another into the confused mass of mailclad horsemen. It seemed at first that they would be completely submerged, but they fought with a cold, silent fury, refusing to recoil when the crested and armoured knights swept down upon them, but keeping shoulder to shoulder, thrusting their spears into the bodies of the chargers, and so bringing horse and rider to the ground. But what Bruce had feared came to pass: the English archers at last struggled clear of the press of knights, took up their position on the flank of the Scots, and sent volley after volley into their ranks. At a word from the King, however, a small body of cavalry which he had kept in reserve dashed among the archers and scattered them like chaff.

Though the Scots fought with an even fiercer fury than before, the issue of the battle was still doubtful, there was still the fear that they might be rolled back by sheer weight of numbers. Suddenly help came from an unexpected quarter: to the surprise of English and Scots alike a host with banners displayed appeared a little to the rear of the Scottish position, and with wild shouts of 'Slay! slay!' advanced to the help of their comrades. It was too much for the sorely pressed English, who did not guess that this terrible new army was composed of the ragtag and bobtail of Bruce's camp, marching to battle under banners of sheets and blankets; at the next surge forward of the reinforced Scottish battalions they recoiled, broke, and fled, or rather, tried to flee.

For they were trapped, pinned down to a narrow wedge of marshy land. Many tried to swim the Forth and were drowned, many sank in the mud, or were trampled underfoot as they

ARCHERS OF THE FOURTEENTH CENTURY

scrambled southward across the shallower stream. Some, including King Edward himself, fled to the castle, but the Governor, faithful to his bargain, shut the doors against them, and the King had no alternative but to make his way to the castle of Dunbar with a handful of knights. Thence he escaped in a small boat to Berwick.

The victory of the Scots was complete; in a few days all the remaining English strongholds in the south, with the exception of Berwick, fell into their hands. Still Bruce was not content; nothing would satisfy him short of Edward's definite recognition of him as the lawful king of an independent country. But, unfortunately for his northern subjects, Edward did not know when he was beaten, and with weak obstinacy he refused to admit Bruce's claim. Bruce retaliated by pounding at the northern counties of England. In 1318 he captured Berwick, and in the following year he countered Edward's attempt to recapture it by sending an army into the heart of Yorkshire. In vain the Archbishop of York, at the head of a hastily assembled force, tried to stop the invaders at Mitton; one yell from the Scots was enough to put the Archbishop's motley army to flight.

Raid followed raid, till in many parts of Northumberland and Cumberland the inhabitants found it wise to make a separate peace with the Scots. In 1322 Edward roused himself to attempt another invasion of Scotland, but, when he had advanced to within ten miles of Edinburgh through a country from which every living creature seemed to have vanished as if by magic, when all the food that his foraging companies could find was one solitary lame cow, he judged it wise to return. Bruce followed him up, came on part of his army near Rievaulx Abbey and scattered it, capturing the King's baggage and pay chests, and sending him flying headlong to York. Edward abandoned the struggle for the time, and in 1323 a truce of thirteen years was arranged.

The accession of the young Edward III in 1327 brought about a renewal of the war: Douglas and Randolph, with a swiftly moving force of mounted Scots, swept down upon the northern counties, played hide-and-seek for nearly a month with the great army which the young King led against them, and slipped away under cover of darkness after they seemed to be securely trapped, leaving the future victor of Crécy to cry his eyes out.

His advisers were convinced that it was folly to continue the struggle; negotiations were opened with King Robert's representatives, and in the spring of 1328 the Treaty of Northampton put an end to twenty-two years of strife. The independence of Scotland and the right of King Robert to the crown were fully recognized, a 'perpetual peace' between the two countries was established, and, to cement this new friendship, a marriage between Prince David, the only son of the King of Scots, and Edward's sister Johanna was arranged.

But the great King had only a few months of life in front of him. He was not old in years, but prolonged hardship and exertion had sapped his strength and aged him before his time. And a more dreadful foe than the English attacked him; he was stricken with leprosy. Still, he required only one thing to make him content: the withdrawal of the sentence of excommunication. Negotiations had been going on ever since Bannockburn; in 1320 the Scottish nobles, assembled in Council at Arbroath, had plucked up courage to write to the Pope and tell him that he had been misinformed. 'It is not for glory, riches, or honours that we are fighting,' they declared proudly, 'but for liberty alone, which no man loses but with his life.' But it was not till 1329, only a few weeks before the King was laid to rest in Dunfermline Abbey, that the sentence was finally removed.

CHAPTER XII

'DARK AND DRUBLIE DAYS': 1329–1406

A theatre spread over with mourning, and stained with blood, where in a revolution many tragedies were acted.

DRUMMOND OF HAWTHORNDEN.

Kings of Scotland			*Kings of England*			
David II (Bruce)	.	.	1329–1371	Edward III	. . .	1327–1377
Robert II (Stewart)	.	1371–1390	Richard II	. . .	1377–1399
Robert III	,,	.	1390–1406	Henry IV .	. . .	1399–1413

WE look on the struggle for national independence as the most glorious chapter in the history of our country. Under the guidance of a leader of genius, himself transformed by some strange alchemy from a selfish adventurer into a statesman and hero, the Scottish people were lifted out of themselves, into forgetfulness of the differences that divided Highlander and Lowlander, baron and bondman, and became for a time a band of brothers, capable of facing the armed might of England with serene confidence in the result. But these few bright years were followed by a long period of gloom, when Scotland seemed destined to become one of the most miserable countries in Europe.

For these bright years were not as bright as they seemed; Scotland gained its independence at a very heavy cost. The loss in human life must have been enormous. Nor was it confined to the battle-field, for in those days, when doctors worked by magic and spells, slight wounds often gangrened and proved fatal; then in the wake of the armies followed famine and pestilence, to devour those whom the sword had spared. The country was much poorer, too; as the most fertile parts were precisely those that were most exposed to the inroads of the invaders, it is little wonder that cornland went out of cultivation and that flocks and herds diminished. But as wool and hides were almost the only commodities that Scotland exported, the Scottish merchants could offer little in exchange for the foreign products which their countrymen urgently needed, and so foreign trade dwindled. The loss was moral as well as material; people became restless and unsettled; the peasant could not be expected to take pains with the building of a farm-house which might be destroyed in the next English invasion; he would not toil at his twenty-six acres with over-much energy when a raid into England might furnish him with half a score of plump cattle.

Among all the evils which followed these years of war, let us chronicle one benefit. Sometime in the course of the fourteenth century, but when or how no one knows, villeinage disappeared from Scotland; the ordinary peasant was no longer a serf but a freeman. He was not emancipated altogether from his lord's control; he had still to appear at his court, render the old services to him at the appointed time, and take his corn to be ground at his lord's mill, but the bond, though sometimes vexatious, was no longer dishonourable.

Unfortunately, Scotland got no chance to recover from the strain of the thirty years of warfare; the 'perpetual peace' established by the Treaty of Northampton lasted for only four years. To the ambitions of Edward III the treaty was only a flimsy barrier; he did not see why he should not repudiate a treaty which had been forced on him by his advisers; besides, he argued that the Scots, by breaking their promise to reinstate certain English barons in the possessions that they had formerly held in Scotland, had virtually repudiated the treaty themselves. He dispatched the dispossessed barons to Scotland with a force of a few hundred men, and sent with them no less a person than Edward Balliol, the son of the luckless King John. King Edward's plan was a simple one: if the expedition failed he would wash his hands of it; if it succeeded

Balliol would be crowned King of Scotland and would straight-way do homage to him for his kingdom.

It came very near to success. By an evil chance the Scots found themselves three years after the death of Bruce without a single one of the great soldiers who had led them to victory in the War of Independence. Edward Bruce had crossed to Ireland in 1315 to drive out the English there, had been accepted as King of Ireland by some of the Irish chieftains, and had fallen in battle three years later. In 1330 Douglas, in accordance with the last wishes of King Robert, set out for the Holy Land, bearing with him his dead master's heart borne in a silver casket. He landed at Seville, however, to help the King of Castile in his struggle with the Moors, and died gloriously in battle with the infidel. Randolph, who since King Robert's death had governed the kingdom on behalf of the child king David II, died suddenly while he was preparing to deal with the threatened invasion.

Balliol and his followers landed at Kinghorn in 1332, marched through Fife almost unopposed, and reached the banks of the Earn, beyond which, at Dupplin, the Scottish army was en-camped. But the Earl of Mar, who had been hastily put in Randolph's place, was a youngster without experience in war. He had omitted to post guards by the river, with the result that Balliol's men forded it unopposed at dawn, and surprised and cut to pieces an isolated detachment of the Scottish army. The Scottish vanguard hurried up, and beat off the English attacks for a time, but Mar lost his head, and sent the main body of his men crashing into the rear of the vanguard. Jammed together in hopeless confusion, the Scots found it impossible to fight, and were slaughtered like sheep. Balliol entered Perth, was crowned King of Scots, and set off on a triumphal tour of his newly won realm.

It came to an ignominious conclusion. At Annan a small party of Scots made a raid on his lodging by night, and he

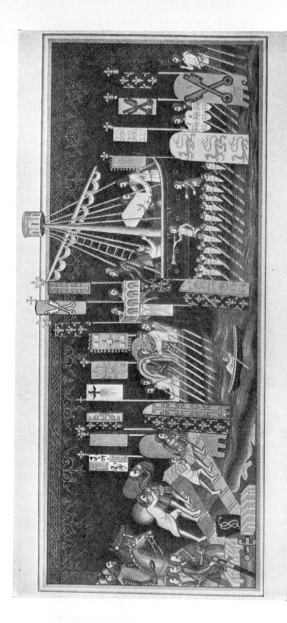

SETTING OUT FOR THE HOLY LAND

Knights of the Holy Spirit embarking

escaped only by rushing out with one boot off and one boot on and flinging himself on a horse that was neither saddled nor bridled.

He came back early in 1333, accompanied this time by Edward of England, who straightway laid siege to Berwick. A Scottish army advanced upon the town and came upon the English at Halidon Hill, but while the Scottish spearmen struggled across a broad and deep valley which divided them from their foes, the English archers shot them down at leisure. This disaster was followed immediately by the surrender of Berwick, which since that time, with one brief interval, has remained an English town.

The melancholy truth was that the Scots, unlike the English, had failed to profit by the lessons of the War of Independence. The Scots remembered only that spearmen fighting in mass formation had been successful against cavalry at Bannockburn; they forgot that spearmen in mass formation had been shot down wholesale by the English archers at Falkirk. The English generals had learned that to send cavalry against an unbroken body of spearmen was simply to ask for trouble; they also saw that a sudden cavalry charge, like the unexpected charge of the handful of Scottish cavalry at Bannockburn, might put their archers out of action, so when they drew up their troops in battle array, they made companies of archers alternate with companies of spearmen or of dismounted cavalry armed with lances. A rapidly moving force of hostile cavalry might elude the cloth-yard shafts of the bowmen, but they would be hurled back by the spearmen; the more slowly moving infantry would probably be shot down before they could come to close quarters. The Scottish leaders did not understand these tactics; time and again they sent spearmen against archers, and always with the same result.

But, as Edward was to find out in France a little later, it is one thing to win battles; it is a very different thing to hold down by force a kingdom that is determined not to submit to alien rule. Though he invaded Scotland in four successive years, though he received the homage of Edward Balliol, though he captured every castle in Scotland, he knew that he had not subjugated the country. The war had become a 'war of attrition'; the Scots, under the direction of a new Guardian, Sir Andrew de Moray, deliberately avoided pitched battles and, by driving their cattle into the hills and letting their lands lie derelict, they tried to starve out the invaders—an attempt to save the country from conquest by making it not worth conquering.

At last the tide turned. Edward's enmity to Scotland became swallowed up in enmity to France—enmity that originated partly from his knowledge that the King of France had openly shown his sympathy with the Scots—and when in the summer of 1339 he began the Hundred Years' War by invading northern France, the pressure on Scotland had already sensibly diminished.

In the previous year the successful defence of the castle of Dunbar by the Countess of Dunbar, a daughter of the famous Randolph, had done much to restore the confidence of the Scots. When the stones from the mangonels sang through the air and crashed against the battlements, Black Agnes, as her admirers called her, infuriated the besiegers by sending a girl with a towel to wipe away the marks. Once the garrison was perturbed when a 'sow', the medieval equivalent of a tank, a great wooden tower upon wheels, rolled up to the castle walls. Black Agnes remained calm. 'Montague,' she called, 'I sall gar thy sow farrow against her will.' She gave the word to her engineers; at once the sow became a target for enormous stones shot from a mighty catapult which had been placed on the battlements; it crumpled up, and Black Agnes smiled grimly as she watched the miserable wretches crawling out from the ruins.

One by one the English strongholds in Scotland were recaptured; in 1339 Sir William Douglas drained the water out of the moat that girdled the walls of Perth and led his troops over dryshod; two years later he captured Edinburgh Castle by an equally clever stratagem.

The long, grim struggle had come to an end at last; two centuries were to pass before an English King again attempted to convert Scotland into a province of England. But the evil effects remained: Scotland was even more impoverished in 1341 than it had been in 1329, and fifty years of warfare made hatred of England second nature to the Scots. The French, too, had learned what an English invasion meant, and so a common hatred drew Scotland and France more closely together; the treaty made by King Robert in 1326 became the foundation of an alliance which endured down to the time of the Reformation—an alliance from which the smaller country did not always gain the greater profit. More than once, in obedience to a hint from a hard-pressed king of France, the Scots marched to disaster in northern England. In 1346, for example, while Edward III was absent in France, David II led a Scottish army southward, only to see it riddled with arrows at Neville's Cross, and to be himself led off captive to London.

The impoverished and disturbed state of Scotland in the fourteenth century was not altogether due to the after effects of the War of Independence; it is to be explained partly by the weakness of the Crown. In those days, when Parliament met only at long intervals to promulgate laws which few ever heard of, when there was no strong body of permanent officials to help the King to govern the country, the character and ability of the monarch counted for much more than they do to-day. With a weak king misgovernment inevitably followed, for the King had formidable rivals; every baron was an absolute monarch within his own territories, exercising the power of life and death over his vassals, who, however, regarded him not as

A 'SOW', THE MEDIEVAL EQUIVALENT OF A TANK

a tyrant but as a protector. They knew well that if any out-
sider brought a complaint against them at their lord's court,
he would have very little chance of obtaining a conviction.
The complainant might lodge an appeal with the sheriff, but
the sheriff was only human, he would hesitate to incur the
wrath of a powerful baron by arresting his vassal. Every one
remembered how in 1342 Sir William Douglas had forced his way
into the sheriff court at Hawick with a body of armed vassals,
seized the Sheriff of Teviotdale, Alexander Ramsay of Dal-
housie, and carried him off to his castle of Hermitage to die
of starvation, and how neither King nor Justiciar had lifted a
finger. In addition, the sheriff was usually appointed, not
because of his knowledge of the law or his zeal in dealing with
law-breakers, but because his father had held the office before
him. Then he might be bound to the neighbouring landowners
by a definite treaty of friendship. For the baron claimed other
kingly privileges in addition to the administration of justice—
the right of levying war on any of his neighbours against whom
he had a grudge, and that of entering into 'bands of manrent',
agreements for mutual support, with those landowners who
were inclined to be friendly to him. Thus a great Earl who
found himself in bad odour with the King could count on the
support, not only of his own vassals, but of other landowners
whom he had agreed to protect, and who, therefore, had to do
their best to protect him. And these quarrels between one
baron and another had a way of developing into hereditary
feuds, which continued long after the original cause had been
forgotten.

Even if the King had succeeded in imposing his will on the
Lowlands, he would still have been confronted by the problem
of the Highlands. The Highland chief was, if anything, more
powerful than the Lowland baron: his rule over his clan was
absolute and unquestioned; the clansmen did not regard him
as a feudal superior but as a father, and he in his turn regarded

them not as vassals, but as children to whom he was bound to give protection and support. Perhaps as a consequence of this, the feuds between chieftain and chieftain, between clan and clan, were even more fierce and obstinate than the feuds that distracted the south.

In general the King thought it wise not to meddle with the Highlands. But the Highlanders would not refrain from meddling with him, or rather, with his Lowland subjects. An

GROAT OF DAVID II

The groat (4*d.*) was introduced into Scotland in 1358, after David's return from imprisonment

invasion on a grand scale they seldom attempted, but they often swooped from their hungry moorlands into the pastures and cornlands of Strathmore, to return in a few hours, or a few days, with a multitude of sheep and cattle.

Unfortunately for Scotland, a hundred years had to pass before a worthy successor sat on the throne of Bruce. It cost the Scots 100,000 merks to release David II from his captivity in England—an exceedingly bad bargain. When, after his return in 1357 his subjects crowded round him as he rode to a meeting of his Council, he damped their enthusiasm by snatching up a mace and shouting 'Stand still, or the most forward of you shall get one with this mace on his head'. A few years later he calmly proposed that if he died without leaving a son, the crown should pass to one of the sons of Edward III, and was furious when his Parliament very properly refused its consent.

When David II died in 1371, leaving no children behind him, the crown was bestowed on Robert the Steward, the son of Walter the Steward, who had married Marjory Bruce, the daughter of the great King Robert. In his youth Robert the Second had been one of the most formidable opponents of Edward III, but advancing years had made him timid and unenterprising, and, conscious that the great nobles regarded him simply as one of themselves, he was more anxious to conciliate them than to contradict them. When in 1385 Jean de Vienne, Admiral of France, arrived at the head of a splendid army of about 2,000 knights and cross-bowmen to co-operate with the Scots in an invasion of England, he came at the invitation, not of the King of Scots, but of his nobles, and when he set out to raid the northern counties, it was not the King, but the Earl of Douglas, who drew up his plan of campaign.

Little good came of this expedition; the raid provoked a much more serious counter-invasion by John of Gaunt, in the course of which both Dundee and Perth were burned down. The French left soon afterwards, utterly disgusted with the poverty of the country and the independent spirit of the ordinary Scotsman. 'Rude and worthless people', they called their allies, 'like savages, who wish not to be acquainted with any one, and are too envious of the good fortune of others, and suspicious of losing anything themselves.'

Another raid which Douglas made into England had a far different result. In the summer of 1388 he led an army up to the walls of Newcastle, within which Sir Henry Percy—Shakespeare's Hotspur—and other northern barons were assembled. Though no serious fighting followed, encounters took place between small bodies of English and Scottish knights, in the course of which Douglas gained possession of

Percy's banner. After announcing that he meant to take it to
Scotland, Douglas set off on his leisurely march home. But
Hotspur had vowed that the banner should never reach Scotland; he followed hard on the track of the Scots, and two days
later, as the sun was setting, he came on their camp at Otterburn, assailed it furiously and drove back the defenders in
confusion. Just when he thought that the fighting was
over, he heard a shout of 'Douglas!' and from the wood on his
flank a body of knights, headed by the Earl himself, bore down
upon his startled troops. Both sides fought valiantly; the
Scots who had fled at the first sudden attack returned to take
their share; the sun went down and the moon shone bright in
an unclouded heaven; the moon in its turn set; still they fought
on under the starlit sky. Not till the stars had faded away into
the grey light of dawn did the English quit the field where they
had so gallantly striven, leaving Hotspur and some hundreds
of his men in the hands of the Scots. Only then did the
Scots discover that their leader had been dead for many hours.
Soon after the fighting some of his knights had seen him fall,
and had rushed up to ask how he fared. 'Right evil,' was his
answer, 'but thanked be God there hath been but a few of
mine ancestors that have died in their beds.' Then, knowing
his wound to be mortal, he charged them to say nothing of his
plight to any one, but to bear his banner aloft confidently, and
shout 'Douglas'.

In this manner did 'a dead man win a fight'.

But the victory of Otterburn was only a transitory gleam in
the darkness, a darkness that grew steadily deeper. In 1390
the old King died, to be succeeded by his son, Robert the Third,
a prince whom ill-luck had pursued from his cradle. Even his
name was not his own: he had been christened John, but before
his coronation his advisers made him abandon the name of the
unhappy Balliol. An injury received in a tournament had made
him so lame that he could not bestride a horse, and so debarred

him from commanding his army in the field, or journeying about his kingdom to administer justice. He was naturally inactive and timid, however; too ready to entrust the business of government to his more active brother the Duke of Albany, and to defer to over-powerful subjects, like Archibald the Grim, Earl of Douglas.

His timidity increased his troubles tenfold. The clans immediately to the north of the Highland line began to get out of hand, and to vary fierce fighting with frequent raids into the fertile plains of Strathmore. Sir David Lindsay, Lord of Glenesk, tried to keep them out, but with slender success. In 1392, along with Sir Walter Ogilvy, Sheriff of Angus, and a body of about sixty horsemen, he attacked a band of the marauders near the banks of the Isla. The Lowlanders had the worst of it; Lindsay escaped with difficulty; Ogilvy refused to budge, and he and his men were surrounded and slain.

Despairing of any other remedy, Lindsay, now Earl of Crawford, resolved to try the effect of blood-letting on a large scale. In 1396 he arranged that the two clans which had caused most trouble by their perpetual feuds should each send thirty representatives to Perth to settle the business by a fight to the death. Barricades were erected on the North Inch to enclose a stretch of level turf, and thither, just as they come to-day to see a cricket match, the burgesses of Perth flocked to watch this grim entertainment. They had no need to be ashamed, for the King himself had come to see his subjects butcher one another. The sixty champions entered, armed with bow, sword, axe, and dagger, dashed together, and fought till only five were left alive on one side, and only two on the other. But the Highlands were not to be pacified as easily as all that.

The King's very anxiety not to offend his nobles offended them all the more. His elder son, David, Duke of Rothesay, had been betrothed to the daughter of the powerful Earl of March, whose castle of Dunbar guarded the eastern approach

A TOURNAMENT

to Scotland, but when the Earl of Douglas demanded that his own daughter should be married to Rothesay, the King weakly gave way. The Earl of March was furious at the insult, and early in 1400 made his way to the court of Henry IV of England, who was even then planning an invasion of Scotland. For the timid and well-meaning King of Scots had succeeded in offending Henry by affording shelter to a pretender who claimed to be Richard II, the rightful King of England. Henry could not strike hard, for he had a rebellious kingdom behind him, but in 1402 the Scots delivered themselves into his hands. Headed by the new Earl of Douglas, 'Tineman'—the Loser—and Murdach Stewart, the son of Albany, they advanced into Northumberland. Near Wooler they came in sight of an English army commanded by Hotspur, and, with an excess of prudence, formed up in dense masses on the slopes of Homble-don Hill to await the English attack. Hotspur was for hurling his troops on the Scottish schiltroms at once, but the Earl of March, who was with him, advised him to send forward his archers only. A handful of the Scottish knights, after appeal-ing in vain to Douglas to order a general attack, charged the English bowmen, but as Douglas remained passive on his hill and sent them no support, they failed to stop the archers, who, as soon as they got within range, sent volley after volley into the serried ranks of the Scots. Only when the schiltroms were riddled with arrows did Douglas order an advance. It was too late; his men were utterly broken, and like Sir Murdach Stewart he was forced to surrender to the English.

A blacker misfortune had already befallen the King. A few months earlier his elder son, the dissolute Duke of Rothesay, had disappeared, starved to death in the castle of Falkland, it was whispered, by order of his uncle Albany and his brother-in-law, Douglas.

The wretched monarch did not know which way to turn, or whom to trust. His Queen had died; men said that his brother had murdered his son. All that he had left in the world was his son James, a boy not yet in his teens. Not knowing what might happen to him, the King resolved at the beginning of 1406 to dispatch him to France. One of the few men he could trust, Sir David Fleming, took the young prince to North Berwick and rowed him over to the Bass Rock, where he embarked on a ship that was waiting for him. On his way back to Edinburgh Fleming was slain. Worse was to follow: the ship with the Prince on board was captured by an English vessel off Flamborough Head.

The King was spared this last and bitterest wound: by a strange coincidence, he died on the fourth of April, the very day on which his son was taken prisoner.

Note.—The title of this chapter is taken from the first stanza of Dunbar's *Meditation in Winter*, which, in modern spelling, runs as follows:

> Into these dark and drublie [dripping] days,
> When sable all the heaven arrays,
>   With misty vapours, clouds, and skies,
>   Nature all courage [liking] me denies
> Of songs, ballads, and of plays.

CHAPTER XIII

JAMES I AND THE SCOTTISH PARLIAMENT: 1406–37

> Ill doom is mine
> To war against my people and my knights.
>
> TENNYSON.

Kings of England

Henry IV 1399–1413   Henry V 1413–1422
        Henry VI 1422–1461

THE death of the old King and the appointment of Albany as Guardian of the kingdom on behalf of the imprisoned James I made no difference to the country. Albany had already acted as regent to the decrepit Robert II, and had been the virtual governor of the kingdom in the reign of Robert III. He seemed to cling to power, and yet to fear to use it; he did not exert himself to secure the release of the young King, though his own son Murdach was liberated in 1415; on the other hand, he was ready to go to any length to secure the good-will of the great nobles. In 1409, for example, he pardoned the traitor Earl of March, and restored him to his estates.

But some of these petty kings were clearly becoming dangerous. In 1411 the great Celtic potentate, Donald, Lord of the Isles, not content with the earldom of Ross on the mainland, claimed the earldom of Mar as well, and marched on Aberdeen with ten thousand Highlanders and Islesmen at his back. It was not a question of a cattle raid this time; it was a war of conquest, which was meant to add to Donald's already vast territories the whole of north-eastern Scotland from the Tay to the Moray Firth. At Harlaw, only twenty miles from Aberdeen, he found his path barred by the burgesses of Aberdeen and all the available fighting men of the region between the Don and the Tay, under the command of the Earl of Mar and the Sheriff of Angus. Both armies fought gallantly, but the impetuous valour of the clansmen could not prevail against the grim determination of the Lowland spearmen, who refused to give way, though their losses were far heavier than those of

JAMES I

their opponents.   In the end Donald led off his men and withdrew baffled to the west.

A triumph of a different kind was celebrated in St. Andrews a little later.   Hitherto the Scottish youth who wanted more learning than he could get at the burgh grammar school, where little more than Latin was taught, had to go to England or to the Continent. In Paris he would even find a Scots College, established for the special benefit of the wandering Scottish student. But the Bishop of St. Andrews, Henry Wardlaw, knowing that in time of war England would not welcome Scottish students, and that the journey to France was long, expensive and dangerous, in 1412 granted a charter establishing a university at St. Andrews.

The old Duke of Albany died in 1419; his son Murdach reigned in his stead; still King James remained a captive in England. But these were not wasted years. To the young prince's complaints that his imprisonment would interrupt his education, King Henry had replied that he knew French and would teach him all that he wanted. The King kept his promise; James grew up to be one of the most accomplished men of his age.

A little under medium height, thick-set, quick in his movements, he looked what he was, an expert at putting the weight and throwing the hammer. But one might be surprised to learn that this athlete was a musician and a really fine poet, and that his zeal for the arts was accompanied by an interest in machinery. What interested James most, however, was not the management of machines, but the management of men. He meant, if ever he returned to Scotland, to be a King in deed as well as in name, to be the mightiest man in his realm; to use his power, not for his own glory, but to make Scotland a safe place to live in. But how was he to make—in his own homely words—'the key keep the castle and the bracken bush the cow'?

Clearly the great noble with his private court of justice was the most formidable obstacle to the maintenance of law and order; clearly the policy of Robert II and his successors— bestowing estates and dignities on nobles who were already dangerously powerful, encouraging them to marry into the royal family, and avoiding a quarrel with them at all costs—

had done the exact opposite of what it had been intended to do : it had diminished the authority of the Crown, and increased the power and arrogance of the nobles.   So no more fair words! The great lord who would not bend to the King's will must be broken.   James knew that he might himself be broken in the process, but it was a risk that he was quite prepared to run.

Though the King saw that over-much reliance on the nobles had proved disastrous to the Crown in the past, he recognized that he could not govern the country single-handed; he must have some body of men to advise and help him. Such a body, he knew, existed in England. Until the second half of the thirteenth century the English Parliament, like the Scottish Parliament, had been identical with the Great Council—an assembly of the great landowners, clerical and secular, but from 1275 onwards it had included representatives of the towns and of the smaller landowners in the counties. Early in the fourteenth century the English Parliament divided into two bodies : the archbishops, bishops, abbots, earls, and barons formed the House of Lords, and the 'knights of the shire'—the county representatives— and the burgesses the House of Commons. This separation in the long run diminished the weight and influence of the great barons. Thrown together as they were with the merchants and craftsmen, the knights of the shire learned to look at questions of state from the point of view of their humbler comrades and the burgesses for their part were not afraid to oppose the Upper House, knowing that they would have the country gentlemen solid behind them. So it seemed to James that a Parliament after the English model, in which the smaller landowners and the burgesses acted as a counterpoise to the nobles, would solve the most difficult of his problems.

There was, indeed, a parliament in Scotland, but it differed in some important respects from the English Parliament. Though the most important Scottish burghs had for long sent representatives to a little parliament of their own, known first

as the Court of the Four Burghs, and later as the Convention
of Burghs, it was not till 1326, at a Parliament held at Cambuskenneth, that burgesses appeared side by side with the
bishops and the barons. The occasion was a special one; the
damage done to the royal demesnes during the War of Independence had diminished the King's revenues, and had forced
him to ask his subjects for money. For some time the burgesses
attended Parliament only when they were specially summoned:
not till the second half of the fourteenth century did they
attend every session of Parliament as a matter of course. Of
another class, the small landowners, Parliament often contained
no representative at all. In theory every 'tenant-in-chief',
however small the parcel of land that he held directly of the
Crown, was required to come to Parliament; in practice, only
these landowners attended who were entitled to hold their own
private courts.

The Scottish Parliament never separated into Lords and
Commons; the three 'estates' or classes, clergy, barons, and
burgesses, sat together in the hall of some royal castle, for as
yet there was no Parliament House, and the capital of the
country was wherever the King happened to be. But there
was a division of another kind: the Parliament of 1367 handed
over its unfinished business to a committee of its own members,
to allow the other members to go home for the harvest. In
1370 a more important change was made: at the beginning of
the session Parliament appointed two committees, chosen from
each of the three estates, one to draft new laws, the other to
deal with lawsuits that had been referred to Parliament for
decision. For the Scottish Parliament, like the English Parliament, was a law-court as well as an assembly for making laws.
If, for example, a man thought that the sheriff had bestowed
his inheritance upon the wrong person, his only remedy was
an appeal to Parliament. Members who were not appointed to
either committee were excused attendance till the end of the

A SCOTTISH BARON OF THE TIME OF JAMES I

Early fifteenth-century effigy in Dunkeld Cathedral. The mutilated effigy on the ground is that of William Sinclair, Bishop of Dunkeld, 1312–1337.

session, when they returned to hear what new laws had been proposed, and to give or withhold their consent.

This became the regular procedure. The legislative committee, known as the Committee of the Articles, and the judicial committee, known as the Committee of Causes and Complaints, was appointed at the beginning of every session. The scheme had serious faults: the Committee of Articles was at once too weak and too powerful; it was small enough to be controlled by one determined man, but in its turn it controlled Parliament. But James saw that this might be to his advantage: only let him govern the Committee of Articles, and he could make Parliament play what tune he pleased.

At last he got an opportunity of translating his purposes into action. In 1424 he was released, after he had promised to pay £40,000, the cost, he was informed, of board and lodging for eighteen years. He wasted no time: on the 5th of April he crossed the border with his bride, the Lady Joan Beaufort, a grand-daughter of John of Gaunt; on the 21st of May, Queen Joan and he were crowned at Perth, and before another five days had elapsed he had persuaded Parliament to pass a number of laws, in which his future policy was clearly defined. War between private persons was forbidden; rebels were reminded that they would lose not only their lives, but their goods; their property, in other words, would go, not to their families, but to the King; timid souls who might hesitate to help the King to suppress a rebellion were encouraged by the declaration that if they stood aside they would be treated as accomplices and punished with death and forfeiture of goods. Only men of property were to be allowed to be sheriffs, because only men of property could be heavily fined if they gave wrong decisions. The hereditary sheriff whose legal skill was not above suspicion was allowed to retain his office only if he found a competent deputy, for whose actions, however, he had to take full responsibility. Unscrupulous barons who had been in

the habit of helping themselves to the customs dues or to the
'burgh mails'—the rents paid by the royal burghs to the King—
were reminded that this money was the property of the Crown.
The King suspected, too, that land which had once belonged
to the Crown had often been grabbed by these same nobles;
he ordered his sheriffs therefore to find out what land had
belonged to the Crown within the last hundred years, and
offended the great landowners by announcing that he meant
to examine the charters by which they held their estates.

Within less than a year James held a second Parliament at
Perth. Perth, he had decided, was to be his capital, and Parliament was now to meet regularly once every year. 'Bands of
manrent' were forbidden by this Parliament, and those who
offered hospitality to rebels were assured that they would be
treated like rebels themselves.

But James knew that it was one thing to make laws, and
another to see that they were obeyed; he knew that more than
one of his barons when asked to produce his charter had defi-
antly produced an old sword, so he resolved to show evil-doers
that he was in deadly earnest. He ordered his greatest subject,
the Duke of Albany, to be arrested on a charge of high treason.
He was tried by a tribunal of his fellow nobles, found guilty,
and executed at the Heading Stone beside Stirling Castle.
With him perished at the same time his two sons and the Earl
of Lennox.

The Parliament which met in Perth in March 1426 had no
such tragic interruption. It made one far-reaching change,
however. It was evident that in the short time between the
opening and the closing of Parliament the Committee of
Causes could not deal with all the cases brought before it, so a
similar Committee—known later as the 'Session'—was ordered
to meet three times a year when Parliament was not sitting.

But James was meditating a fresh stroke: he meant to give
a warning to the turbulent Highland chiefs like that which he

had already given to the Lowland barons; a few weeks later he held a Parliament at Inverness which most of them judged it wise to attend. The story of the 1425 Parliament was repeated; as each chieftain entered the hall he was seized and thrust into a dungeon, while the King entertained the barons who stood about the throne by composing Latin verses, which may be translated thus:

> To the dungeon strong
> Hale the rogues along;
> As in Christ's my hope,
> Well they need the rope.

Of the less important captives some were hanged, some beheaded, and some banished. The Lord of the Isles fared better; the King, hoping to turn him from an enemy into an ally, made him a member of the royal household. But the young chieftain, chafing at what was really an honourable captivity, escaped and burned the town of Inverness. The King marched northwards and defeated his supporters, whereupon the young rebel judged it wise to surrender. He was kept a prisoner in Tantallon Castle till the King had reason to think that he had come to a better frame of mind, when he was summoned to Holyrood. There in the Abbey Church the great chieftain, clad only in his shirt and breeches, knelt before the high altar, surrendered his sword to the King, and humbly begged for pardon. Even with this humiliation James was not satisfied; not till the Queen herself had interceded for the captive was he set at liberty.

The King's audacity had cowed the Highlands for a time, but more than audacity was needed for a permanent solution of the Highland problem.

James could now congratulate himself that he had succeeded in making the creaking machinery of Parliament work more smoothly; but he noticed that the poorer country lairds still regarded attendance at Parliament as a troublesome duty, to be dodged whenever it was possible. The King therefore proposed in 1428 that the much more convenient English system should be adopted: in future the great landowners were each to receive a special summons from the King forty days before the meeting of Parliament; other landowners were to be ordered by the sheriff of their county to assemble on a certain day and elect two of their number to represent them in Parliament. But the latter part of the scheme was wrecked through the apathy of the ordinary country laird, who still persisted in staying away from Parliament, unless the King, by making him a 'Lord of Parliament' raised him above the level of a simple knight.

In truth the King's bright hopes were beginning to be dimmed. He had undertaken a task too great for any single man, and he was left to grapple with it alone; there was no wise and wary counsellor at his elbow, no Kennedy or Elphinstone to tell him when to give soft words and when to strike hard; his bold policy had alienated the nobles without gaining for him the support of any other section of his people.

He had given the nobles ample cause to fear and hate him. In 1431 he had suddenly lodged the great Earl of Douglas in prison and as suddenly released him; in 1435 he stripped the Earl of March of his estates, for no better reason than that his father had gone over to the English more than thirty years before. If a great baron died without leaving a son, the King did not trouble over-much to discover the rightful heir, he calmly added the estate to his own royal demesnes. Nor could the nobles forget that those of their kinsfolk who had gone to England as securities for the King's ransom had been condemned to perpetual banishment by his refusal to pay a penny of the money.

But James held on his course unafraid: in December 1436 he set off to celebrate Christmas at the Blackfriars Monastery at Perth, not knowing that in his own household a plot against his life had already been hatched. The King's Chamberlain,

Sir Robert Stewart, did not love the man who had allowed his
father to die an exile in England; he believed, besides, that
James's claim to the throne was invalid, and that the rightful
king was no other than his own grandfather, the Earl of Atholl,
who was a son of Robert II. He had entered into communication with Sir Robert Graham, a man who had long borne a
grudge against the King because he had deprived his nephew
of the earldom of Strathearn.

On the night of the 20th of February, 1437, everything was
ready: Stewart had laid planks across the moat that surrounded the monastery and had removed the bolts from the
doors. Still the King suspected no evil; at the moment when
Graham and his accomplices were crossing the moat, he was
talking gaily to the Queen and her ladies. Not till the clash
of arms was heard, followed by a scream, did he suspect that
anything was wrong. The conspirators had slain the page
posted at the door of the King's apartment. Before they could
reach the door itself, however, one of the Queen's ladies rushed
up, thrust her arm through the staples, and kept the door shut
till the King had time to wrench up a plank and leap into a
vault below. But she could not keep them back for long;
Graham and his accomplices forced open the door, breaking her
arm as they did so, and rushed into the room, only to find that
the King had vanished.

They retired disappointed, but a noise made them come
back: the King, thinking the danger was past, was trying to
climb back into the room. The conspirators leaped down upon
him, but James, unarmed as he was, sprang at the foremost
assassin, seized him by the throat, and trampled him underfoot. The second he served in the same way, but the struggle
could have only one conclusion, and a few minutes later his
dead body lay in the vault, pierced by twenty-eight wounds.

CHAPTER XIV

STEWART AND DOUGLAS: 1437–1488

And nothing then remained to do
But to begin the game anew.

A. E. HOUSMAN.

Kings of Scotland		Kings of England	
James II	1437–1460	Henry VI	1422–1461
James III	1460–1488	Edward IV . . .	1461–1483
		Richard III . . .	1483–1485
		Henry VII . . .	1485–1509

THE savage tortures inflicted on the murderers of James
the First could not undo the evil they had wrought. They
had destroyed more than the King; they had destroyed the
law and order that the King had established—the bracken
bush no longer kept the cow. The new King, James the
Second, was a boy of nine, a mere prize to be contended for by
the factions of ambitious nobles who would strive to rule the
country in his name and in their own interest. Parliament was
useless without the King; its small size and its practice of
handing over all really important work to small committees
made its control by a baronial clique or a single powerful baron
a very easy business. This would not have mattered so much
if any of the great barons had displayed the qualities of a real
statesman, and used his authority to 'prop the tottering
throne', but every one of them thought only of increasing the
wealth and influence of himself and of his house. The Earl of
Crawford, for example, instead of suppressing theft, turned
thief himself, and pocketed the customs duties levied at the
port of Dundee, and though the Earl of Douglas had been
appointed Governor of the Kingdom, he stirred not a finger to
end the dispute between two of the lesser barons, Sir William

Crichton and Sir Alexander Livingston, for the possession of the King.

The death of Douglas in 1439 made Crichton and Livingston, reconciled for the time, the foremost persons in the kingdom. But they feared the rivalry of Douglas's successor, the young Earl William, and persuaded themselves that they should not be safe till the arrogant youth was removed and his fat, easy-going uncle, James the Gross, put in his place. They therefore inveigled the Earl and his brother to Edinburgh Castle, introduced them to the boy King, and entertained them to dinner in the great hall of the castle. In those days most dinners, even in the halls of kings, consisted of two courses only, but on this occasion, when the custards and other dainties were removed, the servants returned with what seemed to be another dish. It was a bull's head, which they placed on the table before the young earl. Douglas turned pale and started to his feet, for he knew what the bull's head meant—it was the sentence of death. He looked about wildly for some way of escape, but before he could leave his place, there was a movement behind the arras; the armed men who had been hidden there sprang forward and seized not only the Earl, but his brother and the gentlemen who had accompanied him. The young King burst into tears when he saw the rough treatment meted out to his visitors, for he guessed what was to follow, but though he implored Crichton not to put them to death, Crichton answered rudely that Douglas deserved all he was going to get; he was a traitor, and as long as he remained alive the King would never be at peace. With that he gave orders for the Douglases to be taken to the highest part of the castle rock, where they were beheaded a few minutes later. Little did the weeping King think that before ten years had passed he and another Douglas would be the chief actors in a similar scene.

The sluggish James the Gross, as Crichton and Livingston

had expected, continued to pocket the King's revenues, but made no effort to strengthen the King's authority. But when Earl James died in 1443 he was succeeded by a much more formidable person, William, the eighth Earl of Douglas. A fortunate marriage had increased Earl William's already vast possessions; he had estates in ten different counties, and the half-dozen castles which he owned included the powerful fortresses of Bothwell, Threave, and Abercorn. His brothers— Archibald, Earl of Moray, Hugh, Earl of Ormond, and John, Lord Balvany—had great estates in the north of Scotland. That the young Earl could make himself master of Scotland, if he chose, Livingston understood full well; he therefore took the precaution of breaking with Crichton and making friends with Douglas. The King himself for a time came under the spell of the spirited, ambitious youth.

But in his castle on the brink of the sea at St. Andrews the sage and subtle Bishop Kennedy pondered long over the plight of his country. There was little to choose between Livingston and Crichton, he knew; but Livingston was Douglas's jackal, so he judged it prudent to make some sort of alliance with his rival. For Douglas was the real enemy, he considered. He distrusted him for his influence over the young King and for his friendship with the unscrupulous Earl of Crawford, and when in 1445 Crawford and Livingston invaded Fife and harried the lands of the bishopric, Kennedy was sure that Douglas had a hand in the business. As yet he could not strike back except with spiritual weapons; he excommunicated the spoilers, but though he repeated the curse again and again, nobody seemed a penny the worse. A twelvemonth and a day, however, after the curse had first been pronounced, the Earl of Crawford was mortally wounded in an encounter with the Earl of Huntly outside the gates of Arbroath. His own followers were terrified by this apparent judgement from heaven; when their master died they refused to bury him till they had received permission from the Bishop. The effect soon wore off, and in 1449 Scotland was again full of rumours of plots and rebellions.

But the King was no longer a child; long years spent in an atmosphere of plot and counter-plot had changed the tender-hearted boy who wept at the death of Douglas into a ruler with a fearlessness and a ruthless determination worthy of his father himself. Even his appearance was sinister and menacing: from birth one side of his face had been covered with a splash of scarlet, whence his subjects called him James of the Fiery Face.

As yet the King hesitated to strike at the Douglases, though in 1449 he clapped Livingston, with his sons and kinsmen, into prison. In 1450 the two sons of Livingston were executed on the castle hill, near the spot where ten years before the two Douglases had been beheaded; he himself escaped only with the loss of all his possessions. Later in the year the King's chance came; while Douglas and his brothers were carrying themselves like great princes in Rome, attracting the attention of the Pope himself by the nobility of their bearing and the magnificence of their attire, James marched into Earl William's territories and captured the most important of his castles. Douglas hurried home, not to make war, but to surrender his estates to the King and to throw himself on the King's mercy. The device succeeded; the quick-tempered, impulsive Stewart gave him back the bulk of his possessions, and pardoned him for anything he had done amiss.

The King could not lay aside his suspicions altogether. There was trouble in the Highlands, where Livingston, lately escaped from prison, and his son-in-law, the young Lord of the Isles, were besieging and capturing the King's castles. Then somehow or other he learned that the Lord of the Isles had entered into an alliance with the Earl of Crawford and the Earl of Douglas.

James resolved that this coalition must be broken up at once. In February 1452, having first given him a letter assuring him that no harm should befall him, he persuaded Douglas to meet him in Stirling Castle. At first only pleasant words passed between the King and his guest, but after supper the King took him to an inner room, and told him plainly that he must at once break with Crawford and the Lord of the Isles. 'I cannot, and will not,' was Douglas's insolent reply. 'False traitor, since you will not, I shall,' cried the King, as, drawing a dagger, he stabbed the Earl in the throat. One of the courtiers at once smashed in his skull with a pole-axe, and the others who rushed up showed their approval of the King's deed by plunging their daggers into the dead body of his guest.

The Douglases and the Lindsays did not approve. Crawford at once summoned his vassals to march against the King, and while James with a small force lay at Perth waiting for Huntly to join him, the Douglases, headed by the new Earl, dashed into Stirling. They displayed the King's letter to the astonished burgesses at the market cross, then nailed it to a board, which they fastened to a horse's tail and dragged through the streets, and departed, after they had plundered and burned the town.

For a moment the King lost heart; but for Bishop Kennedy's exhortations he would have abandoned the struggle altogether and taken refuge in France. Soon, however, he was rewarded with better news: Huntly, instead of marching to Perth, made for Brechin, where he came upon the Lindsays, all glorious in their new green liveries, and completely defeated them. Encouraged by this success the King harried the Douglas lands in southern Scotland, till Earl James judged it wise to submit to his brother's murderer.

Though Douglas had solemnly promised to lay aside all thoughts of revenge, though he was employed by James as an ambassador to England, he was still carefully watched by the King. In 1453, for no reason at all, it seemed, a horde of

Islesmen sailed into the Firth of Clyde and plundered the
villages that lay along the coast. James knew that Douglas
had visited the Lord of the Isles, and he put two and two
together. It seemed to be only goodness of heart that made
Douglas negotiate for the release of a Scottish prisoner when
he was an ambassador in England. But the prisoner was
Malise Graham, the nephew of that Sir Robert Graham who
had murdered James I, and grandson of Robert II—a man
whose title to the crown was supposed by some people to be
better than that of the reigning King. Again the King put
two and two together: the inevitable Douglas conspiracy must
be faced once more.

According to an old story he went to St. Andrews and told
Bishop Kennedy of his perplexity. The Bishop answered by
laying before him a sheaf of arrows bound by a leathern thong.

'Put the bundle across your knee and break it,' he said.
The King answered that it was impossible. 'I will let you see
that I can break it,' replied the Bishop, as loosening the thong
he drew out the arrows one by one and snapped them across
till every one in the bundle was broken.

The King understood: if he could detach the Earl's supporters from him by promises of pardon and rewards, he would
find it a comparatively easy business to break the Earl.

In the early spring of 1455 the last act in the long drama of
hatred began. The King suddenly appeared with an army before Douglas's castle of Inveravon and ordered the garrison to
surrender. The garrison capitulated, and the castle was completely destroyed. From Inveravon the royal troops marched
through the Douglas country, burning and plundering, till they
struck northward and invested the castle of Abercorn. The
besiegers seemed destined to become the besieged; Douglas,
with one of his most powerful supporters, Hamilton of Cadzow,
hurried to the rescue of the garrison. But the thong which
bound the arrows together had been loosened; Hamilton

unexpectedly went over to the King's side, leaving Douglas with no alternative but to take refuge in England.

It was a fight to the death now. When Abercorn was captured at the end of May its defenders were executed. A few weeks later the Earl's brothers, who had been lurking on the other side of the border, made a last desperate raid into Scotland, but they were attacked and routed at Arkinholm by the Earl of Angus. Moray was slain, and his head brought to the King as a trophy. Ormond fared little better. He was captured, but not before he had been severely wounded. James kept him in prison till his wounds were healed, and then ordered him to be beheaded.

For the next five years Scotland had peace; no other baron dared to bring on himself or his kinsfolk the fate that had overwhelmed the house of Douglas.

South of the border it was different: there a faction of the barons, led by Richard, Duke of York, in an attempt to dethrone the feeble Henry VI had plunged the country into civil war. In an unlucky hour for himself, James moved towards the border and laid siege to the castle of Roxburgh, which had been in English hands since the time of Edward Balliol. The King, who had inherited his father's interest in mechanical contrivances, often amused himself by working the great siege pieces with his own hands. His zeal made him share the fate of many medieval gunners: one of his own guns burst and a flying splinter of metal killed him. Roxburgh, however, surrendered two days later, and in the following year Henry VI handed over Berwick to the Scots.

The new King, James III, was only a boy of nine, but he had the sagacious Bishop Kennedy behind him, and for a time, except for the raids of the Lord of the Isles and his men, the country remained tranquil. But after Kennedy's death in 1465 the old scramble for the King's person and the royal revenues began. Lord Boyd, the head of a hitherto inconspicuous

family, was successful in this dishonourable contest, and dealt
out titles and honours to his sons and kinsfolk as Crichton and
Livingston had done.

At first it seemed that the young King would surmount his
troubles. The fall of the Boyds in 1469 was as sudden and
dramatic as that of the Livingstons had been, and, in the same
year, by marrying the Danish Princess Margaret, James put
an end to the two-century-old dispute about the payment of
tribute for the Hebrides, and gained possession of the Orkney
and Shetland Islands. At first he held them only as security
for the payment of his bride's dowry, but after waiting four
years for the promised 60,000 marks, he annexed them to his
kingdom. In 1474 he strengthened his position further by a
treaty with Edward IV of England, which purported to establish a permanent peace between the two countries, and in 1476
he attacked the territory of the Lord of the Isles by land and
sea, forced that turbulent chieftain to submit to him, and
deprived him of the earldom of Ross.

But the great nobles could not understand the King. He
was not one of themselves. He kept them at arm's length and
spent most of his time in the company of men of low birth who
were interested in the things that interested him—music and
architecture, astrology and alchemy. He did not travel about
his kingdom, but lived sequestered in the castle of Stirling,
planning new buildings with his architect Cochran, or wearing
out his eyes in a vain search for the philosopher's stone. For he
was over-fond of money; stories ran through the realm of his
mysterious black 'kist' and the gold that was hoarded in it,
and the issue from the mint of coins made of copper or billon[1]
instead of the usual silver was looked on as a subtle device to
enable the King to enrich himself at the expense of his subjects.

James, for his part, was jealous of his over-mighty subjects.

---

[1] An alloy of silver with copper or tin, in which the baser metal
predominates.

Like most princes of his time, he wanted to be an absolute
monarch, sharing the work of government with men of low
degree, whom he had made and whom he could unmake, men
chosen simply for their cleverness and their diligence in his
service. To the Secret Council, the little committee chosen by
himself which shaped and directed his policy, he invited busy
clerics like Schevez, who had once helped to buy his clothes,
and Elphinstone, whose only wealth was a subtle brain and
a store of learning amassed in the colleges and law courts of
Paris. He paid them by securing for them preferment in the
church; Schevez, for example, through the King's influence
became Archbishop of St. Andrews,[1] and Elphinstone Bishop
of Aberdeen.

The great nobles liked the Council even less than they liked
the King. It is true that the Council was no new invention:
as the calling together of Parliament was a very slow business
—forty days' notice had to be given to all who were invited to
attend—the Scottish Kings had for centuries referred urgent
business to this smaller body, consisting mainly of the great
officers of state whose duties kept them near the King's person.
But its power, or its pretensions, seemed to be increasing; it
was a committee of the Council now, and not a committee of
Parliament that, under the name of the Session, met three times
a year to settle disputes about property, and this same committee did not hesitate to overturn the decisions of the hereditary sheriffs, and even to inflict punishments on these amateur
judges.

But the Council could not exercise to the full these powers
with which the King was willing to entrust it: the great nobles
had resolved that they would not be at the beck and call of a
handful of upstarts, and spread all sorts of ridiculous stories
about it. Its policy was supposed to be shaped and directed,
not by Elphinstone, who was one of the greatest jurists and

[1] St. Andrews became an Archbishopric in 1472, Glasgow in 1492.

statesmen in Europe, but by Cochran the architect—or mason, as they styled him—and the King's tailor, Hommyl, was reputed to be an influential member. So it is little wonder that the Council could not maintain order, and that civil wars on a small scale raged unchecked in various parts of the kingdom.

From murmuring against the Council the barons proceeded to murmur against the King, and to talk of replacing him on the throne by his brother Alexander, Duke of Albany. The King's suspicions were aroused; in 1479 he imprisoned Albany in Edinburgh Castle and his younger brother Mar in Craigmillar. Mar died suddenly, murdered by the King's orders, the nobles said; Albany slew his guards, clambered down the castle rock with the help of a rope that had been smuggled into his prison, and succeeded in making his way to France.

But the King's troubles were only beginning. War broke out with England, and in the summer of 1482 James set out for the borders, with an army from which most of the barons had absented themselves. He did not know that his brother Albany had already been a guest at the court of Edward IV, and that at that very moment he was marching northward with King Edward's brother, the Duke of Gloucester, resolved on the subjugation of Scotland. For Edward had begun to amuse himself with the old idea of ruling Scotland through a vassal king. Nor did James know that his own barons, moved by no friendly purpose, were hurrying after him at the head of their vassals.

At Lauder they overtook him; then a sudden timidity seized them. They all wanted the King to surrender his power to them, but not one of them dared to face the angry monarch. Lord Gray, seeing them hesitate, told them the story of the cat and the mice. Still they hesitated, then the young Earl of Angus calmly remarked 'I will bell the cat', and set off for the royal tent to demand the surrender of the detested councillors. He came back a few minutes later to their meeting-place in Lauder Kirk with the news that the King had flatly refused.

While they debated what their next step should be, a knock was heard, and the door opened to reveal a gorgeous figure—Cochran, the most hated of all the King's low-born friends.

HERMITAGE CASTLE IN LIDDESDALE
A stronghold of ' Bell the Cat '

The sight of the favourite, all gorgeous in black velvet and gold, with a chain of gold about his neck, and a horn tipped with gold at his side, was too much for the nobles. 'A rope will suit you better,' cried Angus, as he snatched the chain from his neck.

'My lords, is this jest or earnest?' exclaimed Cochran.

'It is good earnest,' was the ominous reply. The nobles rushed from the church to the royal quarters, seized every one who they thought looked like a member of the Council, and hanged six of their captives, including the gorgeous Cochran, over the bridge at Lauder. Cochran died as he had lived, protesting that he should have been hanged in a silken cord, and not in 'ane tow of hemp, like ane thief'.

The King was escorted to Edinburgh and lodged in the Castle. The retreating armies were followed by Albany and Gloucester, who made their way into the capital unopposed. But Gloucester judged it prudent to leave his confederate to fight his own battle, and returned to England, taking care to capture Berwick on his way south.

Now that the Scottish nobles had Albany they were not altogether satisfied with him. They did not like James, but they liked still less a prince who, as they suspected, was in the pay of King Edward, and who had let Berwick slip into English hands. For a short time Albany ruled as Regent, but he was forced to release the King and go through a form of reconciliation with him, and in 1483 he found his position so precarious that he fled to England.

He came back in 1484, accompanied by the long-banished Earl of Douglas. At the head of a company of horsemen they dashed into Lochmaben at fair time, but the burgesses resisted stoutly, till the local lairds, galloping in from the country with their tenants behind them, completed the rout of the raiders. Douglas was captured and brought before the King, but when he looked on the face of the monarch against whom he had hatched so many plots, he turned away his head and said not a word. Only when they told him that he was to be lodged in Lindores Abbey did he mutter 'He that may no better be, must be a monk'. Albany escaped, and made his way to France, where he was killed a year later in a tournament.

Gradually the King put together the ruins of his fallen authority; Elphinstone and the other base-born experts returned to the council-table, and as the hold of the King on his turbulent nobles grew tighter, the old murmurs against royal avarice and the arrogance of the upstart Council began to be heard. In 1488 the nobles again rose in rebellion, seized Prince

James, the King's eldest son, proclaimed him Governor of the country, and marched with him in triumph through southern Scotland. The King, according to an old story, went to Lindores to ask the Earl of Douglas for his support. 'Sir, you have kept me and your black coffer in Stirling too long,' was the bitter reply. 'Neither of us can do you any good.'

The King made his way to Aberdeen, rallied the northern earls to his support, then turned southwards and met the rebel lords near Blackness on the Forth. An agreement was patched up between the two parties, whereupon the King rashly disbanded his army and went to Edinburgh Castle. Almost immediately the nobles rose in rebellion again. The King hurried towards Stirling and came upon them at the village of Bannockburn.

The rebels were victorious, but the victory saddened the young prince more than defeat would have done. His conscience already reproached him for his alliance with his father's enemies, and he had tried to deaden it by giving strict orders that no one should lay hands on the King—but the King had disappeared. A few days later the discovery of the King's dead body in the mill of Bannockburn let the Prince know that he was now King James the Fourth of Scotland. But it was a barren honour: he could not rid himself of the idea that he was his father's murderer. One thing he resolved to do. Till the day of his death he would wear an iron chain round his body, and every year, as the anniversary of his father's death came round, he would add another link to it.

How had the King come to be in the mill? According to an old story, the King's horse had bolted, and had thrown him when he was a few yards from the mill, whereupon the miller and his wife had rushed out and dragged him in. Knowing that he was badly hurt, he asked them to send for a priest. The miller asked who he was. 'I was your King this day at morn,' he sadly replied. On hearing these words the miller's wife ran out crying for a priest for the King. 'Here am I, ane priest,' said a man who was passing by. 'Where is the King?' She took him into the mill and led him up to the wounded man, who implored the stranger to give him the sacrament. 'That shall I do hastily,' said the pretended priest, as he drew a sword and stabbed the King to the heart.

THE MERCHANT
(See p. 198)

CHAPTER XV

SCOTLAND IN THE TIME OF
JAMES THE FOURTH: 1488–1513

No state in Earth here standis sicker;[1]
As with the wind wavis the wicker[2]
So wavis this world's vanitie:—
  Timor Mortis conturbat me.[3]

Unto the Death gois all Estates,
Princes, Prelates and Potestates,
Baith rich and poor of all degree:—
  Timor Mortis conturbat me.

WILLIAM DUNBAR.

Kings of England

Henry VII	.	. .	1485–1509
Henry VIII	.	. .	1509–1547

THE rebel lords soon found that they had not destroyed the monarchy when they killed James III; that, on the contrary, they had made it stronger than it had been since the time of Bruce. It is true that some of them, like Alexander Hume, who became Lord Chamberlain and Keeper of Stirling Castle, and his confederate Patrick Hepburn, who emerged from the scramble as Earl of Bothwell and High Admiral of Scotland, secured estates and offices of profit for themselves and for their kinsfolk, but they were plainly not in a position to govern—or to misgovern—Scotland according to their own devices. They had overreached themselves; the news of the King's death caused a wave of horror and indignation to run through every town and village in Scotland, and made their own position very precarious. They could not afford to be vindictive, and though they banished some half-dozen of the King's associates, within a few weeks they were compelled to admit

---

[1] sure.   [2] willow.   [3] The fear of death disquiets me.

the chief of the late King's supporters, including his Chancellor, Bishop Elphinstone, to Parliament and to the Secret Council.

They had made another mistake: James the Fourth was not altogether the thoughtless, pleasure-loving youngster that they had supposed him to be. It is true that he was an impulsive, high-spirited boy, bent on making full use of the opportunities for enjoying himself which his lofty position offered to him. His boyish restlessness, his insatiable curiosity, his zest for enjoyment never left him; dancers, jugglers, jesters, and story-tellers always found a ready welcome at the royal palaces, and never went empty away. He was a grown man when he sent a gipsy to the King of Denmark with a letter of introduction stating that the bearer was an Egyptian prince, and when he bestowed an abbacy upon a rascally Italian friar who professed to be able to fly from Scotland to France. Equipped with a pair of wings the adventurer attempted a flight from the walls of Stirling Castle, but he 'crashed' and broke his leg; he disarmed the King, however, by explaining to him that he had made the mistake of putting some hens' feathers in his wings, and they had 'drawn him to the midden and not to the skies'.

James spent money profusely, for he liked to go richly attired and to be lodged in a palace that was worthy of a king. But his extravagance was more popular than his father's avarice. The unlettered, hard-riding nobles welcomed the change from the moody recluse to the gallant youth who shared their enthusiasm for hunting and jousting, who liked to have his new-built palaces crowded at Christmas and Easter with a gay company of revellers, and who did not seem to object to losing money to his dutiful subjects at the card-table. The burgesses liked to see him 'come sounding through the toun' at the head of a glittering cavalcade, and noted with approval that the blind and the crippled, even the loathsome lepers clustered outside the burgh port, never asked him for an alms in vain.

But under the cloth of gold lay the iron belt; with all this

JAMES IV
From the drawing attributed to Jacques le Boncq of Artois in the Library
of the town of Arras

avidity for pleasure went an extraordinarily keen sense of duty; restless and changeable as he was, his determination to be master in his own house, to be a terror to evil-doers, never changed. He did not trust the rebel lords who had once made him their tool; he did not break with them, but he shaped his policy to please himself, and when he was in doubt he let himself be guided by the advice of Bishop Elphinstone, the wisest of his father's counsellors.

The administration of justice was tightened up. The justiciars, accompanied sometimes by the King in person, once more went on their rounds regularly from county town to county town, twice every year, to deal out punishments to the malefactors whom the sheriff haled before them. At last the average county laird began to understand that if he plundered the dwelling or drove off the cattle of a neighbour with whom he had quarrelled, he would be lucky if he got off with the payment of a heavy fine to the Justiciar, and that the criminal action before the Justiciar would be followed by a civil action before the Council, to force him to disgorge the goods of which he had despoiled his victim.

But the King knew that there were great stretches of his land where his writ did not run, remote border valleys which no royal messenger dared to enter, islands in the west where the word of the Lord of the Isles, humbled though he had been in 1476, still counted for more than the word of James Stewart.

At the very beginning of James's reign the Islesmen invaded the mainland in an attempt to win back Ross for their master; the King retaliated by declaring that the whole of the vast territories of the Lord of the Isles was forfeit to the Crown, and followed up his declaration by taking a fleet to the Hebrides in the autumn of 1493. Though the Lord of the Isles surrendered a year later, to end his days, as his confederate Douglas had done, in a monastery, it was not till the end of 1505, after James had invaded the Hebrides for the sixth time,

BISHOP ELPHINSTONE (1431–1514)

that he could feel certain that the Islesmen would remain quiet.

Meantime James had achieved a triumph of a very different kind. Though it seemed at one time as if his chivalrous, impetuous character would make him reopen the old, bitter, fruitless struggle with England, though, by raiding the northern counties of England in 1496 on behalf of the impostor Perkin Warbeck he almost forced a war upon the unwilling Henry VII, in the following year he was persuaded by the Spanish ambassador, De Ayala, to agree to a truce with England. In spite of the truce the two countries were again brought to the brink of war a few months later over a scuffle between some Scottish youths and some of the garrison of Norham Castle. James began to ask himself if any good came of these age-long hatreds; if friendship with France must always exclude friendship with England. Even if he were to establish a friendship with England, how could he be certain that it would endure. More than one treaty of 'perpetual peace' had already been signed and broken. But why should he not strengthen the fragile tie that bound the two countries together by marrying Margaret Tudor, the elder daughter of the English King?

Henry VII welcomed the proposal; he was not deterred even by the prospect of a Scottish king becoming King of England at some future date. Better that than the perpetual menace of war, he argued. Besides, as he pointed out to his Council, even if Scotland and England were united the greater would always draw the less, England would always be the predominant partner. So in 1502 another treaty of perpetual peace was signed, and in August 1503, before the high altar in the abbey church of Holyrood, the King of Scots was married to the young English princess.

The autumn was spent by James and his Queen in a triumphal progress through the southern half of his kingdom. He had reason to be pleased with what he saw; once more, over

A SCOTTISH BARON OF THE TIME OF JAMES IV
Effigy of William, Lord Borthwick, in Borthwick Parish Church, Midlothian

the greater part of the country, 'the key kept the castle and
the bracken bush the cow', and farmer and craftsman alike,
freed from the fear of foreign invasion and of civil war, were
giving their whole minds to the arts of peace. 'There is as
great a difference between the Scotland of old time and the
Scotland of to-day', De Ayala had written six years before,
'as there is between good and bad.' But if we could mount
Mr. Wells's 'Time Machine' and transport ourselves back to
Scotland as it was in the year 1503, we should be amused at
De Ayala's raptures.

Progress was slow in this remote northern country; the rural
districts especially had changed little since the time of Alexander III. South of the Grampians the country was still for
the most part bare and treeless, undivided by hedgerow or by
dry stone dyke; marshes and reed-fringed lochs that have long
since disappeared still occupied the undrained river valleys.
Though good stone was plentiful the country folk still dwelt in
smoky, windowless huts of turf, and they tilled the ground in
the old unthrifty way, ploughing the barren hill-sides because
the rich land beside the river was waterlogged, exhausting
their best arable land by never letting it lie fallow, con-
tenting themselves at harvest with plucking off the ears of the
corn and leaving the straw to rot. Like the husbandman of
Alexander's time, they used the clumsy wooden plough,
dragged by a team of eight oxen, for though you might see
hundreds of shaggy ponies at the fairs in Perth or Dundee,
though you might buy one for a shilling or two, heavy draught
horses were both scarce and expensive. Few countrymen had
as many as eight oxen fit to pull the plough, for their farms
were small—twenty-six acres of arable land was quite an
ordinary size—but their holdings were often arranged in groups
of four, and four neighbours would arrange to make up a
plough team between them. Still, they might have made
more use of the little land they had; they might have manured

their fields, and their cottages might have been surrounded by gardens, and shadowed by orchard trees. But they refused to plan for the future. It is true that the ordinary countryman was no longer bound to the soil as he had been in the thirteenth century; his complaint now was that the tie binding him to the

A WOODEN PLOUGH
Second half of fifteenth century

soil was not strong enough. As his land was now leased to him for a period of not more than five years, he would be foolish if he wasted time and labour in building a comfortable house which he might not be allowed to occupy, or in planting an orchard from which he might not pluck a single apple.

The King saw the injustice of this arrangement: in 1504, he announced that he meant to set his own lands in feu farm, and hinted that his barons should do the same with theirs. This meant that the land was leased, not for a short time, but in perpetuity; the landowner virtually surrendered the land to the occupier in return for a fixed annual rent, or feu-duty, and as long as this sum was paid the occupier could look on the ground as his own.

Though the village had changed little, a glance at the baron's castle would have convinced us that Scotland had become a wealthier country. It is true the poorer laird was content to dwell in a single stone tower. The small barred windows set high up in the wall, the iron yett or grille protecting the entrance, which was usually on the first floor, the battlemented parapet which surmounted the tower, all showed that the place was built so that it could resist a sudden attack—a necessary precaution in the days when almost every respectable family boasted at least one hereditary feud.

But the wealthier baron refused to be content with these cramped quarters, he built additions to the single tower, till it became L-shaped or Z-shaped in plan, or expanded it to form a great hollow square, such as we may see at Crichton[1] or at Craigmillar, with a courtyard in the centre. The King set the example; at Holyrood, at Linlithgow,[2] at Stirling, additions were made to the stately buildings which the luckless Cochran had designed for the more luckless James III.

In the towns the wealthy merchants followed where King and barons led; they pulled down the wooden structures that had satisfied their fathers, and built houses of stone, with vaulted basements and crow-stepped gables, often surrounding a courtyard. From the courtyard, which, like the courtyards of the great castles, was approached by a pend or covered passage, a flight of steps led to the first floor, where the principal rooms were situated.

Suppose then that we are in Edinburgh in the year 1503; suppose we enter the pend, cross the courtyard, and climb the stairs of the new house that some prosperous merchant has

¹ See p. 193.   ² See p. 195.

THE HALL OF CRAIGMILLAR CASTLE

In the fourteenth century, Craigmillar Castle, like Crichton Castle,
consisted of one single tower, the interior of which is shown in the
photograph. In the fifteenth century a curtain-wall was built round
this tower, and in the sixteenth and seventeenth centuries buildings
were erected against this wall, thus giving a square courtyard almost
completely surrounded by buildings.

built for himself. If we swung back the heavy iron-studded door at the top of the outside stair, we should find ourselves in the hall, which in those days was not a mere vestibule, but the principal living-room in town house and palace alike. It is not too well lighted, for only the upper halves of the windows are glazed, the lower halves being obscured by wooden shutters, but as our eyes grow accustomed to the dim light we notice that the walls are hung with tapestry, and that the rafters in the low roof are picked out in gay colours. Carpets there are none; rushes or dried grass must serve instead even in the King's palaces. There is very little furniture; a trestle table covered with a green cloth, a counter or table with fixed legs, one chair, reserved for the master of the house, one or two benches or settles with loose cushions, a kist or chest, and an aumrie or cupboard would probably complete the list. Though the arch over the handsome stone fireplace might serve for a bishop's tomb there is no grate, the flaming logs are kept from rolling among the rushes only by metal fire-dogs.

In the profusion of handsome silver plate on the table and counter we notice neither forks nor knives, and only a very few spoons. As every one carried a knife on his person in those days it was not thought necessary to provide him with another for use only at meals. As for forks—the basin and towel placed in a conspicuous position on the table let us into the secret. As the diners held their meat with their fingers, they had to wash their hands immediately after every meal. We should notice other omissions: there is no glass or china; silver plates are used for occasions of state; for everyday use pewter or wood has to suffice. And the food would seem strange to us: we should weary of the everlasting salt beef and mutton, too 'gamey' in flavour for the modern palate, even though it is smothered in mace and nutmeg and other eastern spices. White bread, too, we should find regarded as a luxury, for little wheat was grown in Scotland; barley bread, or oatcakes, baked on a 'girdle' or on the hearth, were used on ordinary occasions.

The bed is the only feature of the bedroom that is worth mentioning—a noble structure, a great swelling feather-bed

CRICHTON CASTLE FROM THE NORTH-WEST

The original castle consisted of a single tower, which is still standing, though in the photograph it is masked by the later buildings. Most of these were added in the fifteenth century, but the great hall at the north-west corner was not built till the end of the sixteenth century

rising from a foundation of wooden boards and surmounted by a canopy, from which hang curtains of heavy cloth. For it was only at night, when he fastened the curtains at either side, and 'kest on claithis threinfauld' that the medieval Scotsman could keep the airs of heaven at bay; even when he sat before the great fireplace the winds whistled through the holes in the shutter and waved the arras till the pictured shapes seemed to come to life.

To his distrust of fresh air—of which he got too much—the average Scotsman added a distrust of soap and water—of which he got too little. Soap was a costly commodity, imported from abroad in small quantities, and even the most comfort-loving merchant did not dream of fitting up a bath in his house. So you might see unwashed faces with jewels and costly raiment, for strangers thought the Scots inordinately fond of fine clothes. And the streets of Edinburgh, as of any other Scottish town, gave evidence of this same disregard of cleanliness.

To one who did not examine it too closely, Edinburgh, rising proudly from the lochs which then almost enisled it, must have seemed a stately and gracious city. In place of the angular mass of barracks one grim, grey tower rose from the castle rock, and at the other end of the town a much more beautiful St. Giles than the St. Giles of to-day thrust its lantern spire into the sky. And St. Giles stood in a street that was not a narrow lane, like most medieval streets, but a great square, round which rose the new stone-built houses of noble and merchant, some of them with arcades underneath, where one found the best shops that Edinburgh could boast. The closes, too, were still closes in the old sense of the word—garden closes—for the long, narrow gardens that stretched behind the High Street to the Cowgate and the Nor' Loch were still unbuilt on; apple and cherry trees still displayed their blossom within a few yards of the Mercat Cross.

But in this beautiful city, set among gardens on its lofty ridge, there were neither water-pipes nor drain-pipes; the refuse from the houses was flung into the streets, where pigs routed among the foul-smelling garbage, and the drinking water was drawn from wells, many of them in the public streets, sunk in the polluted soil. It is little wonder that every few years Edinburgh, like the other towns in medieval Scotland, was devastated by a pestilence against which the medical science of

the day could find no defence. In their despair people tried
strange remedies: the Bishop of Dunkeld—if we are to believe
his biographer—cured those who had been stricken down by
the pestilence with holy water, in which one of St. Columba's
bones had been dipped. The only man who did not recover,

LINLITHGOW PALACE AND CHURCH OF ST. MICHAEL
FROM THE NORTH-WEST

The west front, the oldest part of the Palace, was built soon after 1424:
the Palace was completed in the reign of James IV, though the north front
was rebuilt early in the seventeenth century. As at Crichton Castle, the
buildings completely enclose a central courtyard

says the same veracious biographer, was a shameless wretch
who wished that the holy water had been a pot of good ale.

But it was in those dark ages of medical science, in the year
1505, to be exact, that the College of Surgeons of Edinburgh
received its charter from King James. For though the influence of the Renaissance was not felt in Scotland at this
time, though the bishops and clerks who visited Rome came
away quite untouched by the enthusiasm which they found
there for the newly discovered art and literature of Greece,

some attention was paid to learning. A second University, Glasgow, had been founded in 1450, and in 1495 Bishop Elphinstone founded a third at Aberdeen. These universities were attended for the most part by men destined for the priesthood, but the King and his advisers knew that a sheriff who was ignorant of law could do as much mischief as a priest who did not know the Latin of his service-book, and in 1496 an act was passed to compel country gentlemen to send their eldest sons, first to a grammar school 'till they have perfyte Latin', and then to a university, to get instruction in law.

In those days, of course, one could not be a learned man without Latin, for it was the language of educated people all over Europe, the language in which all scientific books, and most histories, were written. The book of marvels which Hector Boece composed about this time and called a History of the Scots—was written in Latin, like the more accurate work of John Major. These two historians wrote for the continental scholar, their books were printed, not in Edinburgh, but in Paris; but the poets Henryson and Blind Harry, and the forgotten bards whom Dunbar, the greatest of them all, celebrates in his *Lament for the Makars*, wrote in Scots for their own country-folk. For in this bleak northern land, in this too short interval between war and war, poetry had a strange brief blossoming, a spring which no summer followed.

But though people were now thinking of comfort as well as security, and of seemliness and beauty as well as of comfort, their desire for beautiful objects outran their skill; it was not a Scottish 'wright', for example, who fashioned the elaborately carved aumbrie or linen chest which we saw in the dwelling of the wealthy merchant; that was imported from Flanders, like the tapestries on the wall, or the silver ware that glittered on the counter. In fact, if a really good manufactured article of any kind was wanted—from a feather-bed to a tombstone, from a cushion to a candlestick—it had to be imported from

Ioan Stradanus inuent.   Phls Galle excud.

A PRINTING OFFICE OF THE SIXTEENTH CENTURY

abroad. It was the same with books: though in 1507 two merchants, Walter Chepman and Andrew Millar, set up a printing press in Edinburgh, they ceased operations after they had published a few volumes.

In return, Scotland exported no manufactured goods except woollen cloth of poor quality; the staple exports were salt fish, wool, and hides. In other words, Scotland paid in raw materials for the manufactured goods, and for the sugar and wine, spices and sweetmeats which it imported. But this trade was small in bulk and carried on under some curious restrictions. Only merchants in royal burghs were allowed to engage in foreign trade; they were forbidden to take their ships out of harbour in the stormy winter months, and when they did set sail they were all expected to make for the port of Middleburg in the Low Countries. Here the Scottish 'Staple' was established; in other words, the town of Middleburg conferred certain privileges on Scottish merchants on the understanding that it would be granted a monopoly of the trade with Scotland in return.[1] Here the merchants found a hostel, and warehouses where they could store their goods. Usually they did not deal directly with the Dutch merchants, but put their affairs into the hands of the Scottish Conservator—consul, we should call him. To him they sold their wool and their salted salmon, and he in return bought for them the medley of odds and ends which they required.

Though the Scottish merchant was a very small man beside the merchant princes of Bruges or Antwerp, he considered himself an exceedingly important person in his own town. He was tenacious of his own privileges and suspicious of what seemed to him to be the insolence of the craftsmen. For the craftsmen had taken a leaf out of the merchants' book; in every town the members of the separate crafts or trades organized themselves into separate gilds after the model of the merchant

[1] Removed to the neighbouring town of Veere in 1507.

gild. When an apprentice shoemaker became a journeyman, he paid a fee to the boxmaster or treasurer, and was enrolled in the cordiners' gild or craft, the head of which was an official known as the dean or deacon. These craft gilds might be called medieval trade unions, but they differed from the modern trade union in two important respects: they included both masters and men, and they were purely local associations; a member of the baxter craft in St. Andrews, for example, could not open a baker's shop in Cupar or Dundee.

In spite of the rise of the crafts, the merchants, for a time at least, tightened their hold over the towns. In the reign of James III the right of electing the burgh council was taken from the general body of the burgesses and conferred on the burgh council itself; after 1469 there was nothing to keep the retiring council from re-electing itself, and it usually did so. Further, in 1504 it was enacted that only a merchant trading within the burgh could represent it in Parliament. So the craftsman was excluded both from the burgh council and from Parliament, and so the merchants who represented the burghs in Parliament succeeded in securing the enactment of vindictive laws against the crafts and their deacons. But the crafts had come to stay.

Except for these squabbles between merchants and craftsmen, a deep peace seemed to have settled down on Scotland. Even the borders had been quiet ever since that November night in 1510, when the King, at the head of a great force of horsemen, rode out of Edinburgh, rounded up the border cattle thieves, and dealt out the local brand of justice to them at Jedburgh.[1] So law-abiding had the country become that the King would think nothing of riding from Stirling to the shrine of St. Duthac in Tain without an escort of any kind.

James played his part well, but at times he must have looked on Scotland as too narrow a stage for a king of his energy and

[1] 'Jeddart Justice' meant hanging a man first and trying him afterwards.

political talent. The treaty with England was not the last of his diplomatic triumphs; he had succeeded in securing the friendship of England without losing the friendship of France, and in consequence he found himself courted by more than one continental prince. In 1506, for example, he sent a fleet to the help of the beleaguered Queen of Denmark; in 1507 he urged the citizens of Lübeck not to aid the rebellious Swedes in their quarrel with the Danish King Hans; and when in the same year his kinsman the Duke of Guelders appealed to him for help against the Emperor Maximilian and the Spanish King, who were invading his territory, James, without actually fighting, succeeded in extricating the Duke from his perilous position. Even Louis XII of France did not disdain to ask the King of Scots for four thousand soldiers to help him in his invasion of Italy. For a time it seemed as if James were to become the arbiter who would decide the fate of monarchs far mightier than himself.

James knew that he could not play that part unless he had the backing of a powerful fleet. Skilful and daring captains he had: he knew that on one occasion five English ships and on another three had been attacked by Sir Andrew Wood with only two ships, and had been forced to surrender. But he had few ships, and timber was scarce in Scotland. As early as 1506 he informed King Louis that he intended to build a fleet for the defence of his shores, and obtained permission for his agents to fell timber in the forests of Normandy; at the same time Scottish merchants went as far afield as Spain to buy anchors and cordage for the projected fleet.

One of the new ships was put under the command of Andrew Barton, who straightway sailed over to the Dutch coast and waged a vigorous war against the Dutch pirates who had been preying upon the Scottish merchant ships. But Barton leant a little too much towards piracy himself; again and again he captured Portuguese merchant ships, though Scotland and

Portugal were at peace. When King Emmanuel of Portugal complained to King James, he was informed that Barton was quite within his rights, as, thirty years before, his father's ship had been captured in an encounter with a Portuguese vessel,

A WARSHIP OF 1514–15

and, in spite of repeated requests, no compensation had ever been paid for the slaughter of the elder Barton, or for the loss of his ship.

But the Portuguese complaints had not gone unheard at the English court. The Lord High Admiral of England, the Earl of Surrey, who was later to figure in a more momentous contest, resolved to rid the seas of a man whom he regarded as no better than a pirate. In the summer of 1511 he attacked

Barton's two ships in the Downs, as they were returning from the Dutch coast. If courage could have availed against superior weight of metal, Barton would have been victorious; when he lay on deck mortally wounded, with his leg shattered by a cannon ball, he insisted on beating a lively tune on a drum to encourage his men. But the Scots were completely outmatched; their ships were taken into the Thames and the crews lodged in the Tower.

James remonstrated as warmly with the King of England as Emmanuel had remonstrated with him; he could get nothing more than the answer that princes did not dispute about pirates, and had to extract what consolation he could from a contemplation of his newest ship, the *Great Michael*, with its towering castles and innumerable port-holes bristling with guns, the mightiest ship in Europe he believed it to be, to build which all the woods in Fife had been laid low. For already the 'perpetual peace' was wearing thin; the dispute about Barton was only one of several questions, trivial enough in themselves, but serious enough to serve as a pretext for war to a prince who had set his heart on it. Had Henry VII been alive these questions might have been shelved, but Henry VII had died in 1509, and the ambitious and confident Henry VIII did not seem to care greatly whether James made war on him or not.

In 1512 came the test that strained the 'perpetual peace' to the breaking point: the French King found himself confronted by the Holy League—a coalition organized by the Pope, in which England was a partner—and appealed to the King of Scots for help. Not for long did James hesitate between the old alliance with France, never definitely abrogated, and the 'perpetual' friendship with England. Elphinstone counselled peace, but the King, still romantic and adventurous at forty years, rejected Elphinstone's policy of caution for the flashy and dangerous schemes of Andrew Forman, the clever, restless Bishop of Moray. In the summer of 1512, acting on Forman's advice, he renewed the alliance with France. He did not know that Forman had been bribed by Louis XII with the promise of the Archbishopric of Bourges.

But Louis wanted more than expressions of friendship. In the early summer of 1513, when Henry was on the point of setting sail for France, an envoy from Louis was admitted to an audience with James and his Council at Edinburgh. To the King he presented, along with the letters from Louis, a turquoise ring and a letter from Queen Anne, in which she hailed him as her knight, and asked him to advance into England and strike a blow on her behalf.

The King forgot that he was a King and thought that he was simply a knight-errant; the young nobles, who had never looked on the nameless horrors of the battle-field, clamoured for war, and shouted down Elphinstone when he tried to plead for peace. He could not make the gallant, adventurous King and the hot-brained nobles see what he saw only too clearly, that a Scottish victory would bring advantage only to France, and that the consequences of a Scottish defeat were almost too terrible to be thought of. The King had no brothers; the heir to the throne was a child only a year old; if the King perished in battle, there would be no one to take his place. Parliament could not do it, for James, like many other sixteenth-century monarchs, believed in keeping Parliament in its place, which often meant no place at all. No, if the King perished the whole structure of law and order which Elphinstone and he had built up would be in jeopardy.

Long afterwards stories were told of the strange and ominous happenings in the time of waiting which followed—how when the King knelt in his stall in the Church of St. Michael at Linlithgow an old man clad in a robe of blue appeared before him, uttered a solemn warning, and suddenly vanished, and how 'there was a cry heard at the market cross of Edinburgh at the hour of midnight', a cry from ghostly heralds come from the realm of the dead to summon earls and lords, barons and burgesses, to appear before their Master within forty days.

All went well at the beginning of the campaign. On the 22nd of August James crossed the Tweed at the head of the most splendid army that a King of Scotland had ever commanded, and before the month was out he had captured three of the great border castles. But the Earl of Surrey was hurrying north at the head of a formidable army. 'The crooked old carle' had not learned his tactics from romances of chivalry, but he knew how to deal with those who had: before he got within striking distance of the Scots he sent on a herald to ask James to remain for another three days in his camp on Flodden Hill, and James, like a simpleton, agreed. Then, instead of marching straight on the Scottish position from the south, he crossed the River Till, recrossed it a few miles farther down at Twizel Bridge, and so put himself between the Scots and Scotland.

He hoped by doing this to tempt James down from his apparently impregnable position on the heights; but as, on the afternoon of September 9, he watched for some sign of a forward movement tongues of flame began to ascend from the Scottish camp, and in a few minutes the Scottish army was completely hidden from him by a dense bank of smoke. He could guess what this meant, the Scots had set fire to their tents and the heaps of rubbish that had accumulated in the camp, and meant to attack under cover of this smoke screen. Soon the thunder of the Scottish guns confirmed his suspicion, but they did little damage, and when the English gunners replied they not only silenced the Scottish batteries, but sorely galled the infantry who, drawn up in five compact divisions on the hill-side, were waiting the signal to advance.

About half-past four in the afternoon the Scots broke through the smoke and charged down on the four divisions of the English.

They all, even the King and his household in the centre division, fought on foot, and that they might move more easily over the slippery turf, they had taken off their shoes.

At first it seemed that they were to be victorious: though the Highlanders on the right wing were flung back in confusion, Lord Hume and the borderers on the left routed the English division opposed to them, and in the centre the King clove a way through Surrey's division to the English commander. His advisers had often found fault with him for exposing himself unnecessarily in battle, and his answer had always been that if his subjects risked their lives for him, it was only fair that he should risk his life for them. For once, however, his 'young adventurousness' did not carry him through; he was struck down, no one knows by whom, when he was only a spear's length from Surrey himself.

A stupor seemed to seize upon the Scots when they saw their King perish; though the centre fought on valiantly they got no help from the other divisions and perished almost to a man. At length the merciful darkness came and put an end to the fighting, though the plunderers were busy all night, stripping the slain and sparing neither King nor bishop. For one archbishop, two bishops, and thirteen earls had died beside their King. And with them perished a great multitude of 'the mere uncounted folk'. No chronicle preserves their names, but one heart-breaking old tune, still played as a dirge in Scottish regiments, echoes the wail of anguish that arose from every town and hamlet as the news of the disaster spread over the land. For it was not the youth of Ettrick Forest only that lay cold in the clay, and Selkirk was not the only town to which only one survivor returned out of a great and gallant company.

206

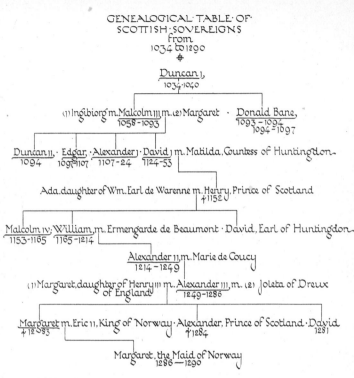

GENEALOGICAL·TABLE·OF·
SCOTTISH·SOVEREIGNS
from
1034 to 1290

Note.—Duncan II was the son of Malcolm III and his first wife, Ingibiorg.

GENEALOGICAL·TABLE·OF·
THE·KINGS·OF·SCOTLAND
from
1306 to 1513

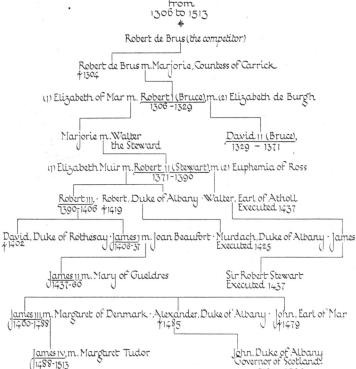

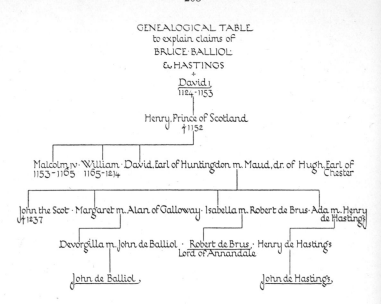

GENEALOGICAL TABLE
to explain claims of
BRUCE·BALLIOL·
& HASTINGS
+
David I,
1124-1153

Henry, Prince of Scotland
† 1152

Malcolm IV· William · David, Earl of Huntingdon m. Maud, dr. of Hugh, Earl of
1153-1165 1165-1214   Chester

John the Scot · Margaret m. Alan of Galloway· Isabella m. Robert de Brus· Ada m. Henry
† 1237   de Hastings

Devorgilla m. John de Balliol · Robert de Brus · Henry de Hastings
                    Lord of Annandale

John de Balliol,   John de Hastings,

CHAPTER XVI

KING JAMES THE FIFTH: 1513–1542

In lack of justice this realm is shent,[1] alas!

(From a poem attributed to Dunbar.)

Scotland		*England*	
James V	1513–1542	Henry VIII . . .	1509–1547

NOT all at once did the Scots become fully aware of what had been lost at Flodden. The English army had been too badly mauled to venture north of the Tweed. The white-haired burgess of Edinburgh waited in vain for the bell that would warn him to grasp his rusty spear in his unaccustomed hand, and sally out to guard his town against the slayers of his son. For a time he tried to believe the comforting rumour that the King had not really been killed, that he had gone at last on that long-contemplated pilgrimage to the Holy Land, from which he would soon return. But for King James, as for that legendary king who sleeps under the Eildons, there could be no return; the country must fare as best it could with a boy-king seventeen months old.

Had Elphinstone been younger, had those great nobles who survived the wreck of Flodden, men like the Earl of Arran, the head of the great semi-royal house of Hamilton, and the Earl of Angus, grandson of old Bell-the-Cat, cared more for their country than for themselves, the Highland clans might have thought twice before they harassed the depopulated Lowlands, and the border reiver might have herded his own, and not his neighbour's cattle. But Elphinstone was too old. After Flodden, says his friend and biographer Hector Boece, 'he was never again seen to laugh, to enjoy jests or to make even the most modest pleasantry.' He died in Edinburgh in October 1514,

---

[1] lost.

too soon, one trusts, to know that at the beginning of the month Louis XII of France, the king for whom his master had sacrificed his life and wrecked his kingdom, had married the younger sister of Henry VIII.

The marriage of Angus to the Queen Dowager, in the autumn of 1514, again made a Douglas virtual master of Scotland, but in the moves and countermoves of Angus and his rival Arran, Scotsmen soon ceased to look for any trace of a disinterested motive. They expected more from the great noble who appeared in the kingdom in the summer of 1515 and who was almost immediately appointed Governor or Regent of Scotland. This was John, Duke of Albany, a son of that adventurous and over-ambitious prince who had been forced to flee from the kingdom in the reign of James III. Their hopes were disappointed. Albany, it is true, had inherited his father's courage and his kingly presence, though he never at any time tried to imitate his father by ousting the rightful king from the throne. But his heart was in France. He had been born in France, had spent all his days in France and could speak no language but French. And the man who sought to govern a turbulent kingdom could not govern himself; if he was contradicted, he flung his hat in the fire, and dared any of the company to rescue it. It was soon obvious that he really cared nothing for Scotland; the cost of maintaining his French servants and his falconers, his private company of actors and his Italian trumpeters, emptied the already impoverished treasury; by the Treaty of Rouen in 1517 he light-heartedly bound Scotland to go to war with England should England go to war with France.

It is little wonder, then, that Scotland was as disturbed after his coming as it had been before. An insolent jest by the Regent lost him the support of Alexander Lord Home, and brought about a rebellion on the borders—a rebellion which ended in the execution of Lord Home and his brother. In 1517 Albany sailed to France, for the prolonged holiday which he deemed necessary, leaving one of his French comrades, Antony de la Bastie, to be Warden of the East March, the country of the Homes.

De la Bastie knew that the Homes would make trouble if they could, and when in the autumn of 1517 he heard that their confederates had seized the castle of Langton, he galloped out at the head of a few horsemen, his long hair streaming in the wind. But the castle would not yield, and he was forced to withdraw. As he rode off at some little distance from his men, the thunder of hoofs behind him told him that something was amiss. He looked round, to see a party of the Homes, led by David Home of Wedderburn, riding hard after him. For a time it seemed that he would outstrip his pursuers and reach the castle of Dunbar, but his horse fell and the Homes overtook him and slew him. The death of Lord Home had been avenged ; the Laird of Wedderburn rode back in triumph, with the head of the murdered man tied to the saddlebow by its flowing hair.

Nor were strife and bloodshed confined to the borders ; less than three years later a pitched battle was fought in the very High Street of Edinburgh. Albany's prolonged absence had allowed Angus and Arran to resume their old manœuvres— manœuvres in which Angus, who had gained control both of the King's person and of the town and castle of Edinburgh, had hitherto got the better of Arran, so when in the spring of 1520 a large party of the Hamiltons and their confederates, headed by Arran and his ally James Beaton, Archbishop of Glasgow, came to Edinburgh and lodged in the Canongate and those parts of the city outside the Flodden Wall, Angus and his friends judged it prudent to close the Netherbow Port and the other gates and remain on the alert all night. In the morning, while Angus drew up his forces in the High Street, his uncle Gawain Douglas, now Bishop of Dunkeld, went to the Black-friars Monastery, where Beaton was, and urged him to put matters right before trouble began, for he knew how to do it.

'My lord, by my conscience, I know not the matter,' cried Beaton, laying his hand on his bosom. There was a tell-tale clash as he did so, for under his clerical robes he wore an unclerical suit of armour.

'I perceive, my lord, your conscience be not good, for I hear them[1] clatter,' remarked the bishop, calmly.

Sir Patrick Hamilton, however, moved by the bishop's words, went to his brother the Earl and urged him to abandon his perilous enterprise. Arran had almost consented when his ferocious young son taunted Sir Patrick with being afraid. In a moment the peacemaker was transformed into an infuriated warrior. With a shout of 'I shall fight this day where thou dare not be seen', he rushed out and, with a few score other Hamiltons at his back, hurled himself upon the spears of the Douglases. Sir Patrick was the first to fall; the Douglases stood firm and gave better than they got, and after a grim struggle the Hamiltons broke and sought refuge in the wynds and closes that opened off the High Street. Arran himself escaped only by flinging himself on a collier's horse and fording the Nor' Loch. Neither clerical rochet nor unclerical plate armour would have saved Beaton from the enemies who dragged him out from the altar in the church of the Blackfriars, had not Bishop Gawain magnanimously interceded for him. Altogether seventy-two combatants perished in this brawl, which the burgesses of Edinburgh long remembered under the name of 'Cleanse the Causeway'.

The return of Albany in 1521 constrained Angus to cross the border, but when Albany left Scotland for the last time in 1524, after involving it in an unsuccessful war with England, Angus promptly returned and played his old game of misruling the country in the name of a captive king.

So far every one had left the King out of his calculations.

---

[1] The plates of armour, not the Archbishop's conscience, as Sir Walter Scott supposed.

Soon after Albany's departure, James had been told that he was now king indeed. He was delighted, because the announcement brought release from what an old writer calls 'correctioun at the schools', which in the sixteenth century was a formidable and painful business, even for a prince. But the ambitious

FALKLAND PALACE

youth of sixteen refused to be contented with the gilded captivity which had satisfied the boy of twelve. In the summer of 1528 he escaped by night from the Castle of Falkland and rode to Stirling, where he was joined by those lords who desired the downfall of Angus. A few weeks later, at the head of an army of 2,000 men, he advanced against the great Douglas stronghold of Tantallon, where Angus had taken refuge. The threat of a siege was enough; Angus and his kinsmen fled to England.

The wild, gallant stripling promised to develop into an excellent king, for if he had inherited something of his father's prodigality and love of adventure for adventure's sake, he also inherited his fierce passion for law and order. If his weakness for roaming about the country in disguise under the name of the Gudeman of Ballangeich got him into curious scrapes, it also taught him much about the people whom he ruled, and, when he went on a hunting expedition into Yarrow or Teviotdale with some hundreds of armed horsemen at his back, the deer was not always the only quarry that he sought, as John Armstrong, one of the most formidable of the border freebooters, discovered. When in the summer of 1530 Armstrong heard that the King and his huntsmen were riding over the moors into Teviotdale, he rashly assumed that he had to deal only with a simple boy, and with more than two score followers behind him set out from his tower of Gilnockie to pay his respects to the King. James was not deceived by this sudden show of loyalty; he ordered Armstrong and his companions to be seized and hanged on the nearest convenient trees. Armstrong begged for mercy, but he looked in vain for any sign of relenting in the smooth young face of the prince. Then, the old ballad writer tells us, when he saw that his death was inevitable, he broke into a last hopeless taunt:

> To seek het water beneath cauld ice,
>   Surely it is a great folie;
> I have asked grace at a graceless face,
>   But there is nane for my men and me.

James's zeal for justice did not stop with the hunting down of robbers; he knew that the courts engaged in the less thrilling task of dealing with disputes about money and property could not possibly overtake their duties. There were two such courts which dealt not only with complaints brought straight to them but with appeals from the burgh and sheriff courts; the one was the Committee of Causes, a sub-committee of the Parliament, which met only when Parliament was in session, and the other the Session, a sub-committee of the Secret Council. Both the Lords Auditors, who sat on the first, and the Lords of Council, who sat on the second, were expected to perform their duties without payment; the result was that they sometimes accepted from the suitors that payment which they could not obtain from the King. Further, as knowledge of law was not too common in Scotland, the few legal experts were overworked, and had to be both Lords Auditors when Parliament was in session and Lords of Council when it was not. In both courts the same scenes were witnessed, crowds of bawling suitors at the door, each holding out a paper and demanding that his case should be held first. It was rude of them, but then some of them had heard the macer announce not once, but twenty times, that the hearing of their cases was postponed.

James knew the hardships of the ordinary suitor, he also knew that his own greatest hardship was a lack of money, so in 1531 he persuaded the Pope to allow him to impose a tax on the bishops and abbots of £10,000 a year, to be used to found and maintain a College of Justice—a body of expert judges who would be paid for their services and who would always be available for duty on the bench in a supreme civil court. There were to be fifteen of them, it was afterwards ordained, eight clergymen, one of whom was to be President of the Court, and seven laymen, and this new Court of Session was to sit regularly in Edinburgh all the year round. The bishops reluctantly consented; the original £10,000 was soon whittled down to a more convenient sum, and in 1532 an Act of Parliament was passed establishing the new court.

James's action had consequences of which he had little dreamed. The prelates, to raise the necessary money, set their lands in feu farm and in so doing often dispossessed the original tenants in favour of new-comers who offered to pay a larger sum, thus loosening still further the bond, already dangerously slack, between the clergy and the poor country-folk. At the same time the bond between the King and the bishops was drawn dangerously tight. He knew that if his attitude to the great questions which were now agitating Christendom failed to please them, they could, by refusing to pay the new tax, bring to naught his schemes for the better administration of justice.

Though fifteen years had passed since Luther had nailed his theses to the door of the church in Wittenberg, though northern Europe seemed already lost to Catholicism, though Henry VIII had even now definitely broken with the Pope, to all outward appearance the position of the Roman Church in Scotland seemed stronger than it had ever been before.

But even among those who detested the new doctrines of Luther, who looked on King Henry as a traitor to the faith which he had undertaken to defend, there were many who recognized that all was not well with the Church. There was no more bitter opponent of the new opinions than John Major, the Lothian youth who had become the most famous theologian in the colleges of Paris, but Major did not hesitate to say that the Church was far too wealthy and that it would have been better if David I had not lavished lands and money upon his newly built monasteries. 'That wealth was indeed the offspring of a truly pious sentiment,' he said, 'but the wanton daughter ended by strangling her mother.' Men entered the priesthood for what they could get out of it, and preferment in the Church went not to the man who was most worthy of it, but to the man who could call a powerful noble his kinsman or who could spend money more lavishly than his rivals at the court of Rome. Even the King was far from scrupulous in the use of the influence which he possessed with the Pope; if he could not have a bishop who was both saint and statesman, he chose a statesman rather than a saint. Sometimes, too, he wanted to provide for a needy kinsman without expense to himself; this explains why in 1492, James Duke of Ross, the brother of

James IV, was made Archbishop of St. Andrews, and why he was succeeded in 1504 not by Elphinstone, but by Alexander Stewart, a boy of thirteen, whose only recommendation was his close kinship to the King.

The royal example did not lack imitators; the great nobleman provided for his younger sons by securing rich benefices for them, and by arranging that while they studied philosophy and theology at Paris or St. Andrews, their clerical duties should be performed by a poorly paid substitute. That was not all: there was nothing to prevent a priest being parson of two parishes, even though one might be in Tweeddale and the other in Caithness.

So it was almost inevitable that often the bishop or abbot should forget what he was supposed to be, and should sink to the level of a secular baron. John Major mildly suggested that twelve or fourteen servants would be a suitable number for a bishop; St. Columba had one. And when the bishops neglected to visit the parish churches in their dioceses, when they did not care who knew that their manner of life was no better than that of the ordinary self-indulgent, pleasure-loving landowner, it is little wonder that laziness and ignorance were the least of the faults of which the mass of the inferior clergy were accused.

Of one thing Major was assured: the fault lay not in the doctrines of the Catholic Church but in the fact that these doctrines had been flouted by the very men who professed to be its servants. The remedy for the evils which he deplored was simple: complete obedience to the precepts of the Church. So thought the old theologian, when in 1524 he returned from the turmoil of Paris to the courtyards of Bishop Kennedy's College at St. Andrews. So did not think the fiery young scholar, Patrick Hamilton, who in the same year came to the same quiet haven, but found no quiet there.

One could not purify the Church without changing the

doctrines of the Church. The imaginations of medieval theologians must be swept aside; each man must shape his conduct and his beliefs, not according to the code of instructions laid down by the Church, but according to his own independent interpretation of the Bible.

So Hamilton thought, and what he thought he did not hesitate to declare openly. He was exiled, but in his banishment he talked with Luther himself face to face, and he returned to St. Andrews in 1528, more ready than ever to declare that his was the only faith in which to live and die. But he had walked into a trap; his enemies were watching him; at the end of February 1528 he was arrested by the command of James Beaton, now Archbishop of St. Andrews, adjudged to be a heretic, and burned in front of St. Salvator's College. The people of St. Andrews long remembered how in all the slow six hours' torment his courage never failed him, how when the flames leaped round him he disdained to save his life by calling upon the Virgin, and how the Dominican friar who had accused him went mad with horror when he saw what he had done. The burning of Hamilton did not have the effect that Beaton intended; in defiance of the Act of Parliament of 1525 Protestant books were smuggled into the country, and the discussion of the new doctrines was by no means confined to the professional theologians at the universities.

But whatever his subjects might think, the King, dependent as he was on the support of the clergy, showed no disposition either to follow the example of some of the North-German princes and become an out-and-out Protestant, or to take the middle course pointed out to him by his uncle Henry VIII. In 1531 Henry definitely repudiated his allegiance to the Pope, without, however, making any attempt to alter the doctrines or ceremonies of the Church within his kingdom, and in 1535 he had begun to plan an attack on the English monasteries.

Like many people of lesser rank both north and south of the

border Henry not only doubted if the monasteries were ful-
filling the purposes for which they had been founded, but
wondered if they had any purpose to fulfil at all. For the
monks did not consider themselves obliged either to preach or
to teach; preaching they left to the parish clergy and to the
friars, teaching they left to the grammar schools, which were to
be found in almost every Scottish burgh, and to the three
universities. Schools, it is true, were to be found in some of the
monasteries, but their main function was to train the young
novices who would afterwards become monks, or the boys who
sang in the choir of the abbey church. What was more, the
efficiency of the parish clergy was impaired by the fact that
the revenues of the parish churches were often diverted to
the monasteries. For example, the tithes of fourteen parish
churches, including the church of Dundee, were paid to the
Abbot of Lindores. And Lindores was not one of the exceptionally wealthy abbeys; to the Abbey of Arbroath came the
revenues of thirty-three parish churches, to the Abbey of
Kelso the revenues of thirty-seven; in fact, it was reckoned
that two-thirds of the parish churches of Scotland were
annexed to abbeys or priories.

That was not all: the very seclusion in which the monks
lived encouraged the spread of scandalous stories about them;
nor can it be denied that in the sixteenth-century monasteries
one found too many men who were fond of ease and good living
and too many who were fond of low pleasures.

Henry VIII knew what he meant to do with his own monks:
he meant to prove that not only one or two monasteries in his
kingdom, but one and all were sinks of iniquity, to turn the
monks adrift, and annex their property. Some of it he would
keep; the remainder he would sell or give to lay landowners
who, knowing that they owed their new-gotten wealth to the
King and to his change of faith, would be eager to support him
through thick and thin. What is more, Henry had determined

that James must follow his example. One would think that what James did or did not do to the Scottish monasteries was no business of his; but Henry was looking far ahead; he saw that if he went ahead with his policy of hostility to the Pope he might have need of an ally; he saw too that if he could persuade James to commit himself to an attack on the Catholic Church, James would find himself at loggerheads with the King of France, and would become the permanent ally—and in time the vassal—of England.

In vain was the net spread in the sight of the bird. Though ambassador after ambassador went north in 1535 and 1536, James, instead of crossing the border to discuss theology with Henry and plan a combined attack on the monasteries, set sail for France, where, on the first day of the year 1537, he was married to the Princess Magdalen. But the fragile beauty of the tender-hearted girl withered away in our cold Scottish summer; only two months after she had bent down to kiss the soil of her husband's kingdom, she lay in her coffin in Holyrood. James married again before the year was out, and again his bride was a Frenchwoman, Mary of Guise.

Even these two marriages, even the declaration of the Scottish Parliament in 1541 that no one was to impugn the Pope's authority under pain of death, failed to convince Henry that James had not the slightest intention of taking his advice; he tried to entice James to York, but after staying there for a few weeks he had to return south without his nephew. He was convinced now; in the summer of 1542 the fleet sailed for Scotland and at the same time the border villages and farm steadings began to go up in flame to heaven. The English raiders burned their fingers badly; a strong force of them commanded by Sir Robert Bowes was intercepted and captured by the Earl of Huntly at Haddonrig, and though a larger army crossed the border a few days later its only achievement was the destruction of the beautiful abbey of Kelso.

The King, delighted with his success, urged Huntly and the other nobles to follow up the retreating invaders. But the nobles thought that they had done enough; they had no mind to obey a 'priests' king', and though they knew that Henry had despoiled the English monasteries, they did not see why their king should quarrel with him over a policy which had brought wealth to many a needy baron and knight. Though a Scottish army crossed the border in November the King did not go with it, and the nobles were furious when they learned that the chief command had been delegated, not to one of themselves, but to the King's favourite, Oliver Sinclair. While they were disputing, while some of their men had begun to move off homewards, they were hotly attacked by a small body of English cavalry. They fled in panic, only to find themselves trapped among the stagnant pools of Solway Moss. Many of the nobles surrendered without striking a blow.

Almost mad with grief, with a mortal disease upon him, the King rode from Lochmaben to Holyrood and from Holyrood to his pleasant hunting-seat of Falkland. For the moment it seemed as if his melancholy might be lifted; news came to him from Linlithgow that a child had been born to his Queen. He asked anxiously if it was a boy. 'A fair daughter,' said the messenger. The King, remembering how the Scottish crown had come into the Stewart family through the marriage of Marjorie Bruce with Walter the Steward, murmured, 'Adieu, farewell, it came with a lass, it will pass with a lass,' then, in the words of the old chronicler, 'he turned his back unto his lords, and his face unto the wall'.

CHAPTER XVII

THE REFORMATION AND THE END OF THE
FRANCO-SCOTTISH ALLIANCE: 1542–1560

> The sticks break, the stones crumble,
> The eternal altars tilt and tumble,
> Sanctions and tales dislimn like mist
> About the amazed evangelist.
>
> R. L. STEVENSON.

Scotland		*England*	
Mary 1542–1567		Henry VIII . . . 1509–1547	
		Edward VI . . . 1547–1553	
		Mary 1553–1558	
		Elizabeth 1558–1603	

OF the prelates and nobles who looked at one another fearfully as they stood beside the body of their king, probably there was not one who thought of that scene when, on the morning after the great tempest, the frightened searchers gathered round the dead Alexander. Yet, in the two hundred and fifty-six years separating the death of Alexander III from the death of James V, the wheel had come full circle. In 1542, as in 1286, a king had died suddenly, leaving only a little girl to succeed him ; in 1542, as in 1286, a hard, strong, efficient king, a great-uncle, moreover, of the child Queen of Scots, sat on the English throne. The same ambition which had burned in Edward I flamed up in Henry VIII : he would unite Scotland to his own kingdom, and he would do it in the same way, by securing the consent of the Scottish leaders to the marriage of their queen with Prince Edward, the heir to the English throne.

Henry's task seemed an easy one. His policy of hostility to the Roman Catholic Church had many admirers in Scotland ; even the Governor of Scotland himself, the changeable Earl of Arran, had become something of a Protestant, more through hatred of his rival the great Cardinal Beaton than through zeal for reform in the Church. And in some of the too-willing prisoners from Solway Moss, the Earls of Cassilis and Glencairn and their fellows, Henry found Scotsmen who were ready to act as English ambassadors in return for their liberty. Early in 1543 he sent them to Edinburgh in the company of the Earl of Angus, lately a refugee at the English court, pledged to do their utmost to secure the consent of the Scottish Government to the treaty of marriage.

They succeeded; in July 1543, the Treaty of Greenwich was signed, by which the Scottish Government gave its consent to the marriage of the young Queen to Prince Edward, and to her removal to England as soon as she reached the age of ten. In their ecclesiastical policy, too, the Governments of the two countries seemed to be drawing closer together; the same Parliament that appointed ambassadors to discuss the treaties with the representatives of the English Government also announced that any man who chose might now read the Bible in an English translation without fear of punishment.

Then something happened: before the end of the year the Scots realized that Henry VIII, like Edward I in his day, was aiming at nothing short of the complete incorporation of Scotland into his own kingdom. The Scottish Parliament promptly repudiated the treaty, and Arran, in his desperate need for the counsel of a wiser man than himself, found it necessary to make friends with his former rival, Cardinal Beaton.

Henry was furious. Still, as Edinburgh was far from London, the Scots thought that they had no cause for fear, and when in the early summer of 1544 a great fleet appeared in the Firth of Forth the Governor and the Cardinal persuaded themselves that it was only a fleet of fishing-boats returning from Iceland, and the burgesses of Leith who had paused to gaze at the strange spectacle on their way from church, sat down to their Sunday dinners with an easy mind. Most of them, however, left the meal untasted, when they heard the clash of weapons in the streets outside and commands shouted in the unfamiliar southern tongue. The English had come. But their commander, the Earl of Hertford, aimed at a bigger prize than Leith. On the morrow, when he had been reinforced by two thousand horsemen, he forced his way through the Canongate into Edinburgh and let his troops loose in it to burn and plunder as they pleased. At the end of a week nothing was left of the stately city but a heap of smouldering ruins.

This was not the way to win the hearts of the Scots. Even the Scottish Protestants, who had shrunk from the Cardinal's policy of firm friendship with France, began to wonder if it might not be the lesser of two evils; even the Douglases lost their enthusiasm for the English alliance when, in 1545, they found their lands laid waste and the tombs of their ancestors in Melrose Abbey desecrated by English raiders. When on Ancrum Moor, in the half-light of a February afternoon, a strong force of English borderers, blinded by the smoke of their own guns, fled in panic from the terrible Scottish spears, the Scots knew that they had been successful because Angus, that master of shifts and stratagems, had for once consented to give his country the benefit of his skill. But Henry persisted in his rough wooing: in the autumn of 1545 Hertford appeared on the border once again; once again plundered monasteries and flaming towns advertised to the Scots the benefits of the English alliance and the merits of the faith that Henry had embraced. Such arguments only confirmed the obstinate Scots in their errors.

Henry was not the only clever man who blundered. To his cleverest antagonist, David Beaton, Cardinal, Archbishop of St. Andrews and Bishop of Mirepoix in France, Protestantism and treason seemed to be one and the same thing. Questions of doctrine did not interest Beaton—why should he want to change the Church that had made him what he was? He did not see that the elevation of a man of notoriously evil life like himself to the ranks of the princes of the Church supplied the critics of that Church with a most damaging argument.

Of the few Scottish preachers who had dared openly to denounce the Cardinal and the Catholic Church none wielded

JOHN KNOX
After the engraving in Beza's *Icones*

more influence than George Wishart. Those who were not moved by his preaching were moved by his courage; all Scotland knew how, when the pestilence broke out in Dundee, he had hurried back to the stricken town, and from the top of the East Port of the city had preached to the sick and dying without the gate, and to those still untouched by the pest within. Of him Beaton resolved to make an example. He was arrested at Ormiston House, near Haddington, taken to St. Andrews and lodged in the Castle there. Wishart seems to have had some premonition of the fate that was in store for him. He had narrowly escaped assassination in Dundee, and from that time, whenever he preached in public, a grim-visaged, black-bearded schoolmaster, John Knox by name, had stood on guard beside him, grasping a great two-handed sword. An hour or two before he was arrested Wishart ordered his friend to lay aside his sword and leave him, and when Knox protested, he quietly replied, 'Nay, return to your bairns, and God bless you! One is sufficient for one sacrifice.'

Wishart was found guilty of heresy, and early in 1546 was burned in front of St. Andrews Castle. The two greatest prelates in Scotland, the Cardinal and the Archbishop of Glasgow, sat at a window in the Castle to watch his dying agonies. Men who detested Wishart's doctrines were constrained to admire his calm and cheerful courage. Even the executioner knelt and asked his pardon before he bound him to the stake. 'Lo, here is a token that I forgive thee,' said Wishart, kissing him on the cheek; 'my heart, do thine office.' But no sign of compunction came from the Cardinal.

This was not forgotten: three months later a party of Wishart's friends assembled near the Castle early in the morning, rushed over the drawbridge before the affrighted porter could pull it up, knocked the porter on the head and made their way to the Cardinal's room. 'I am a priest; I am a priest,' cried the terrified Cardinal, 'ye will not slay me.' 'The blood of Wishart cries a vengeance upon thee,' said one of his murderers coldly as he raised his sword to strike, 'and we from God are sent to revenge it.' 'I am a priest,' moaned the dying man again as he fell to the ground, 'fie, fie, all is gone.'

During the next twelve months St. Andrews Castle became a city of refuge to all those upon whom the hand of the Governor had pressed too heavily. Here, for example, at Easter in 1547,

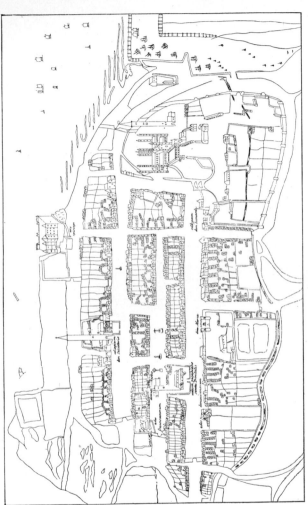

BIRD'S-EYE VIEW OF ST. ANDREWS ABOUT A.D. 1530

The Cathedral stands in the great walled enclosure to the east of the town. Notice the Castle (*arx episcopi*), St. Salvator's College (*collegium divi Salvatoris*), the Town Hall (*domus urbis*) with the market cross and the tron standing beside it, and the three ports guarding the western entrances to the town came John Knox. As yet he had never preached in public ; now, urged by his friends, he not only attacked the doctrines of the Church from the pulpit, but administered the Communion in the manner advocated by the continental reformers. 'Master George Wishart spoke never so plainly,' said one of his hearers, 'and yet he was brunt ; even so will he be.' Knox was not burned : the clergy, threatened by the guns of the Castle, did not dare to lay hands on him.

In the meantime events of the greatest importance had happened elsewhere. Henry VIII died in January 1547, two months before his great rival, Francis I. The death of Henry made no difference to the relations between England and Scotland : though the nominal governor of England was the boy-king Edward VI, Hertford, now become Duke of Somerset and Protector, was the real ruler of the country. But if England had not grown any less hostile, with the accession of Henry II France became almost embarrassingly friendly.

It was not altogether sympathy for a small nation, faithful ally of France though it had been, that moved the French King to interest himself in Scottish affairs. It was something much less laudable : Henry of France had begun to think that he might succeed where Henry of England had failed ; he would do his best to keep Scotland from becoming a province of England that he might ultimately make it a province of France. One advantage he had : the mother of the child-queen was a Frenchwoman, the sister, moreover, of the Duke of Guise and the Cardinal of Lorraine, the greatest men in France next to himself ; he could count on her, therefore, to favour the marriage of her daughter to his son, the Dauphin Francis.

The defenders of the Castle became aware of this new activity on the part of France when, in the summer of 1547, a French fleet sailed into St. Andrews Bay and opened fire upon them. At first they were not dismayed, for the first broadsides only dislodged a few slates ; even when they saw the brazen guns being pulled up the slope from the harbour and planted on the roofs of the Cathedral and of St. Salvator's College they still boasted that they would 'keep their Castle against England, Scotland, and France all three'. 'Your walls shall be but egg-shells,' was Knox's grim comment. Six hours after the bombardment had begun in real earnest a breach yawned in the wall through which a horse and cart could have been driven, and the garrison had no choice but to surrender. Their lives were spared, but they were taken to France to toil at the oar in the galleys.

So Knox disappears for a time from Scottish history. On his release from the galleys in 1549 he settled in England, where he gained so much fame as a preacher that he was appointed chaplain in ordinary to the young Edward VI, and was asked to become a bishop. With the accession of the Catholic Mary Tudor in 1553 Knox judged it wise to take refuge in the free city of Geneva. Here he heard the great French reformer, John Calvin, explain his religious beliefs—a creed as austere, majestic, and terrible as the great snow-clad mountains that stand about Lake Leman; here too he saw a city governed as he would fain have Scotland governed. From Geneva he went to Frankfort, to be minister of the congregation of exiled English Protestants there; but wherever he went contention seemed to follow, and after a few months he returned to Geneva to wait for news from Scotland.

Meantime much had happened in Scotland. In 1547, a few weeks after the sails of the French fleet had sunk below the horizon, an English army, led by Somerset, crossed the border and, keeping in touch with the fleet, advanced up the east coast towards Edinburgh. On Saturday, 16th September— Black Saturday—they came upon the Scottish army at Pinkie, about six miles east of the capital. For a time it seemed as if the Scots might prevail; the spearmen in the Scottish vanguard stood like a wall against the charges of the English and drove them back in disorder. But some of the lighter English ships, creeping close inshore, opened fire on the left flank of the Scottish army, and when the English field batteries joined in, the Highlanders, terrified by the unfamiliar noise, broke and fled. The vanguard, after waiting in vain for reinforcements, retired on the main body, but their comrades, blinded by the rain that was driving over the battle-field, mistook them for the enemy and attacked them fiercely. The English, encouraged by the evident panic and confusion in the Scottish ranks, laid aside their fears and advanced. At once the panic became general; in the biting words of an old Scots historian, his countrymen 'fled but[1] order, like beasts'. Many in their panic leapt into the River Esk and were drowned, many were so paralysed with fear that they allowed themselves to be cut down without attempting to defend themselves. Only when Somerset ordered his trumpets to sound and cried 'Kill no more!' was there any slackening in the pursuit.

Somerset found, like many an English commander before him, that to defeat a Scottish army in battle was a very different thing from subjugating Scotland. The disaster of Pinkie, far from persuading the Governor and his advisers to consent to the marriage of their Queen with King Edward, convinced them that they must not only send her to France, but also give their consent to her marriage with the Dauphin, should that marriage be the price of the French King's support.

It was in vain that a few weeks after Pinkie an English expedition captured Broughty Castle at the mouth of the Tay and bombarded Dundee; it was in vain that in the spring of 1548 the English seized Haddington and used it as a base of operations for pillaging the surrounding country. The girl-queen was sent to France; companies of French, German, and Italian mercenaries crossed from France to Scotland; in the autumn of 1549 Haddington was recaptured; in the early

[1] without.

spring of 1550 Broughty Castle surrendered to the Governor and his French auxiliaries.

Scotland had no more to fear from Somerset; the failure of his Scottish schemes had brought the great Protector low; he had fallen from power, and death on the scaffold was fated soon to be his portion. What is more, by the Treaty of Boulogne, which put an end to the war which had broken out in 1549 between England and France, the English Government undertook to withdraw its garrisons from Scotland, to refrain from attacking Scotland in the future, and to raise no objection to the proposed marriage of the Scottish Queen and the Dauphin.

France had saved Scotland from England; who was now to save Scotland from France? Henry II could now boast that Scotland was as much subject to him as his own kingdom. Steadily the weight of the gilded chains increased, till in 1554 Arran, bribed by the offer of the French dukedom of Châtelherault, resigned the office of Governor to the Queen-Mother.

Mary of Guise had no lack of courage or of womanly charm; she could soften the hearts of her most stubborn opponents with tactful speeches, framed in the prettiest of broken English; but more than courage and charm was required in her new position. The Scottish nobles, seeing the French King change from an ally into an overlord, grew restive; in 1557 they protested strongly against being dragged into a war with England simply because Philip of Spain, the husband of the English Queen, had dragged an unwilling England into war with France, and though a Scottish army crossed the Tweed in October, it refused to risk another Flodden and had to be disbanded. But before the end of the year the Scottish Parliament had given its consent to the marriage of the young Queen Mary with the Dauphin of France and had appointed eight ambassadors to be present at the ceremony in Paris.

The chains were being drawn tight, tighter than the ambassadors knew. As they stood under the grey towers of Notre-

Dame and gazed at the flower-like figure and candid face of their Queen, they could not know that this girl of fifteen had already played them false. She had signed one paper bequeathing her kingdom unconditionally to the King of France should she die childless, a second putting her kingdom in pledge to him for the sum of 1,000,000 crowns—the cost of her education—and a third declaring that no document which she might sign thereafter could cancel the other two. Though the ambassadors knew nothing of this, and though they had already agreed that the Dauphin should take the courtesy title of King of Scotland, they saw something sinister in the proposal that he should be allowed to wear the crown as well, and refused to grant this request without consulting the Scottish Parliament. Something still more sinister happened after their refusal: four of them died suddenly on their way home before they had left France.

Men whispered that they had been poisoned, but the rumour did not keep the Parliament from allowing the Dauphin to wear the crown. To outward appearance the two countries had never been more friendly; the French King had conferred an unheard-of privilege on his allies; Scots who came to France were to be treated as naturalized Frenchmen and were not to be debarred from any benefice or office, or from inheriting any property in France because of their foreign blood, and the Scottish Parliament retaliated courteously by conferring a similar privilege on Frenchmen living in Scotland. In spite of her daughter's marriage, in spite of this generous naturalization law, the Regent's position become more difficult every day. What was she to make of the Scottish Protestants, who were steadily gaining in numbers and becoming louder in their complaints ? At first they had not absented themselves from the ordinary services of the Church, but in 1555 John Knox had paid a secret visit to Scotland and had succeeded in persuading many of them to stop attending Mass. The Regent was no persecutor, nor did she want to do anything that would make the French alliance unpopular; on the other hand she was an orthodox Catholic, and she knew besides that in the past the Catholic prelates had supported the alliance with France through thick and thin. So, though she was not unwilling to let the Protestants worship in their own way, provided they did it in secret, she would admit of no alteration in the organization, ceremonies, or doctrine of the Roman Catholic Church in Scotland.

But the Protestants would not be content with mere toleration; at the end of 1557 certain of the Protestant Lords had signed a bond or agreement by which they declared that they forsook the Roman Catholic Church and pledged themselves to apply their whole power, substance, and very lives to establish and maintain a reformed Church in Scotland.

And though the Queen Regent was averse from persecution herself, she could not control the prelates; in the spring of 1558 Hamilton, the Archbishop of St. Andrews, a half-brother of Châtelherault, ordered Walter Myln, an old man of eighty-two, to be burned at the stake as a heretic.

A thrill of horror ran through Scotland. The Protestants had been assured by the Regent, only a short time before, that she would not molest them; now they found it hard to believe either her original promise or her declaration that she had not consented to Myln's death. In vain the Lords of the Congregation tried to get their way by negotiation; neither the Parliament which met at the end of 1558 nor the Provincial Council of the Scottish clergy which met in March 1559 would listen to their demand that the services of the Church should be in the vulgar tongue and that the reformed Communion service with the Communion in both kinds[1] should replace the mass. The Scottish clergy, galvanized by fear into an unwonted activity, passed many much-needed laws for stiffening up the discipline

---

[1] Communion in which the wine as well as the bread is administered to the lay worshipper.

of the Church, but steadfastly refused to alter its doctrine, its ceremonies, or its organization. And the Regent became suddenly less conciliatory; she knew that as peace had been signed between France and Spain, she could now count on the support of French troops should any serious trouble arise in Scotland. So when she heard that the people of Perth had suddenly gone Protestant she ordered the Provost to make them Catholic again, only to be told that 'he could make their bodies to come to Her Grace . . . but to cause them to do against their conscience he could not promise'. She learned too that on Easter Sunday, despite her express commands, the people of Perth and Dundee stayed away from mass altogether. It was too much; she peremptorily ordered the four preachers whom she considered responsible for this defection to appear before her at Stirling on the 10th of May.

To the Protestants the summons seemed a declaration of war. The country gentlemen of Angus and the Mearns assembled at Dundee, resolved that if the preachers went to Stirling they would go with them. To Dundee too came John Knox, who after waiting for many months at Dieppe, had at last decided to put his fiery eloquence and rude but effective wit at the service of his brethren.

From Dundee the Reformers went to Perth, and in the Parish Church, on the second Sunday of their stay, Knox preached a rousing sermon, in which he declared that the sacrament of mass was an idolatrous rite. Undeterred by the preacher's vehemence, a priest stepped forward to the high altar when the sermon was over, intending to celebrate mass as usual. 'This is intolerable!' shouted a boy, only to be promptly cuffed by the priest. The youngster thereupon retired to a safe distance and threw a stone at the priest; it missed him, but smashed an image on the altar. Other bystanders joined in the stone-throwing and soon they had succeeded in demolishing every image in the church. Word spread that mischief was afoot, but the preachers and the country gentlemen prudently remained indoors at dinner and the 'rascall multitude', as Knox called them, soon served the beautiful buildings of the Charterhouse, even though its chapel contained the tomb of a king, and of the Franciscan and the Dominican monasteries as they had served the parish church.

The Regent replied by getting an army together and advancing against Perth; but she could not be altogether sure of her followers. Two of them, the ambitious Lord James Stewart, a half-brother of Queen Mary, and the young Earl of Argyll, were really heart and soul with the Reformers, and before she could summon the city to surrender, the Protestant lairds and burgesses of the west, led by the Earl of Glencairn, had appeared on the scene. Neither side was over-anxious to come to blows; the Lords of the Congregation withdrew from Perth on the understanding that the Regent should not garrison it with her French mercenaries, and advanced on St. Andrews. There the same sorry story was repeated; the crowd, lashed into a frenzy by the reckless eloquence of Knox, sallied forth to the Cathedral, the fairest and greatest church in all Scotland, and smashed and battered to their hearts' content till only the bare walls were left. The Regent was powerless, Argyll and Lord James had deserted her; though her army advanced against the Protestant forces, it found them strongly posted at Cupar and retired without risking a battle. From Cupar she withdrew to the capital, but even there there was no safety; the victorious army of the Congregation, after it had turned aside to capture Perth, after it had sacked the churches in Stirling and Linlithgow, was now heading for Edinburgh. The Regent retreated to Dunbar; hardly was her rearguard clear of the capital when the disorderly forces of the Protestants poured in at the gates. Even now the Regent did not lose heart. Her small, well-disciplined professional army held together in defeat; the motley hosts of the Congregation melted away in the hour of victory. Her sudden advance on Edinburgh three weeks later found the Lords of the Congregation with only a handful of followers ; they were forced to promise that they would no longer molest priests or destroy churches, and to retire to Stirling.

The Regent's forces straightway occupied the town of Leith. Every day her position grew stronger ; in the closing months of 1559 reinforcements from France poured into the fort at Leith, and though the Lords of the Congregation accompanied by no less a person than Châtelherault again occupied Edinburgh and prepared to lay siege to Leith, their forces were mauled so badly in a chance encounter that they again retired to the west. Emboldened by this success, the Regent sent a detachment of her army into Fifeshire. So at the end of 1559 the cause of the Scottish reformers seemed hopeless. But help was at hand. In November 1558 the Protestant Elizabeth had ascended the English throne ; in the following year the death of Henry II made Francis and Mary King and Queen of France. But to faithful Catholics who did not regard Elizabeth as a lawful daughter of Henry VIII, her kinswoman Mary was not simply Queen of Scotland and France, she was Queen of England as well. And the Scottish Queen did not hesitate to make this claim ; when she heard of the death of Mary Tudor she promptly assumed the coat of arms of England in addition to those of Scotland and France.

The French occupation of Scotland, then, might be but a step to a French invasion of England. On their side the Lords of the Congregation were forced to recognize that their volunteer armies were no match for the disciplined French mercenaries, that they must look outside Scotland for help, and that only from their old enemy England was help to be expected. They despatched the cleverest of their number, the wily Maitland of Lethington, to the English court with their appeal for help. His was no easy task ; the help might be given at too great a price ; if he called in the Englishman to expel the

Frenchman, the Englishman might stay. But he was successful; by the Treaty of Berwick, signed in February 1560, the English Government agreed to send an army to Scotland to co-operate with the Lords of the Congregation, and to continue the struggle until the French were driven completely out of Scotland.

Even before the Treaty was signed a fleet of English ships appeared in the Forth—to look for pirates, their commander said—and early in April a strong English army joined the forces of the Lords of the Congregation before the walls of Leith. The plight of the French garrison was desperate. In France, too, Catholic and Protestant were now involved in open war, and the King did not dare to send forces sufficient to break through the English blockade. The Queen Regent lay in Edinburgh Castle stricken with a mortal sickness. But the French mercenaries fought stoutly, beat off attack after attack, and made more than one murderous sally into the lines of the besiegers. The Regent's death in the early summer made no difference to them; they fought on even when the English cannon had destroyed their stores and magazines and reduced them to scanty rations of horseflesh. The French king's advisers saw that the struggle was hopeless, and ambassadors were dispatched to the English court, whence, accompanied by two English ambassadors, they proceeded to the camp of the allies.

The Treaty of Edinburgh, which the representatives of the three countries signed early in July, put an end to the French attempts to dominate Scotland. Only six score French soldiers were to be allowed to remain in Scotland ; the French officials, too, had to go ; in future no foreigner was to hold any office under the Scottish crown. There were to be no more French Regents; in the sovereign's absence the country was to be governed by a council of twenty-four, of whom only seven were to be appointed by Francis and Mary. Finally, the Scottish Queen must remove the three lions of England from her royal insignia and so declare to the world that she considered Elizabeth to be the rightful Queen of England.

So with the signing of the Treaty of Edinburgh the Auld Alliance came to an end: the events of the previous ten years had convinced the patriotic Scot that France was no longer the champion of Scottish independence, but its foe. That the alliance should have ended when it did was clearly the fault of Mary of Guise and her over-ambitious kinsmen; that it would have developed into a permanent partnership if they had been content to go slowly cannot, however, be maintained. Apart from the common fear of England, there was no real bond of union between the two peoples; the difference of language, even without the five hundred miles of estranging sea between the pier of Leith and Calais harbour, was sufficient to keep them apart. Some trade there was between the two countries, it is true, but it was Veere in Holland, and not Bordeaux or Havre de Grace, that attracted the bulk of the Scottish merchant ships. To one small though influential class the end of the old friendship made a change; though the Scottish soldier of fortune still took his sword and his valour to France, the Scottish scholar, to his loss, now forced himself to be content with such learning as he could get in St. Andrews or Glasgow or Aberdeen. The cultured Scotsman had no longer, as it were, one foot in Paris and one in Edinburgh; his horizon was contracting; in time he would become almost, though not quite, as insular as his English neighbour.

Though the Treaty of Edinburgh made no mention of religious matters it put the Scottish Protestants in an unassailable position. In August 1560 the Scottish Parliament met in Edinburgh to repudiate the supremacy of the Pope, to condemn mass as an idolatrous rite, to forbid its celebration even in secret, and to repeal all acts in favour of Roman Catholicism. Hamilton and Wishart had not died in vain.

CHAPTER XVIII

MARY QUEEN OF SCOTS: 1560–1568

> Consider the way she had to go.
> Think of the hungry snare,
> The net she herself had woven,
> Aware or unaware,
> Of the dancing feet grown still,
> The blinded eyes.—
> Queens should be cold and wise,
> And she loved little things,
> Parrots
> And red-legged partridges
> And the golden fishes of the Duc de Guise
> And the pigeon with the blue ruff
> She had from Monsieur d'Elbœuf.
>
> MARION ANGUS.

	Scotland			*England*	
Mary	. . . .	1542–1567	Elizabeth	. . .	1558–1603

TO us the signing of the Treaty of Edinburgh and the denunciation by Parliament of the Roman Catholic Church mark the end of a chapter in the history of Scotland. But to the thoughtful Scotsman of that day, everything must still have seemed dark and uncertain. The Treaty of Edinburgh had indeed been signed, but Queen Mary would not ratify it; in other words she still maintained that she and not Elizabeth was the rightful Queen of England. The Parliament of 1560 had indeed repudiated the authority of the Pope and prohibited the celebration of mass, but how could a Parliament which had not been expressly summoned by the sovereign be a lawful assembly? Besides, it was doubtful if Parliament had the bulk of the nation behind it; though the burgesses and country lairds of Angus, Fife, and the Lothians were now solidly Protestant, Catholicism was strongly entrenched in the north-east and the south-west.

The divisions among the leaders of the Protestant party made the outlook still more uncertain. Everything was clean-cut and definite in John Knox's dreams: dreams of a country kept free from the taint of Catholicism by fear of the prison and the gallows, dreams of a Church not unlike the Anglican Church, with bishops—only he would call them superintendents—and with a prayer book—the English Book of Common Prayer would serve till he framed a simpler one. If Knox had his way there would be no more ignorant clergy; he would cover the whole land with a network of schools. Every parish would have one, and so a clever boy, however poor he might be, would be able to proceed from the Parish School to the Burgh School, where he would learn Latin and Greek, and perhaps Hebrew, and thence to the University, till in the end he exchanged the scarlet gown of the student for the black Geneva gown of the minister. A noble dream; easy of realization if the revenues of the old Church could be handed over intact to the new. But the nobles and country lairds had different views. It is true that their zeal for the overthrow of the old order seemed to be equal to that of Knox himself; but it was sometimes hard to distinguish hatred of the Roman Catholic Church from love of the lands which had belonged to it; and the needy country laird, newly enriched with the revenues of the neighbouring abbey, had no mind to disgorge them to provide a minister for the derelict parish church, or a schoolmaster for the school that was yet to be built.

And what of Lord James Stewart, half-brother of the Queen, what dream floated before his eyes? Wealth perhaps—the revenues from the broad lands of Dryburgh Abbey flowed into his coffers—but power still more. If the accident of his birth had kept him from being crowned King of Scotland he could still be the uncrowned king, and perhaps—who knew?—something more. And his new ally Châtelherault. What had made him change from a half-hearted Catholic to a half-hearted

Protestant? He too cherished ambitions, he could not forget that he was the great-grandson of James the Second and that he stood next in the line of succession to the crown. He himself might never wear it, but could Elizabeth be persuaded to marry his son, the Earl of Arran, Mary's claims could be brushed

'stately white châteaux . . . trembling poplars' (p. 242)
Le Château d'Azay-le-Rideau

aside and a Hamilton would become ruler of both kingdoms. There were others besides Châtelherault and his kin who favoured this scheme; the inscrutable, changeable Lethington toiled hard to bring it about, not because he wanted to see a Hamilton seated on the throne of England and Scotland, but because he believed that only through a voluntary union with England could his country ever gain lasting security and prosperity.

This project came to nothing; before the year was out

Elizabeth let it be known that she would not consent to marry Arran, and in the autumn of 1561 Mary herself arrived in Scotland. Bereft of her husband, conscious that she had become an unwanted stranger at her own court, she had resolved to leave France with its clear skies, its broad green plains, its stately white châteaux—palaces rather than castles—mirrored in placid silvery streams shadowed by trembling poplars, and seek the grey skies, grey seas, and grim grey towers of the north. Seldom had Edinburgh looked more gloomy than on the day when she landed in Scotland: 'The verray face of heavin,' said Knox, 'did manifestlie speak what confort was brought unto this cuntrey with hir, to wit, sorow, dolour, darknes and all impietie.' Her heart must have sunk within her as she splashed through the rain with her bedraggled cavalcade, and saw the towers of Holyrood loom ominous through the mist. Her loyal subjects, some five or six hundred of them, came to serenade her that night, but the monotonous cadences of the psalms which they sang and the melancholy wail of fiddles none too well tuned, plunged her French attendants into even deeper gloom.

But in those days the shadows did not rest on her long. She was only nineteen, with a schoolgirl's zest for enjoyment, with a gay confidence in her power to charm both friend and foe. The tap of dancing feet, the stately strains of pavane and coranto were heard once more in Holyrood, and sober citizens shook their heads when they heard how the Queen and her four ladies-in-waiting—the four Maries—had appeared at one of these dances disguised as swaggering young gallants, and how the Earl of Arran, mad enough already, had come near to losing what remained of his five wits for love of his sovereign.

But as Catholic ruler of a Protestant country, or a country where the Protestants were in the ascendant, Queen Mary had a difficult part to play. On the very first Sunday after her return some of the more extreme Protestants, having heard that mass was to be celebrated in the chapel at Holyrood, made their way into the Palace, and would have broken into the chapel and slain the priest had not Lord James Stewart stationed himself in the doorway. The storm blew over; the Queen issued a proclamation declaring that she had no intention of changing the religion that she found established in Scotland, although she demanded liberty to worship in the ancient way for herself and for her household. Knox might declare in the pulpit that one mass was more fearful to him than ten thousand armed enemies; the ordinary man saw nothing to fear from a ruler who made no attempt to shelter her Catholic subjects from the rigours of the anti-Catholic laws, and who in 1562 accompanied Lord James Stewart in an expedition against the Earl of Huntly, that expedition which ended in the death of the great Catholic earl on the field of Corrichie.

But Mary's thoughts ranged far beyond the walls of Holyrood, far beyond the boundaries of Scotland. She had been Queen of France once, could she not still be Queen of England? She was Elizabeth's kinswoman, the daughter of Margaret Tudor's only son, and she knew that in the eyes of the Catholics, who refused to regard Elizabeth as the lawful daughter of King Henry VIII, she was the rightful Queen of England. If only she could marry some great Catholic prince who would put his fleets and armies at her disposal, then—but only then— could she wrest her heritage from Elizabeth. But no great Catholic prince appeared; the long-cherished project of a marriage with Don Carlos, the eldest son of Philip II of Spain, had to be abandoned by her because of the opposition of England and France. She might try another way: by tact and fair words, by accepting a husband whom her rival had chosen for her, she would persuade Elizabeth to acknowledge her as her successor.

But Elizabeth was adamant; she saw that if she acknowledged Mary's title to succeed to the throne, she would remove the only objection that the English Catholics could have to her rival, and pave the way for her own deposition. It took long for Mary to recognize that there was no getting past this refusal, but after four years' fruitless efforts she realized that tact and patience would avail nothing, that Elizabeth had made up her mind to thwart her at every turn.

Unluckily for Mary, in the early months of 1565 Henry Stewart, Lord Darnley, appeared in Scotland. The Queen saw him at a dance, straightway fell in love with the tall slender youth who carried himself like a king, and made up her mind that she would marry him. The match had little to commend it; it is true that Darnley was, like Mary, a grandchild of Margaret Tudor, and, like Mary, a Catholic; it is true that the English Catholics regarded him with more favour than they did Mary, because, in spite of his Scottish descent, he had been born and educated in England; but Elizabeth could not view with equanimity the marriage of her two most dangerous rivals, and the Protestant nobles in Scotland feared that the marriage would be the first step to the destruction both of their power and of Protestantism in Scotland. Encouraged by Elizabeth, the Earl of Moray—to give Lord James Stewart his new title— and the other Protestant lords prepared to take up arms. Mary held to the course that she had chosen; in July 1565 Darnley and she were married in the Chapel of Holyrood according to the Catholic rite, then, after declaring that she had no intention of attacking the Protestant religion, she gathered an army together, hunted the rebels all over southern Scotland, and finally forced them to retire across the border. Moray went to seek counsel of Elizabeth, but this Queen, who objected to his rebellion, not because it was a rebellion, but because it was unsuccessful, ordered him to 'pack out of her presence'.

This Chaseabout Raid, as people called it, was Mary's last success. Too soon she learned that she had thrown away her

affection on a foolish and petulant youth, one who, not content
with being hailed as King Henry, grumbled perpetually because

QUEEN MARY AND LORD DARNLEY

Mary would not give him the kingly authority which he was
incapable of using. It was not to him that the Queen turned
when she wanted advice, but to David Rizzio, 'a merry fellow
and a good musician', who had come to Holyrood in the train

of an Italian ambassador and had remained behind to be the Queen's French secretary. Soon the supple musician became an all-powerful favourite, and though the haughty nobles might frown on him and thrust him aside, he bore himself with all the more arrogance, 'disdaining all danger and despising counsel'.

Darnley's jealousy of the foreign favourite gave the exiled rebels and their confederates the chance of striking a blow at the Queen. Early in 1566 he was persuaded to join in a plot against the favourite, and he formed one of that band of armed men who in the dusk of a March evening beset the Palace of Holyrood, barred all the doors, made their way by a secret stair to the Queen's little supper-room and seized the unfortunate musician. It was in vain that the Queen stormed and wept, it was in vain that the terrified wretch clung to his mistress; his enemies dragged him out of the room and butchered him, leaving the King's dagger in his body for a sign.

The Queen found herself a prisoner in her own Palace, with a man who had insulted her beyond all hope of forgiveness. It is little wonder that she went almost mad with rage and grief; but knowing that wild outbursts of anger would be useless, she set herself to study revenge. It was an easy matter for Mary, consummate actress as she was, to throw her spell once more over the shiftless Darnley, and detach him from his fellow-murderers; it was an easy thing for her to greet Moray, suddenly come from England, as if she thought it was solicitude for her and not ambition for himself that had made him return. When, two nights later, Moray and his confederates waited on her in her room in Holyrood to ask that she should pardon the murderers, she agreed to do it on the morrow, drank to the health of each of them and asked that the keys of the Palace should again be entrusted to her. When the morrow came, she and Darnley were thirty miles away at Dunbar, and the news that she was gathering an army soon sent the murderers of

Rizzio scurrying across the border. At the same time she won over—to outward seeming at any rate—Moray and the other lords who had taken refuge in England after the Chaseabout Raid. She had ridden out the storm, and a season of calm weather seemed to be in front of her. The birth of a son, too, in the summer of 1566, should have strengthened her position. But her reconciliation with Darnley was a hollow sham : she was no longer merely indifferent to him, she despised and hated him.

Her hatred of her treacherous and contemptible husband, now smitten with a horrible disease, grew more intense when she compared him with one among her nobles, the brave, impetuous, arrogant Earl of Bothwell, whom men might hate, but could not afford to despise. If only Bothwell could be her husband! It was a mad and wicked dream ; not only would Mary's fellow-Catholics regard her as a traitor to their cause if she married a Protestant, but Catholic and Protestant alike would be horrified at the union of two persons both of whom were already married. The ecclesiastical courts might be cajoled into declaring Bothwell's previous marriage null and void, but a divorce from Darnley would not satisfy Mary, for she feared that it would damage her infant son's claim to the throne. But if not divorce—what ?

Bothwell too wanted Darnley away, so did Moray and Lethington, and so did the actual murderers of Rizzio, whom he had first supported and then attempted to betray. Before the end of the year the Queen and these other enemies of Darnley met in council in Craigmillar Castle. Darnley must be got out of the way, they decided ; the Queen consented to leave the precise manner of his removal to the nobles, provided they did it in such a way as to lay no spot on her honour or conscience.

Would we could say that her honour was unspotted! Early in the year 1567 the Queen journeyed to Glasgow, where her husband lay sulking and sick, coaxed him into a good humour and persuaded him to return to Edinburgh with her. Lest he should infect the young prince with his disease she lodged him, not in Holyrood, but in the Kirk o' Field,[1] an abandoned monastery just outside the walls of the city. Here, too, the Queen spent most of her time till the night of the 9th of February, when after chatting with Darnley, and telling him, as if nothing lay behind her words, that almost a year had passed since Rizzio had been murdered, she suddenly announced that she had promised to dance at the wedding festivities of one of her servants, and returned hastily to the Palace. An hour or two later the crash of an explosion shook the sleeping city ; the Kirk o' Field had been blown up 'so that there remained not one stone on another undestroyed'. The affrighted citizens, stumbling about the ruins in the first glimmer of dawn, came upon the dead body of the King in a garden close at hand. There was no mark of burning on him ; the murderers had strangled him first and then blown up the house.

Even if there had been none to say that soon after the Queen's return they had seen Bothwell, arrayed as if for battle, steal out of the Palace, there would have been little doubt about the identity of the prime mover in the affair. But though rumours flew about Edinburgh, though placards accusing him of the murder were placed on the walls by night, though the Earl of Lennox, the father of the murdered man, cried out for vengeance, no one dared to touch him, knowing that he stood higher in the Queen's favour than ever. The Queen was persuaded to appoint a day for his trial, but nothing came of it, for knowing that Bothwell had packed the town with armed men, Lennox prudently stayed away. Moray, too, saw that he had raised a demon whom he could not control, and judged it best to leave Scotland for a season.

Worse was to follow : as Mary was returning from Stirling, where she had been visiting her young son, she was waylaid by

[1] The older buildings of Edinburgh University now occupy the site.

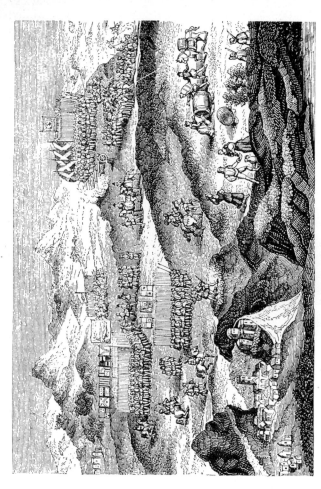

THE SURRENDER OF MARY QUEEN OF SCOTS AT CARBERRY HILL

From an old engraving by Vertue

Bothwell at the head of a party of horsemen and borne off to
Dunbar Castle. People suspected that Mary was a willing
captive, and the manner in which Bothwell's divorce was
hurried through the courts, the spectacular entry of the Queen
into Edinburgh, with Bothwell holding her bridle to make the
crowd think she was his prisoner, and the dukedom which the
Queen conferred upon him, served to confirm their suspicions.
In truth, the Queen had fallen madly, blindly, in love with
Bothwell; she was ready to fling the crown of Scotland after
the crown of England, to alienate the minds of Catholic and
Protestant alike, if only she could be united to him. In vain the
minister who proclaimed the banns declared that the marriage
should not take place; on the 15th of May in the Chapel at
Holyrood, before a handful of the nobles, the Queen of Scots
and the new Duke of Orkney were married 'with neither
pleasure nor pastime'.

Mary was left without a friend in Scotland; even those who
had striven to believe that she had no part in Darnley's death
were horrified at her hasty marriage with her husband's
murderer. That her subjects should rise in rebellion was
inevitable; in Moray's absence the Earl of Morton acted as
leader, and Bothwell and Mary were forced to flee to Dunbar.
They raised an army and marched again towards the capital,
but when they reached Carberry Hill, not far from where the
battle of Pinkie had been fought, they found their way barred
by a stronger force under the rebel lords. The rebels protested
that they had no quarrel with the Queen, but that they must
have the traitor who had murdered her husband. Bothwell
hotly denied that he was a murderer and offered to fight to the
death with any one who charged him with the crime. Kirkcaldy
of Grange and Murray of Tullibardine at once took up the
challenge, whereupon Bothwell protested that one of his degree
could not fight with a simple country laird. To Lord Lindsay's
challenge he could not give the same reply; but the Queen,

fearing for her lover's safety, gave him her purse and ordered him to flee to Dunbar, and then, as soon as she knew that he would be safe from pursuit, she surrendered to the Laird of Grange. From Dunbar Bothwell took ship, and, though closely pursued, escaped to Norway.

A different and a harder fate awaited the Queen. She entered Edinburgh that night, not as she had done a few weeks before, with a proud lover at her bridle; there was no look of triumph on her dusty and tear-stained face; instead of a royal banner a flag with a picture of her murdered husband was borne before her, and instead of the salvoes of welcome from the guns of the Castle, she had to listen to the curses and insults of angry women. From Edinburgh she was hurried a few days later to Lochleven Castle, where she was forced, under threat of death, to abdicate in favour of her infant son James, and to consent to Moray's becoming Regent.

For almost a year Mary remained a prisoner in Lochleven Castle. But the Hamilton faction, though not for any love that they bore to Mary, resolved to secure her release: if they rescued her they might either force her to marry Lord Claude Hamilton, the fourth son of Châtelherault, or else kill her and gain the crown for Châtelherault himself.

It seemed impossible that Mary could escape from her island prison; all the gates of the Castle were locked before dusk every evening, and even though she might have got into a boat unobserved during the day, she would have been seen long before she reached the shore of the loch. But escape she did; one evening, after supper, her guards discovered that though the doors were still locked, the Queen had disappeared. They broke open the gates and hurried down to the waterside. Away out on the loch they could hear the plash of oars; they pushed off their boats in pursuit, only to discover that the rowlocks had been removed, and that, try as they might, they could not overtake the Queen. A party of horsemen was waiting for her at the water's edge and with this escort she rode off to Hamilton.

Mary had barely another fortnight of freedom, if to be in the hands of the Hamiltons could be called freedom. The Regent flung all the troops he could muster—only four thousand—into Glasgow; when the Queen and her allies attempted to march from Hamilton to Dumbarton, keeping a little to the south of Glasgow, they found their way barred by the Regent's troops at Langside. The Regent's horsemen were easily scattered, but his foremost company of spearmen stood fast for the space of half an hour, their spears interlocked with those of the Queen's vanguard. Even when their spears were shattered they fought on, attacking their opponents with stones or with anything on which they could lay their hands. The half-hearted soldiers behind them, encouraged by their example, came up on their right, charged the enemy and broke their ranks. Mary, seeing her followers flee in hopeless confusion, gathered a body of horsemen about her and galloped from the field. Dumbarton was barred to her now, and with Dumbarton the road to France; there was nothing for it but to go to England and throw herself on the mercy of Elizabeth. A few days later, at the Abbey of Dundrennan, on the shores of the Solway, she bade farewell to her followers and embarked on the vessel that was to bear her to England. She never returned. Elizabeth could not afford to be generous to a clever and ambitious princess who considered herself, and was considered by many of Elizabeth's Catholic subjects, to be the rightful Queen of England, and Mary, who had come expecting to be treated as an honoured guest, found that she was to all intents and purposes a prisoner. As the years passed, as plot after plot formed round her, her confinement grew straiter, till in 1587, having been found guilty of complicity in a plot to slay Elizabeth, she was executed in the hall of Fotheringhay Castle.

CHAPTER XIX

THE PARTING OF THE WAYS: 1568–1603

And thus do we of wisdom and of reach,
With windlasses and with assays of bias,
By indirections find directions out.

SHAKESPEARE.

Scotland		*England*	
James VI	1567–1625	Elizabeth	1558–1603

THOUGH Queen Mary never set foot in her kingdom after 1568, for long her unquiet spirit seemed to trouble Scotland. None knew better than Moray, who continued to rule the country on behalf of the infant King James, how treacherous was the calm that followed her departure. In the west the Hamiltons, in the north the Catholic Huntly, threatened rebellion. Some of his former allies too, envious of the wealth and power to which they had helped him, began to curse the folly which had made them drive Mary out only to put Moray in; others, who had objected to Bothwell more than to Mary, asked why the Queen, who had now completely recovered from her mad infatuation, should not again wear the Scottish crown. With most of the malcontents, jealousy of the Regent and the party in possession, with some, loyalty to their former sovereign, led to the formation of a coalition which had for its object the securing of Mary's return to Scotland and her restoration to the throne.

Moray knew that behind all this plotting and planning of the Queen's Lords, as the malcontents were called, was the cunning brain of the chameleon Lethington. In the autumn of 1569 he caused Lethington to be arrested on a trumped-up charge and lodged in a citizen's house in Edinburgh. But Lethington's confederate, Kirkcaldy of Grange, the Governor of the

Castle, promptly arrested him a second time and refused to give him up. War soon broke out—a war on which more depended than either King's Lords or Queen's Lords dreamed. The triumph of the Queen's Lords would have been a disaster for Scottish Protestantism. It is true that many of the Queen's Lords were Protestants, and that they aimed, not at the restoration of Catholicism, but simply at the restoration of a Catholic queen. Still, with a Catholic monarch on the throne a national Protestant Church would be in an exceedingly precarious position.

No story of chivalrous deeds brightens the sordid record of this 'war of religion'. It began with assassination: in January 1570 Hamilton of Bothwellhaugh, knowing that the Regent was to pass through the town of Linlithgow, concealed himself in a house on the main street, in front of which sheets were stretched as if an innocent washing had been hung up to dry. As the Regent rode slowly past, delayed by the pressure of the crowd, Hamilton shot him in the stomach, then flung himself on a horse and escaped. Moray was able to walk to his lodging, but died a few hours later.

Both the house and the horse were the property of another Hamilton—the reverend father in God, James Archbishop of St. Andrews. The friends of the murdered Regent did not forget this. When, more than a year later, they captured the Archbishop in Dumbarton Castle, neither his white hair nor his eighty-five years saved him from being tried and found guilty of murder. So the last Catholic Archbishop of St. Andrews was hanged at the market cross of Stirling, on a gibbet on which some wit had inscribed:

Cresce diu, felix arbor, semperque vireto
Frondibus, ut nobis talia poma feras.[1]

The Earl of Lennox, the grandfather of the young King, whom Queen Elizabeth had persuaded the King's Lords to

[1] Grow, lucky tree, thy leaves be ever green
That on thy boughs such fruit may oft be seen.

accept as Regent, fared no better than his predecessor. In 1571 the King's Lords had been compelled to abandon the town of Edinburgh, swept as it was by the guns of the Castle, and to make Stirling their headquarters. So it came about that in the month of August two Parliaments, one in Edinburgh and one in Stirling, denounced each other as treasonable assemblies, and pronounced sentence of death and forfeiture on offenders who refused to be arrested. But the Parliament at Stirling was graced with the presence of the five-year-old king, attired in gorgeous robes, with a brand-new crown on his head—the old one being at Edinburgh. As he entered the unfamiliar building he asked what place this was, and was told that it was a Parliament. His eyes roved round the hall while his grand-father made a speech, then rested on a gap in the roof. 'I think there is ane hole in this parliament,' remarked the youngster solemnly.

Five days later something happened which made the super-stitious remember the boy-king's idle remark. Between three and four in the morning shouts of 'Ane Hamilton! Ane Hamilton!' followed by the crackle of musketry and the crash of splintering timber roused the sleeping burgesses. Lord Claude Hamilton and the Earl of Huntly had broken into the town with four hundred horsemen at their backs. In the dark-ness and confusion few cared or knew how to resist; within a few minutes Huntly had captured not only the Regent but every one of the King's Lords. Having done all that he meant to do, he prepared to ride back with his prisoners to Edinburgh, but his men were not satisfied; leaving the prisoners all but un-guarded they roamed through the town in search of plunder, and began to break open shops and stables. Meantime the burgesses, having collected their scattered wits, sallied out, fell on the handful of men who had remained with Huntly, and rescued the prisoners. The alarm spread; soon cannon from the Castle were thundering through the darkness, soon the raiders were streaming in disorder along the road to Edinburgh, but not before one of Huntly's men had mortally wounded Lennox.

The death of Lennox did nothing to shorten the war; the Earl of Mar was elected in his place, and the weary struggle went on. It was like stalemate in chess: the Queen's Lords were not strong enough to smash the King's Lords, but, as long as the Queen's Lords held Edinburgh Castle, the King's Lords could not pretend to govern the country. And the Castle seemed impregnable; it was bombarded, but the besiegers feared to follow up the cannonade with an assault; it was blockaded, but provisions and reinforcements slipped through as before; appeals were sent to Elizabeth for guns and engineers, but only fair messages came from the parsimonious Queen.

In the autumn of 1572, when a truce gave a few months' rest to the combatants, Mar died—heart-broken it was said, because he could see no end to the struggle. His death opened the way for the more vigorous Earl of Morton. But the cause of the Queen's Lords was already lost: hitherto the douce burgess had looked on King's Lords and Queen's Lords alike as dangerous nuisances whose broils forced him to leave his booth and promenade the streets of his little burgh equipped with helmet and spear. The news of the Massacre of St. Bartholomew let him see what might happen in his own country if the Queen's Lords were victorious. In a moment indifference disappeared: the great mass of Scotsmen in the Lowlands ranged themselves behind the King's Lords. At the same time the announcement of the English Government that Mary would never be allowed to return to Scotland left the Queen's Lords with nothing to fight for.

But though most of the Queen's Lords made their peace with the Regent early in the following year, though Queen Elizabeth had at last granted the request of the Scottish Government and had sent engineers and artillery northward to Edinburgh, though Lethington was weakened by a deadly disease, the Castle still

held out. Not till the end of May, after the English guns had
bombarded it continuously for a week, killing more than a
third of the scanty garrison, bringing down King David's
Tower and another great tower, and pounding the battlements
into sand, did Kirkcaldy consent to surrender. Respect for
a gallant foe counted not at all with Morton; he ordered Kirkcaldy to be hanged, and would have served Lethington in the
same fashion had not Lethington cheated him by dying.

There were none who loved the cold and avaricious Regent,
but he gave Scotland the peace which it required; he kept it
clear of quarrels with England and entangling alliances with
France, and maintained the new national church. Though his
enemies forced him to resign the Regency in 1578, his eclipse
was only temporary; a few weeks later he was back in the
Secret Council once more. But in the following year a fascinat-
ing stranger, Esmé Stuart, Seigneur d'Aubigny, arrived from
France. He quickly gained the heart of the young King, who
made him Lord High Chamberlain and Earl of Lennox and
admitted him to the Council. But Lennox, it was whispered,
wanted more than titles and offices; he had come to bring
Scotland back to the French alliance and to the Catholic faith,
not by deposing James, but by making the young King and his
mother joint sovereigns. Morton, though he saw the ground
crumbling beneath him, could do nothing. In 1581 he was
accused by Captain James Stuart, one of the associates of
Lennox, of complicity in the murder of Darnley, and arrested
and beheaded, despite the vigorous protests of Elizabeth.
Lennox, no longer an Earl but a Duke, was now the master of
Scotland. But the Duke's vigorous repudiation of the Catholic
faith failed to convince; in 1582 the Earls of Gowrie, Mar, and
Glencairn, convinced that his influence over the King meant
no good to either Church or State, lured the King to Ruthven
Castle, made him a prisoner, and for a twelvemonth governed
the country in his name. Lennox judged it prudent to flee to

France, where he died a few months later. The risk of a back-ward swerve to Catholicism and of a French alliance had not yet disappeared, for in 1583 James escaped from Ruthven, and the attempts of the Earl of Gowrie to bring the King under subjection once more resulted only in Gowrie's death on the scaffold and the flight of his supporters to England. The young King found in Captain James Stuart, now Earl of Arran, a counsellor whose aims were identical with those of Lennox. But, save for the King, Arran had few friends ; the pestilence which smote the country in 1585 was looked on as a sign of the Divine wrath at his misgovernment, and so when the lords who had taken refuge in England returned with an army behind them, Arran followed the example of Lennox and fled.

Whatever may have been the King's private thoughts a year or two earlier, there seemed no likelihood now that he would renounce his policy of friendship with England and the maintenance of Protestantism. It is true that his subjects thought him unduly generous to the three Catholic Earls, Huntly, Errol, and Angus, whose plots and rebellions disturbed the north of Scotland between 1589 and 1595 ; but he had excellent reasons for remaining a Protestant, the same reasons that made Henry of Navarre repudiate his Protestant faith to become King of France. Elizabeth of England was unmarried, she had now neither brother nor sister ; the imprisoned Mary Queen of Scots was her next of kin. But the English would not have Mary at any price ; they could not forget the other Queen Mary and the red glare of the fires of Smithfield. James, on the other hand, had only to stay Protestant, insinuate him-self into the good graces of Queen Elizabeth, persuade her parlia-ment to set aside the obnoxious will of Henry VIII, which barred the descendants of Margaret Tudor from the succession, and the rarest and juiciest of plums would drop into his mouth.

He had only to pay the price, and when Elizabeth died the crown of England would be his. A permanent alliance with

England was the first instalment; in 1585 a treaty was signed whereby each country promised to come to the help of its neighbour if its neighbour should be invaded. At the second instalment James hesitated for a little—only a little—it was his mother's life. He knew what to do. When the sentence of death was pronounced against Mary he protested vigorously, and threatened to invade England, but he assured Elizabeth privately that there was nothing in his threats. One twinge of remorse he seems to have had: he ate no supper on the night when he heard of his mother's death, but though his subjects clamoured for war with England, they clamoured in vain.

But the will of Henry VIII was not set aside; never, till the end of her life, did Elizabeth declare that she wanted James to be her successor. On the other hand, she never declared that she did not want him to succeed her: she simply left the subject alone, unable to face the thought that at some time there would be an England, but no Elizabeth Tudor. But the King took comfort from the pension and the gracious letters that Elizabeth sent him, and lived in hope.

The years that followed the flight of Arran were comparatively peaceful. For one thing, until 1595, the young King allowed himself to be guided by Sir John Maitland of Thirlestane. Thirlestane, unlike his more brilliant brother the unfortunate Lethington, did not ' steer too nigh the sands to boast his wit '; he directed his energies to the humdrum work of repairing the broken machinery of government. James might grumble at the advice which his Chancellor gave him, especially in ecclesiastical matters, but he always took it in the end. In 1587 an attempt was made to restore the prestige and authority of the Parliament—which had tended to become simply a meeting of whatever faction happened to be uppermost at the time—by fining heavily every member who had been summoned and who failed to attend. A more important Act was passed at the same time. Almost every one had forgotten that at one time any landowner

who was entitled to hold a court of his own, however narrow
his lands might be, was entitled also to attend Parliament;
almost every one had forgotten the Act passed in 1428 which
ordained that the freeholders of each county were to send
two representatives to Parliament: when, indeed, in 1560 the
country gentlemen insisted on being present at the Parliament
which established Protestantism in Scotland, their action was
looked on as something new and altogether exceptional. It was
now decreed that the forgotten Act of 1428 was to be put into
execution; before a Parliament assembled the freeholders (landowners) in each county were to meet together and choose 'twa
wise men . . . of gude rent, and weel esteemed' to be their
representatives in Parliament. But the privilege of voting for
Commissioners of the Shire was confined to a comparatively
small class: farmers who paid an annual rent for the land
which they occupied, and freeholders who owned less than a
forty-shilling land—reckoned to be about 104[1] acres—were
alike excluded from taking any part in the election. The
Commissioners of the Shires were to have the same number
of representatives on the Committee of Articles as the other
three sections of the Parliament, prelates, nobles, and burgesses.

It had always been a comparatively easy business to get
Parliament to pass sensible laws: it was still as difficult as it had
ever been to secure obedience to these laws when they were
passed. The long period of civil strife had interrupted the
administration of justice, the circuit courts had fallen into
abeyance, and serious crimes were tried only at Edinburgh.
To remedy this the justice aires were re-established in 1587;
the country was divided into four districts, to each of which
two competent judges were assigned. These judges were to
perambulate their districts in April and October, halting at
every county town to pronounce judgement on the criminals
whom the sheriff of the county haled before them. But it was

---

[1] The old Scottish acre was equal to about 1¼ English acres.

not always easy to get competent and honest judges even in the Court of Session; in 1579, Parliament, moved by the complaints that the King had often chosen 'young men, without gravity, knowledge and experience' and that some of them had taken bribes, found it necessary to ordain that any Lord of Session found guilty of taking bribes should lose his office and all his movable goods, and further, that any judge whom the King appointed in future must pass an examination conducted by the other Lords of Session before he could be admitted to the bench. The Parliament which met in 1592—the first Scottish Parliament to which Commissioners of the Shires were admitted—supplemented this Act by declaring that no one who was under 25 or who had not a private income of at least 1,000 marks was to be appointed a Lord of Session.

The contempt into which the King's courts had fallen was not due simply to incompetent or corrupt judges; the wisest and most upright of judges found it difficult to make himself a terror to evil doers. If one gentleman had a dispute with another he usually settled it out of court, 'à la mode d'Édimbourg', as people said on the Continent, a fashion which involved the use of swords and pistols. If he killed his opponent he was summoned at the market cross of the nearest county town to deliver himself up and stand his trial. If, like a sensible man, he refused to come and be killed, nothing happened to him. There were no police to fetch him, and the score or two of soldiers who made up the royal bodyguard had their hands full protecting their own master. He would be outlawed, of course, but outlawry meant nothing to a laird whose country-house was built like a fortress and who could muster a body of stout retainers to defend it. What made it worse was that most of the disputes were senseless feuds inherited from a previous generation. In 1587, when James was still young enough to believe that men would always listen to reason, he tried one ingenious plan for composing those endless quarrels. He invited the more troublesome of his nobles to a banquet in Holyrood, at which he drank their healths thrice, and urged them to live at peace in future; next day he marched them two by two— each pair a brace of mortal enemies—up the Canongate to the Market Cross, where they found a large table prepared for them. There the performance of the previous day was repeated; to the blare of trumpets, the booming of cannon and the wild cheering of the astonished burgesses, the King drank the health of his nobles and made them drink to one another, then, as an appropriate conclusion to the ceremony, came a burst of fireworks in which the gallows crashed to the ground.

Neither this ceremony, nor the Act passed a few weeks later, establishing justices of the peace after the English model, could break the Scottish country gentleman of his habit of taking the law into his own hands. And too often the King and his judges, while they punished friendless malefactors with furious severity, avoided a trial of strength with a powerful offender; in 1592, for example, the Earl of Huntly, hearing that his enemy the Earl of Moray was at his house at Donibristle with a handful of servants, galloped there at the head of forty horsemen, and slew the Earl as he tried to escape in the darkness. James decided that eight days' imprisonment was sufficient punishment for the murderer.

But the timorous, undignified pedant who now sat on the throne was just as determined as the most heroic of his ancestors had been to establish the reign of law and order in Scotland, and what seems stranger still, he came nearer to success than any of them had done. In some ways his task was easier: there was no longer a hostile government south of the border, ready to stir up rebellion and to offer fugitives from justice a convenient refuge, there was no ambitious Douglas or Albany capable of leading a coalition of nobles against the King. When in 1593 a wild Earl of Bothwell, after three unsuccessful attempts, broke into the King's bedroom and demanded his release from the sentence of treason, when in 1600 the Earl of Gowrie lured James to his house in Perth and attempted to make him prisoner, each was fighting for his own hand, with no backing from the other nobles. The nobles had every reason to be contented; in the scramble for the Church lands they had got almost everything, the Crown and the new Reformed Church practically nothing; what possible cause of quarrel then could they have with the King? If he attempted to make them disgorge their spoil it would be a different story, they might talk of rebellion then, but since he let them digest it in peace there was no need for them to interfere with his experiments in kingcraft.

Though the central regions of Scotland became more peaceful, James's attempts to maintain order in the Highlands and the Borders by Act of Parliament met with little success: the hungry clansman still deemed it a virtue to raid the sheep and cattle that grazed in Strathearn and Strathmore; a long gallop through the darkness to some peaceful farm in Tweeddale or Annandale enabled the border reiver to restock his empty larder. The union of the two crowns in 1603 and the stricter patrolling of the frontier which was a sequel to it was to make the border cattle-raider's trade a more precarious one, but the Highlander remained a problem and a danger.

James's success was not altogether due to the weakening of the opposition to the Crown, it was due in large part to the ability of the monarch. For James was no mere conceited and bewildered pedant, drawing strange theories from half-understood books; he had a whimsical, but a clear and vigorous mind, sharpened by much painful experience. With little money, with no army behind him, James had learned to live by his wits, to read the character of those about him, to get by persuasion, intrigue, and bluff what he knew he could not get by an appeal to the sword. Timorous he might be, but his fears could not turn him from his goal, though he might approach it by devious courses; he might appear to relinquish a scheme; usually he had only postponed it to a more convenient season. And his goal was the establishment of absolute monarchy. It must be remembered that when he worked for it he was moved not by selfish ambition but by the conviction that it was the only thing that would save the country. A sensible king would call in honest and efficient servants to help him in his task of government, but he must be the sole judge of their honesty and efficiency; he would consult Parliament, but he must be free to reject its advice, or the advice of any other assembly, if he did not approve of it. Further, cases which concerned the King, problems which demanded an immediate solution, would be submitted, not to Parliament, but to the more manageable Secret Council, the members of which were appointed by the King.

In 1603 came the news for which James had waited so long. A little before midnight on Saturday, 26th March, a horseman galloped into the courtyard of Holyrood and aroused the sleeping household. Though he was bespattered with mud and reeling with fatigue—he had ridden from London to Edinburgh in less than three days—though the King had retired for the night, he insisted that he must see him at once. When he was admitted, he fell on his knees before James and saluted him as King of England, Scotland, France,[1] and Ireland. The King asked for a proof that Elizabeth was dead, whereupon Sir Robert Carey, for that was the horseman's name, showed him a ring that his sister had drawn from the finger of the dead Queen. James recognized it; it was a ring that he himself had given to Elizabeth. Even then he hesitated to believe his good fortune; not till he received a dispatch from the English Privy Council two days later informing him that he had been proclaimed King of England did he allow the news of his accession to the English throne to be made public in Edinburgh.

[1] The claim to the crown of France, first made by Edward III, was not abandoned till the time of George III.

MEDAL OF THE UNION OF THE ENGLISH AND SCOTTISH CROWNS

CHAPTER XX

KIRK AND KING: 1559–1638

Sweet Teviot! on thy silver tide
   The glaring bale-fires blaze no more;
No longer steel-clad warriors ride
   Along thy wild and willow'd shore:
Where'er thou wind'st, by dale or hill,
All, all, is peaceful, all is still,
   As if thy waves, since Time was born,
Since first they rolled upon the Tweed,
Had only heard the shepherd's reed,
   Nor started at the bugle-horn.

SCOTT.

James VI 1567–1625   Charles I 1625–1649

AT last the dream of Edward I had come true, though in a fashion that would have seemed marvellous to him; the two kingdoms had been united, not by an English monarch succeeding to the throne of Scotland, but by a Scottish monarch succeeding to the throne of England. In such a union there could be little to wound, and much to swell the pride of the patriotic Scotsman. Scotland gave up her King to England, but she kept her Parliament, her Privy Council, her laws and law courts, and her own peculiar ecclesiastical organization. What is more, James's English subjects, far from showing any desire to absorb the smaller in the larger country, strenuously resisted James's attempts to bring about a closer union. In 1606 the English Parliament rejected James's proposals for the establishment of free trade between the two countries and for counting all Scotsmen as naturalized Englishmen. In 1607, however, the English judges decided that the 'post-nati', those born in Scotland after the accession of James to the English throne, should enjoy all the rights and privileges of English subjects.

But though the English Parliament made no attempt to pass laws applying to Scotland, though no disappointed suitor ever dreamt of appealing from the judgement of the Court of Session to that of the House of Lords, the fact remains that Scotland was now governed not from Edinburgh but from Whitehall. The most important work of the Scottish Parliament, the drafting of new laws, was done not by the whole Parliament, but by a committee known as the Lords of the Articles; whoever controlled the Lords of the Articles controlled the Parliament. Originally each estate had chosen its own representatives; James now introduced a new plan: he sent down a list of those members whom he wished to see on the Committee with a request that they should be appointed, a request which Parliament did not dare to refuse. A year or two later he refined on this plan; he arranged that on the first day of Parliament the bishops should choose eight nobles to sit on the Committee; they in their turn chose eight bishops, the sixteen then chose eight burgesses and eight commissioners of the shires. The Committee was completed by eight of the great officers of state. In appearance, the Parliament appointed the Committee without outside interference; in reality, since the bishops, like the officers of state, owed their places to the King, the Committee was still appointed by James himself.

James found his Privy Council an even more useful instrument than a subservient Parliament. It was always in session;

its ordinances had the weight of Acts of Parliament; it was a law-court as well, which never hesitated to deal with offenders who were too powerful or cases which were too difficult for the other courts to tackle. As the members of the Council were all royal nominees—capable judges and administrators perhaps, but men who did not dare to contradict the King—James was able to make the proud boast to his English Parliament, 'Here I sit and govern by my pen; I write and it is done, and by a clerk of the Council I govern Scotland now—which others could not do by the sword'.

In fact, James was more feared and respected by his Scottish subjects when he dwelt in Whitehall than when he dwelt in Holyrood. But they did not look on him as a tyrant, they looked on him as one of themselves, a prince who knew what was good for them and would let them have it if he could. The law-abiding Scot had only one quarrel with his sovereign. But it was a serious dispute, one that in time would make the glaring balefires blaze once more.

To see what the quarrel was about we must go back to the year 1559, when the Scottish Protestants, who had taken up arms against the Catholic Queen Regent, appealed to England for assistance. They knew that the passing of the Act of Uniformity a few months before marked the end of the Roman Catholic Church as the national Church of England. But there were some who would have denied the name Protestant to the Church which was established in its stead. It is true that the supremacy of the Pope and the doctrine of transubstantiation were repudiated, and that an English Book of Common Prayer replaced the Latin Service Books, but much of the organization and ceremonial of the ancient Church was retained. The Church of England was still an episcopal Church; the new archbishops and bishops had the outward appearance and many of the powers and privileges of their Roman Catholic predecessors; like them too, they were members of the House of Lords. But indirectly the sovereign controlled the government of the Church: though a new bishop was nominally elected by the chapter—the cathedral clergy of his diocese—the members of the chapter knew that they must appoint only that man whom the sovereign had given them permission to elect. Many of the prayers in the Prayer Book, too, were simply English versions of the Latin prayers in the old service-books, and while many of the festivals celebrated by the older Church were allowed to lapse into oblivion, some were retained. The very appearance of the ordinary English parish church showed this unwillingness to break completely with the past: the figures of saint and Virgin still glowed in the storied windows though prayer to them was now forbidden; the images that the medieval craftsmen had carved stood undisturbed in their niches; the illustrations of monkish legends with which he had adorned the interior walls had not yet been obliterated by a coating of puritanic whitewash.

But the Scottish reformers felt no tenderness towards anything associated with a Church which to them was altogether evil. The sacrament of the mass, they argued, was an idolatrous rite, therefore the worshipper must not kneel at Communion lest he should seem to be adoring the consecrated bread and wine; pictures and images were idols, therefore, whatever their beauty, they must be ruthlessly destroyed; most of the great festivals of the Church were really survivals of pagan festivals, therefore the burgess must on no account shut his shop on Christmas Day, and the minister must on no account administer Communion on Easter Sunday. So with the organization of the Church: in the first Book of Discipline, submitted to the Scottish Parliament in 1561, Knox and his friends sketched the plan of a Church governed not by bishops and archbishops, but by representative assemblies. For the whole country there was the General Assembly, composed of both ministers and laymen, and presided over by a

Moderator appointed by the Assembly and holding office only
for the duration of that special assembly. The country was
further divided into districts or provinces, corresponding
roughly to the old Roman Catholic dioceses, the ecclesiastical
affairs of which were regulated not by a bishop, but by a Provincial Assembly, or Synod as it was later called, composed like
the General Assembly of both ministers and laymen. Finally,
each parish church had its Kirk-Session, where the minister as
moderator presided over the deliberations of half a dozen elders
chosen by the congregation.

As yet, however, the Scottish Protestants did not show that
hostility to printed service-books and set forms of worship that
they were afterwards to display. In some parish churches the
English Book of Common Prayer was used, though it was
gradually ousted by Knox's Book of Common Order, which
prescribed a much less elaborate form of worship. But minister
and congregation alike regarded the sermon as the most
important part of the service, in fact people spoke not of going
to church, but of going to the preaching. And though sermons
were lengthy, the man who objected to sermons that lasted for
more than an hour seldom dared to stay away from church,
knowing that he ran the risk of being summoned before the
kirk-session and being solemnly reprimanded, or perhaps even
sent to the town prison, there to think over his sins on a diet
of bread and water.

Altogether the differences between the Church of Scotland
and the Church of England were not strongly marked in Knox's
lifetime, and in 1572, the year of his death, bishops were
actually reintroduced into the Scottish Church, though with
none of the powers of their Roman Catholic predecessors. But
they were not wanted; their flocks saw too plainly that they
were only 'tulchans',[1] agents for transferring the Church

---

[1] A 'tulchan' was a calf-skin stuffed with straw put beside a cow whose
calf had died, to make her continue to give milk.

revenues to Morton and his associates, and so the Second Book of Discipline, drawn up in 1578, completed the plan of a Church organization from which bishops were definitely excluded. All ministers were to be of the same rank ; there must be moderators, of course, for the various assemblies, but they were appointed by the assemblies and at the end of their limited period of office they became ordinary ministers once more. Some of the most important functions of the pre-Reformation bishop were taken over by a new body of ministers and laymen, the Presbytery, which administered a group of about a dozen parishes. It was the presbytery, for example, that had examined candidates for the ministry and ordained them when they proved their fitness. It was the presbytery, too, that decided which ministers and elders were to represent the district in the General Assembly.

At first it is difficult to understand why James should have objected to this Presbyterian system. But James found, like Milton after him, that 'new presbyter is but old priest writ large', that he must disentangle again the old problem which had perplexed Alexander I and William the Lion, the problem of the relations of Church and State. What was he to make of this new General Assembly, which was more truly representative of the nation than the old Parliament, and which already enjoyed an equal prestige? It met when it pleased, without any reference to the King's wishes, and before it dispersed appointed a Committee or Commission of Assembly to deal with any problem that might arise before the next assembly was summoned, so that in a sense it was always in session. This would not have mattered if it had shown an accommodating temper, but it seemed to be careless whether it thwarted the King or not. For to Presbyterian divines like Andrew Melville, the outspoken scholar who knew neither timidity nor tact, the problem of Church and State admitted of a simple solution, the solution propounded in the Second Book of Discipline. Let Church and

State confine themselves to their own special provinces; let the Church confine its attention solely to religious matters and the State to secular matters. It was a doctrine familiar to the medieval Popes. But where was one to draw the line between the 'external things' which were the exclusive concern of the State, and 'the matters of conscience and of religion' with which the State was forbidden to deal? It seemed to the King that the Presbyterian divines drew it wherever it happened to suit themselves, that they wanted to have a finger in every pie, to make their churches echo one Sunday with denuciations of his clemency to his Catholic subjects or his suspicious friendliness with Catholic states, and the next with outspoken criticisms of his personal faults, such as his habit of profane swearing.

In 1584, when the Raid of Ruthven had shown the King to what lengths the Presbyterian leaders were prepared to go, James succeeded in persuading the Parliament—already jealous of the growing power of the Assembly—to pass what were known as the Black Acts. No man, whether minister or layman, would in future be exempt from the judgement of the ordinary courts, whatever the charge against him might be. Any one who criticized the King—even in the pulpit—would be punished for spreading slanderous lies, and no ecclesiastical court was to sit in judgement on any case, ecclesiastical or otherwise, except with the express consent of the King. But James was not yet strong enough to challenge the claims of the Presbyterian divines; in 1592 he had to give his consent to an Act which definitely established the Presbyterian system and admitted the jurisdiction of the ecclesiastical courts in spiritual matters.

After the death of Thirlestane in 1595 James felt himself free to follow a bolder course. Convinced that a Church governed by bishops who owed their places to him would not impede and contradict him as a Church governed by independent assemblies had done, he resolved to overthrow the Presbyterian system and introduce Episcopacy. But James loved devious ways; he feared to alarm his subjects and provoke a rebellion, so he moved forward cautiously at first, attempting as far as it was possible to get the consent of the Assembly to measures which in the long run would bring about its destruction. A riot in Edinburgh during the closing days of 1596, which broke out because James insisted on the trial of a minister who had called Queen Elizabeth an atheist, gave the King the chance for which he had waited. His threats that he would move the court to Perth rather than be bullied in his own capital, and his refusal to restore the city to favour till it had paid him a sum of 30,000 marks, convinced many a burgess and many a minister too that the Presbyterian divines had gone too far in their claims to direct the policy of the State. James took care that during the next few years the General Assembly should meet not at Edinburgh, but in remoter towns like Dundee or Aberdeen, where it could be more easily attended by the lukewarm Presbyterians of the north. Interviews with royalty and grants of liberal allowances for travelling expenses weakened the objections of many of the ministers to Episcopacy; the General Assembly of 1600 agreed that the Church should be represented in Parliament just as the pre-Reformation Church had been. At first the Assembly was unwilling to give the name of bishop to these representatives or to appoint them for more than one year, but in 1602 James succeeded in overcoming its scruples and the thirteen Scottish bishoprics were once again filled.

The King was not yet content, for the new bishops were bishops only in name; the government of the Church was still in the hands of the General Assembly and its subordinate synods and presbyteries. But the General Assembly was no longer in a mood to defy the King. In 1605 some ministers who had disregarded a royal edict postponing a meeting of the Assembly were found guilty of treason and banished for life. A few months later the King got rid of his most formidable

opponent, Andrew Melville. Melville had visited London on
the King's invitation and had been tactless enough to write
some satirical Latin verses on the furnishings of the Chapel
Royal. For this he was imprisoned in the Tower, and at the end
of four years banished to France, where he died in 1622. In

AN ORGAN OF THE EARLY SEVENTEENTH CENTURY

1609 Parliament restored to the bishops their right to act as
judges in all disputes about wills and divorces, as well as in all
purely ecclesiastical cases, and in 1610 a tamed and subservient
Assembly consented to the Scottish bishops being granted
all the powers and privileges that belonged to their English
brethren.

So Episcopacy had supplanted Presbyterianism. But James
had succeeded largely because his innovations concerned only

a small minority of his Scottish subjects; the country gentleman did not worry himself as long as James asked no questions
about the land which he had filched from the Church; the
ordinary worshipper did not worry himself as long as he saw
no break in the accustomed routine of the service. On Sunday
he sat in a building which contained nothing to remind him
that it had once been a Catholic church. Whitewash covered
the paintings on the walls, the windows were filled with plain
glass, the great crucifix had been thrown down from its place
above the rood-screen and the niches stood empty of their
saints, the carved seats in the chancel had been burned for
firewood, and on the site of the demolished altar stood a great
wooden pulpit, with a sounding-board overhead. The organ
had disappeared at the same time as the altar; the only music
which one heard during the service was the unaccompanied
singing of a metrical version of the psalms.[1] Throughout the
greater part of the service the worshippers sat on their folding
stools with their hats on; during the prayers, however, they
stood with uncovered heads. But though ministers and people
alike went to absurd lengths in their anxiety to avoid anything
that could remind them of the Roman Catholic usage, there
was nothing trivial, nothing ridiculous about the service in the
ordinary Scottish parish church: its very plainness seemed to
make it all the more solemn and awe-inspiring.

When James visited Scotland in 1617—his one and only visit
after he ascended the English throne—it became evident that
he aimed at modifying the established forms of worship. An
organ costing £400 was fitted up in the Chapel Royal at Holyrood, and when James attended divine service the organ music,
the chanting of the boy choristers, and the appearance of the

[1] The psalms now used in the Church of Scotland were written by Francis
Rous, a Cornishman, and were not introduced into Scotland till 1647. One
or two of the psalms used in King James's time, like the famous Old 124th,
are given in the Psalter as alternative versions distinguished by the heading
'another of the same'.

officiating ministers, not in the black Geneva gown, but in the
white Anglican surplice, grieved the more scrupulous Presbyterians. No voice, however, was raised in protest, and in 1618,
after his return to England, he persuaded a General Assembly
meeting at Perth to pass five Articles making important innovations in the ritual of the Church. Services, to be attended
by all, were to be held on Christmas Day, Good Friday, and
Ascension Day[1] as well as on Easter Sunday and Trinity
Sunday,[2] communicants were to kneel when they received the
Sacrament, those who wished to become communicants were in
future to be confirmed by a bishop. James had gone too far:
it was impossible to enforce the Articles of Perth; a mere
handful of people attended church on Christmas Day; shop-
keepers not only opened their booths but strutted about in
front of them during the service; and there were few ministers who dared to bar from the communion table the devout
worshipper who refused to kneel.

Worse followed with the accession of Charles I in 1625.
James understood his people through and through; Charles,
though he was born in Dunfermline, had left Scotland when he
was three years old and was now to all intents and purposes a
foreigner. With James ecclesiastical questions were matters
of policy; he wanted Episcopacy because it buttressed the
royal power: with Charles they were matters of conscience; he
wanted Episcopacy because he believed that a Church without
bishops was no Church at all. James had made no attempt to
get the Church lands from those who had appropriated them,
though he knew that the ministers were miserably poor;
Charles, a few months after his accession, announced that all
Church lands belonging to lay proprietors must be surrendered
to the Crown, that they might be again used for the support
of the Church. This Act of Revocation was soon whittled
down, but the mischief was done; Charles had alarmed the

[1] The sixth Thursday after Easter.   [2] The eighth Sunday after Easter.

nobles, and they now began to think of making common cause with the ministers who had opposed the King's ecclesiastical innovations.

In 1633 Charles visited Edinburgh to be crowned King of Scotland, but the pageants and processions with which he was welcomed, even the sight of the provost, bailies, and councillors dancing hand-in-hand in the High Street, could not reassure his more precise subjects. They noticed that an altar with candles upon it was erected in the Chapel Royal of Holyrood for his coronation, and that when he went to St. Giles' surpliced clergymen read the ordinary Anglican service. After the King's departure their fears were realized; in 1635 the publication of the Book of Canons, or rules for the Church, which every minister was obliged to say he accepted, let them see exactly where the King stood. Those who questioned the King's right to shape the organization of the Church or criticized the Episcopal system and the Book of Common Prayer were to be excommunicated. All parish churches were to be fitted up like Anglican churches, with the communion table where the altar had been; ministers might hear confession, but were not to utter extempore prayers. Further, ministers must undertake to use a Prayer Book which was being prepared, but which none of them had seen.

Ministers and people alike were indignant, partly at what Charles was doing, partly at the way in which he was doing it. James had tried to carry his people with him if it was at all possible; he secured the co-operation of carefully tamed Assemblies for his reforms, but Charles seemed to be absolutely careless of the feelings and convictions of the ordinary minister and the ordinary worshipper. Bishops and Prayer Books, he argued, were necessary to their spiritual welfare, though they did not know it; therefore bishops and Prayer Books must be forced upon them. It was only natural that the Scot should resent the King's attempt to take charge of his conscience, but

behind his resentment at Charles's high-handed action lurked
something else—the fear that the King's real aim was the
restoration of Roman Catholicism. This fear was strengthened
in 1637 by the publication of the new Service-Book, in the
composition of which it was known that Archbishop Laud had
assisted: it was based on the English Book of Common Prayer,

The Arch-Prelate of S.t Andrewes in Scotland
reading the new Service-booke in his pontificalibus
assaulted by men & women, with Crickets stooles
Stickes and Stones.

FROM A CONTEMPORARY PAMPHLET

but to the excited minds of the people it bore a suspiciously
close resemblance to a Roman Catholic service-book.

The King had gone too far; few even of the bishops wanted
the book; when the Dean of Edinburgh attempted to read it in
St. Giles' Cathedral[1] he was at once interrupted by shouts and
yells from the female worshippers. The Bishop stepped into
the pulpit and tried to quiet the tumult, only to be greeted with
cries of 'Wolf!' 'Beastly belly-god!' and 'Crafty fox!' But
worse followed; the ladies began to hurl bibles and folding

[1] St. Giles', till then simply a parish church, was made the Cathedral
Church of the newly created diocese of Edinburgh in 1633.

stools at his head, so that, to quote an old writer, 'jouking became his safeguard'. No better fortune awaited the Archbishop of St. Andrews when he intervened; he was forced to appeal to the provost and bailies to restore order. Even when the brawlers were driven from the church they battered at the doors and threw stones at the windows, and when the Bishop emerged he was at once mobbed by a furious crowd.

Charles could not realize that every section of his people, laird and noble as well as peasant and petty craftsman, was opposed to his ecclesiastical policy; the riot, far from convincing him that he must retreat, only confirmed him in his determination to force the Prayer Book on a country that would not have it at any price. The news that the King did not intend to abandon the Prayer Book provoked another riot in Edinburgh later in the year, and the Privy Council was at its wit's end when the Lord Advocate suggested that the malcontents, instead of plunging the whole of Edinburgh into an uproar, should appoint a committee to confer with the Council and then disperse. His suggestion was acted on at once; four nobles, four lairds, four ministers and four burgesses were at once elected, and the Lord Advocate realized when it was too late that by giving an organization to the King's opponents he had made them doubly dangerous. The Tables, as this committee was called, resolved that a definite protest should be made, and early in 1638 the famous National Covenant was framed. We have seen how in earlier times private persons, like the Earls of Douglas, Crawford, and Ross in the reign of James II, often entered into 'bands' or engagements to support one another against any one whatsoever. The National Covenant was a band to bind, not one or two individuals, but the whole nation: those who signed it bound themselves to defend the King with their lives, but to have nothing to do with his ecclesiastical innovations until they were approved by a free Assembly and by Parliament.

The Covenant became a standard round which the nation

rallied; all day long Greyfriars Church in Edinburgh was besieged by multitudes eager to sign it; some wept as they took up the pen, others even signed it with their blood. Copies were carried to every quarter of the kingdom, and everywhere, except in the north, were signed with the same enthusiasm.

At last Charles gave way; he announced that a General Assembly was to be held in Glasgow in November. Before ever the Assembly met the result of its deliberations was a foregone conclusion; the presbyteries were instructed not to elect any minister who showed any sympathy for Episcopacy; the ministers, moreover, were to be accompanied by an equal number of lay elders, though laymen had not sat in a General Assembly for almost forty years. The bishops, who knew that their colleagues had no intention of dealing kindly with them, protested that such a gathering, elected by laymen and consisting largely of laymen, was no true Assembly. Their arguments convinced the Lord High Commissioner, the Duke of Hamilton, who dissolved the Assembly. But the Assembly refused to be dissolved; under the guidance of the Moderator, Alexander Henderson of Leuchars, it proceeded to demolish the whole structure which Charles and his father had erected. Episcopacy was abolished, the bishops were deposed and some of them excommunicated, and with them disappeared the Five Articles of Perth, the Book of Canons and the Service Book. At last peace had been reached in the Scottish Church.

So it seemed. But near the Loch of Skene, in Aberdeenshire, men said phantom drummers had been heard drumming all through the night.

CHAPTER XXI

SCOTLAND BEFORE THE CIVIL WAR

Here are no Serean[1] fleeces, Peru gold,
Aurora's gems, nor wares by Tyrians sold;
Towns swell not here with Babylonian walls.

DRUMMOND OF HAWTHORNDEN.

THE drumming will sound louder and louder yet in the next few pages, but before the sword is unsheathed, before the blue-bonneted companies again take the old road to the border, let us look for a moment at the sleepy towns where the roar of besieging cannon has not been heard within the memory of man, at the cornfields that have never been trodden by charging cavalry.

It was a Scotland that, to outward appearance, differed little from the Scotland of 1513. Travellers from England, usually quick to criticize, admired the great unenclosed fields of oats and barley in Fife and the Lothians, but in reality very little additional land had been brought under the plough, and the old-fashioned, wasteful methods of cultivation still persisted.

Nor was there much change in the houses of the country folk; few of them could boast any better dwelling than the low-roofed hut of turf, where the only flooring was trodden earth or clay, and where the smoke from the hearth in the centre of the floor escaped through the unglazed windows, as well as through the chimney of clay in the thatched roof overhead.

Altogether, even in the well-cultivated, long-settled Lothians, it was not a smiling landscape that presented itself to the traveller from the south. Save in the neighbourhood of the houses of the country gentlemen, no trees or hedgerows

[1] Chinese: Serean fleeces = silks.

gave variety to the monotonous expanse of cornland and pasture, and even the laird's new mansion-house, with its iron-barred windows and pepper-box turrets, looked as grey and grim as a medieval fortress. For in Scotland civil strife was not

A SEVENTEENTH-CENTURY MANSION HOUSE
Newark Castle, in Fife, the home of General David Leslie

the far-off forgotten thing that it had become in England. A closer inspection of a seventeenth-century mansion would, however, have revealed some signs of an increasing regard for beauty and comfort, though the panelled walls seemed more gloomy than the old variegated tapestries. One or two pictures —mostly family portraits—added a little colour here and there. A ceiling, covered with frescoes or, more usually, intricate ornamentation in plaster-work, replaced the open rafters. Carpets now covered the floor in the principal rooms; chairs were more plentiful, and also more comfortable, for they were padded and upholstered in leather and tapestry; the beds were now vast structures with four elaborately carved wooden posts supporting a wooden canopy, from which heavy curtains depended.

Other changes were taking place in the country house. The hall now stood empty or was abandoned to the servants: the master of the house had dinner with his family or his guests in the smaller but more convenient dining-room; then, after the dishes of meat were removed from the table, he retired to the new withdrawing-room,[1] where dessert was served. Earthenware dishes now appeared on the table, though it was long till the old-fashioned pewter and tin plates disappeared; and since the establishment of a glass-works at Wemyss in 1619 drinking-glasses were quite common, though even the most fastidious hostess did not think it necessary to set forks before her guests.

Similar changes in the direction of increased comfort were taking place in the houses of the wealthy burgesses. There was one 'improvement', however, that we can hardly admire—the bedrooms were now fitted with box-beds. The English traveller too, though his own standards of cleanliness were not too high, was shocked at the indifference to dirt and foul smells which the average Scotsman seemed to display. He was not astonished that he should be expected to convey his meat to his mouth with his fingers, or that all the water used in the house should be conveyed from wells in the street, or that the house should be devoid of drains and baths—it was what he was accustomed to at home—but he thought that the water might be fetched from the wells oftener than once in two days, that garbage should not be allowed to accumulate in the sink until the whole

---

[1] The modern form 'drawing-room' began to displace the older form about 1642.

house reeked of it, and that the pewter platters need not
appear with traces upon them of the previous meal—or previous week's meals! The visitor thought this carelessness either
amusing or disgusting; the home-keeping Scot never thought
about it at all; neither of them dreamt of connecting with it
the pestilence which every few years devastated the crowded

A Seventeenth-century Plaster Ceiling in Binns Castle

and noisome towns. To the pious, the pest was a judgement
from heaven, sent to warn them against the Popish tendencies
of their rulers; they observed a solemn fast, but made no
attempt to cleanse their polluted highways and houses.

With the smell of Edinburgh in his nostrils the traveller
found it difficult to do justice to the appearance of the town.
It was now enclosed by the lofty Flodden Wall, pierced here
and there by fortified ports or gates. The wall kept the town
from spreading outwards, but it could not keep it from spreading upwards. The newer buildings rose six or seven stories
into the air, and towered high above their predecessors.

The 'closes' too, had ceased to be garden closes, and had become the closes that we know to-day—narrow covered passages leading through the older houses facing the street to the newer houses that now covered the sites of the vanished gardens. But among the dark and evil-smelling wynds and closes there was one noble thoroughfare ; just as the modern visitor admires Princes Street, the seventeenth-century travellers admired the spacious street, lined with lofty stone houses, that stretched from the Castle to the Netherbow Port—a great fortified gateway guarding the lower end of the High Street—and thence, under the name of the Canongate, to the outer courtyard of Holyrood. They lamented, however, that the burgesses should spoil their houses by building projecting wooden galleries in front, which they usually boarded up to form additional rooms, with the result that the handsome stone buildings seemed to be only ramshackle structures of wood. Only one new church had been built in Edinburgh since the Reformation ; when the economical Scot wanted a new church he usually built a partition across an old one. But a stately Parliament Hall was rising a few yards to the south of St. Giles', and the ruins of the Kirk o' Field had been cleared away to make room for the buildings of the new College, for since 1582 Edinburgh had been a University town.

There was little of the repose and quiet that one expected of a University town in the crowded wynds and streets of Old Edinburgh. The scholar who did not wish to be distracted by the skirling of fish-wives, the brawling of caddies or street porters, even the occasional clash of weapons, would find the quiet which he desired in—Glasgow! Travellers seemed to find some peculiar charm in this quiet little town, with its few streets set among gardens and orchards, its Bishop's Palace and its University, above which rose the stately Cathedral in almost all its ancient beauty. It reminded one visitor of Oxford. It is true that the trade of Glasgow had increased

A SEVENTEENTH-CENTURY MARKET CROSS

Aberdeen

rapidly since the beginning of the century, and that it was destined to outstrip Dundee in a year or two, and become the most important town in Scotland next to the capital; as long, however, as the river on which it stood was so choked up with sand that no vessel of more than six tons could reach the wharf, it seemed impossible that it could ever be a port of any consequence.

It seemed impossible, too, that Scotland would ever be able to support its six hundred thousand inhabitants. To the Englishman, the Scot of this period seemed to be cautious and unenterprising; at a time when the English trader had taken his friezes and kerseys to the very ends of the earth, the Scottish trader cautiously followed the old trade routes to Veere and Bordeaux. And he had little to bring to market except salted salmon, coarse woollen cloth, and coal, for the Scottish craftsman was as unenterprising as the Scottish trader, and, like him, was bound hand and foot by the rules of his gild. When we remember that the stagnation in trade was matched by the stagnation in agriculture, we cannot wonder that Scotland was confronted with an apparently insoluble unemployment problem.

In those days there was no Canada to beckon to the workless Scot. It is true that in 1621 Sir William Alexander had founded the colony of Nova Scotia, but this 'New Scotland' was not seven days' but seven or eight weeks' voyage distant, and besides, in 1632 it had passed into the hands of France. So the wandering Scot kept on this side of the Atlantic; if his tastes lay in the direction of trade, he made his way to Poland, which was then a great kingdom, and, with a stock of merchandise small enough to be carried on his back, trudged from village to village. But he kept his Scottish pride; however small his pack, he called himself not a pedlar, but a merchant. The more adventurous Scot found employment of a different kind waiting for him on the Continent. In 1618 war had broken out between the Emperor[1] and the Protestant Elector Palatine, the son-in-law of James VI. It developed into a great struggle between the Catholic and Protestant Princes of Central Europe, which dragged on for thirty years. During this period, Scottish soldiers crossed the seas in thousands—more than 3,000 left Scotland in 1626 and 6,000 in 1631—some to fight in the armies of the Emperor, some, like Dugald Dalgetty, to zigzag from one side to another, going where pay and rations seemed most attractive, most of them to follow the banner of Gustavus Adolphus of Sweden, the Protestant Champion. In the next chapter we shall hear something of two Scottish generals who learned their trade in the Thirty Years' War. But few Scottish troops ever returned: disease slew most of those who escaped from the battle-field.

Still there remained crowds of unemployed at home, drifting about the country with strange tales on their lips: those dark-complexioned folk who called themselves 'Egyptians',[2] and announced that they could see into the future—for a consideration; vagabond students requiring money to enable them to continue their studies; sailors, lately shipwrecked—if their story was to be believed; jugglers, minstrels, and story-tellers—all that joyous crowd for which there was no room in a Scotland that had grown serious. In 1579 Parliament had declared that all such vagabonds were to be arrested, flogged, and burned on the ear with a hot iron, but the Act had little effect. In 1616 the Privy Council complained bitterly that countless beggars lay in the Canongate, bawling for alms, or rising and crowding round any passer-by who chanced to stop for a moment, so that

[1] The (Holy Roman) Emperor, in theory the successor of the Roman Emperors of the West, and of Charlemagne, was in practice the elected head of a loose confederacy of states, occupying in the seventeenth century much the same territory as Germany, Austria, and Czecho-Slovakia to-day. It became customary for the Emperor to be chosen from the Royal House of Austria. But the Hapsburg Emperors ruled Austria and Hungary as absolute monarchs, not merely in their imperial capacity. [2] Gipsies.

decent people were 'fashed and wearied by them', but it could think of no better remedy than ordering the magistrates to expel them from the burgh. The gipsies met with sterner treatment. In 1636, for example, when the Privy Council heard that some gipsies had been lodged in the prison at Haddington for a month, it ordered the men to be hanged, and the women to be drowned, 'because the keeping of them longer there is troublesome and burdenable to the town'.

Parliament showed itself much more considerate to those whom it called aged, poor, impotent, and decayed persons. It was only fair that it should take some thought for them, for the Protestant nobles had reformed many of the medieval hospitals and almshouses out of existence altogether, and, though they had acquired the lands and buildings of the monasteries, they kept no open guest-house to receive the penniless wanderers, nor had they among their servants an almoner to give food to their poorer neighbours. The Parliament of 1579, which thundered against persons 'able in body, living idly and fleeing labour', gave orders that beggars who could not work were to return to their own parishes, which were now authorized to tax themselves for the relief of their own poor. In 1597 the levying of the tax was entrusted by Parliament to the kirk-session of each parish. But few parishes were heroic enough to impose an adequate tax on themselves; in most places the kirk-session was content to draw upon the weekly collection in the plate at the church door, and when it proved insufficient, as it usually did, to issue licences to the poor people, allowing them to beg from house to house.

If we blame the Reformation for diverting into the pockets of the wealthy landowners money meant for the relief of the poor, do not let us blame the reformed clergy. Knox and his fellows, whatever their faults may have been, were not out for plunder; they simply desired that wealth which they thought

had been misused should be restored to its proper uses. Had
they got their way, the revenues of the hospitals would not have
been destroyed or diminished, but increased.

The bulk of the surplus revenue of the pre-Reformation
Church Knox meant to devote to another purpose—the building up of a great educational system. At the time, nothing
came of Knox's plan; the men who had got the Church lands
had no intention of giving them up; and so the Reformation
left the Scottish schools and colleges poorer, if anything, than
they had been before. But the plan was there; others in
succeeding generations reared the noble structure of which
Knox had dreamed. Almost every burgh, however, had its
burgh school, and the founding of Edinburgh University in
1582 gave Scotland four Universities to England's two. Nor
was the University barred against the poor man's son. At the
beginning of November, when he had finished helping his
father with the harvest, the poor student came up to college,
there to 'cultivate the Muse on a little oatmeal', till the end of
the session in April, when he left his books and returned to the
plough and the harrow. But the Universities had comparatively little to offer. Without money, they could not attract
scholars of European renown to be their professors, nor build
up a library like the Bodleian, in which the student, weary of a
ten times repeated lecture, could explore the realms of knowledge for himself. If the libraries were small and badly stocked,
laboratories did not exist at all, for though lectures on science
were given, they were based on the teachings of Aristotle, who
had died more than two thousand years before, and neither
lecturer nor student thought it desirable to check Aristotle's
statements by actual experiment. Altogether, what Dr.
Johnson said of the eighteenth-century Scots might justly be
applied to their seventeenth-century ancestors: 'Their learning
is like bread in a besieged town; every man gets a little, but
no man gets a full meal.'

The seventeenth-century schoolboy would have challenged this statement. He went to school at six in the morning, and, although he was allowed to go home for breakfast and dinner, he was not dismissed finally till prayers had been said at six at night. Saturday was like other days, though once or at most twice a week the boys were allowed to go to some convenient field and play games under the watchful eye of one of the doctors, as the assistant masters were called.

Even on Sunday they did not escape from the prison-house: they had to go to school before the morning service, to be catechised by the head master, and then conducted by him to the parish church. Holidays were given grudgingly, and the Protestant suspicion of the old festivals of the Church tended to make them fewer and shorter. And even when he played with his fellows in the school yards, the schoolboy could not be quite at his ease; he was required to speak Latin all the time. If he used his own Lowland tongue, his words would be noted by one of the 'lupi', or secret censors, and carried to the head master, who would promptly apply the rod. For Latin was still a spoken language. All the lectures in the Universities, both in Britain and on the Continent, were delivered in Latin; scientists and philosophers still wrote in Latin, and so in those days the man who knew Latin had a tremendous advantage over the man who did not.

There was too much Latin altogether in their school curriculum. It was not the business of the Grammar School to deal in such vanities as Art and Science, French or Mathematics, and one shudders to think of what would have happened to any venturesome 'doctor' who put English play-books into the hands of his pupils, and made them study *The Merchant of Venice* as carefully as they studied Terence's *Phormio*.

For there was no room for plays and poetry in seventeenth-century Scotland; in the words of a famous Scottish writer, she had 'received the Reformation without the Renaissance. The revival of the World of Greece brought to her not peace, not beauty, not joy in life, but a sword and ill-will to men.' To pull up the tares, the Reformers too often pulled up the wheat as well. Because miracle plays had been performed at certain festivals of the Roman Catholic Church, miracle plays must be abolished; because ordinary stage plays were sometimes ugly and coarse, even innocent and charming plays like *Twelfth Night* or *The Tempest* were prohibited.

With the ecclesiastical festivals, too, disappeared some ceremonies which were older than the Church. The people of Aberdeen no longer went in procession to the woods on the first Sunday in May to bring Summer home in triumph. The Summer King, Robin Hood, and the Abbot of Unreason, characters in these May-day games, had vanished with the Maypole and the jingling morris-dancers. The mystic bonfire no longer blazed on the hill on Midsummer Night; when Midwinter came no guisers or carol-singers lightened the gloom of the sombre little burghs.

It is little wonder that in an atmosphere like this poetry and the drama did not flourish, that against the mighty array of English writers headed by Shakespeare and Milton we can put only the figure of Drummond of Hawthornden, a true but not a highly original poet. But there were places where, in spite of the decrees of the Assemblies and Kirk-Sessions, the old magic of earth still exercised its spell. It is strange to think that the most beautiful of the weird, wild-hearted border ballads were probably composed in the period between the Reformation and the Civil War. But in the towns there was the kirk-session, quick to pounce on any guiser or caroller, ready to point out to the bailies what their duty was, if the burgh council seemed too easy or too tender-hearted.

The kirk-sessions felt that they had to deal with more dangerous enemies than the morris-dancers or carol-singers.

Were there not in every town and village warlocks and witches, men and women who had sold themselves to the Devil ?

Probably in the confused warfare of Catholic and Protestant, some old pagan creed that had lain half-remembered in the minds of men for centuries had come to the surface again. Probably there were places like the parish of Woodilee in Mr. Buchan's romance, *Witchwood*, where the dark forgotten deities were worshipped with strange barbaric rites. Certainly there were people who professed to have some magical power, spae-wives who assured their dupes that they could see into the future, find stolen goods, cause winds to blow or cease, crops to flourish or wither at their pleasure. Usually they were guilty of nothing more than obtaining money under false pretences. It made no difference : should the minister suspect one of his parishioners of dealing in magic and spells, she was haled before the kirk-session, and, if possible, bullied into an admission that she had gained her skill from the Devil himself. The kirk-session then reported to the Privy Council, which commissioned special judges, usually local lairds or magistrates, to go on with the case. If the accused had confessed nothing, cruel and senseless tests were employed. She might be bound and flung into a pond ; if she floated, it was a sign that the pure element would not receive her guilty body, so she was taken out, strangled, and burned.

No one was safe, for an accusation of witchcraft was discovered to be a convenient way of getting rid of an inconvenient enemy. And the shadow showed no sign of passing. The triumph of the Church in 1638 over the tyranny of Charles I increased instead of diminishing the tyranny of superstition ; in 1643 thirty witches were burned in Fifeshire alone.

I wonder if, from the terror-laden streets of these Lowland towns, people sometimes looked curiously to the blue Highland hills, to the land where the new religion sat on men as lightly as the old, and where murder never masqueraded as zeal for the purity of the Church. Probably they did not: to them the Highlands was still an alien and hostile land that they would never dream of visiting. Scotland was to all intents and purposes two countries; there was more difference between a burgess from Perth and a MacGregor from the braes of Balquhidder than there would be between a burgess of Perth and a burgess of Paris. Let us imagine them standing together. There is the man from Perth in his broad blue Scots bonnet, his close-fitting doublet, with a narrow linen collar at the neck, his voluminous breeches, rather like the modern 'plus fours', stockings of cloth, and buckled shoes. Beside him stands the Highlander; his chief garment is a tartan plaid wrapped round his body and held in place by a belt at the waist, his legs are bare, on his feet are shoes of untanned deerskin. They cannot communicate, for the Highlander speaks nothing but Gaelic. Should the burgess invite the Highlander to spend the night with him, if we can imagine such a thing happening, his guest would scorn the box-bed. He would place the mattress on the floor, and even then be uneasy because of the unusual comfort. For to the most luxurious feather-bed in the world the Highlander preferred his own couch made of bundles of heather, though, when he had no choice, he could sleep out of doors in the winter snow, with his plaid wrapped tightly round him. In other ways he was more of a Spartan than the burgess; he could march for a whole day on a mouthful of oatcake or barley-bread. Work at the loom or the bench he despised, and he preferred fishing or hunting or rounding up the cattle of the Lowland laird to handling the spade or the sickle.

Furthermore, while the bond between baron and vassal had slackened in the Lowlands, the bond that united the Highlander to his chief was as strong as it had ever been. For the Highlander could not think of himself as a solitary individual, fighting for his own hand; he belonged to a special community —the clan—all the members of which bore the same surname and even dressed alike in the same pattern of tartan. And just as he regarded his fellow clansmen as, in a sense, his kinsmen, so he regarded the chief of his clan as more worthy of respect than his own father. To obey him without question was the first and plainest of his duties, to die for him the highest of privileges. The chief, for his part, knew that something was expected of him in return. He had to keep open house; to suffer scores of idle clansmen to live within the walls of his castle and to eat at his table. It was a sad expense, but wealth in fighting-men was preferable to wealth in money or cattle, when one had to do battle with a rival chieftain.

As yet the Lowlander saw no danger in the existence of this other alien Scotland beyond the Highland line. Occasionally rumours would reach him of clan battles, of wild and fantastic deeds of vengeance, but they were no concern of his—'he kept his ain breath to cool his ain kail', and the memory of ancient feuds would keep the clans from ever co-operating in an invasion of the Lowlands on a large scale. So it seemed. But what would happen if a great soldier, not of their own race, appeared among them ? This the unfortunate Lowlanders were soon to discover.

CHAPTER XXII

SCOTLAND AND THE CIVIL WAR

The Solemn League and Covenant
Cost Scotland blood, cost Scotland tears.
Lines attributed to BURNS.

While Darwen stream, with blood of Scots imbrued,
And Dunbar field, resounds thy praises loud,
And Worcester's laureate wreath.
MILTON.

Charles I 1625–1649   Charles II 1649–1685
The Protectorate . . 1653–1659

THE abolition of Episcopacy by the Glasgow Assembly in 1638 and the Restoration of the Presbyterian system were an open challenge to the King. Charles must either give way or fight, and, as he sincerely believed that a Church without bishops was no true Church, he could not give way. But could he fight ? For he had neither a standing army nor money to hire mercenary troops, unless he summoned his English Parliament and asked it to finance the campaign, and he knew that any parliament which he summoned now would be much more critical of his actions than the very unfriendly parliament which he had dismissed in 1629. He did succeed, however, in raising an army of 20,000 men in the early summer of 1639, and getting it north to the border, only to find that the road into Scotland was barred by a force, equal in numbers, but far superior in discipline, commanded by Alexander Leslie, a general who had won renown in the Swedish service. Charles made one half-hearted attempt to advance into Scotland, and then, before any serious fighting took place, he brought the campaign to an end by signing the Pacification of Berwick. This Treaty seemed to promise the Scots all that they wanted, for though Charles refused to recognize the Glasgow Assembly,

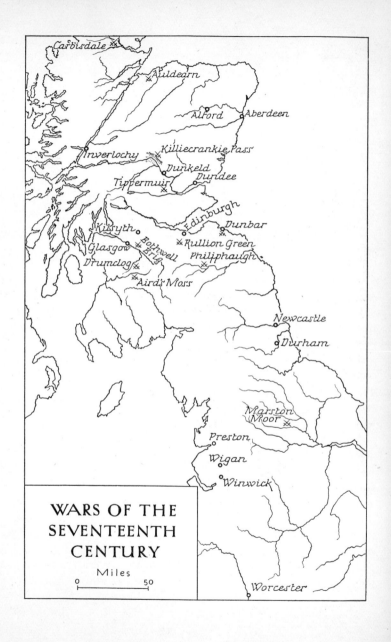

Carbisdale ✕

✕ Auldearn

Alford ○ ● Aberdeen

Inverlochy ○——○ Killiecrankie Pass
✕✕

Dunkeld ✕
✕ Dundee

Tippermuir ✕

Edinburgh ○ ● Dunbar

Kilsyth ✕
✕ Rullion Green

Glasgow ○✕ Bothwell Brig
Drumclog ✕ Philiphaugh ●

✕ Aird's Moss

● Newcastle

○ Durham

Marston
Moor ✕

Preston ○

Wigan ○

Winwick ○

WARS OF THE
SEVENTEENTH
CENTURY

Miles
0   50

Worcester ○

he agreed that all disputed questions should be referred either to another General Assembly or to Parliament. Thus the First Bishops' War came to an end. But the Second Bishops' War followed speedily. When the General Assembly which Charles had sanctioned met a few weeks later, it simply re-enacted all the acts of the Glasgow Assembly. The Parliament would have gone further, if the Lord High Commissioner[1] had not pro-rogued it before it could ratify the proposals made by the Committee of Articles. At length, in June 1640, after ten separate prorogations, Parliament met in defiance of both King and Commissioner, abolished Episcopacy, and freed itself from royal control by setting its own house in order. Hitherto new laws had been drafted, not by Parliament as a whole, but by the Committee of the Articles, to which men who were known to be critical of the King's policy had very little chance of being appointed. Now it was enacted that only when Parliament judged it necessary was a Committee of the Articles to be appointed, and further, that each estate, nobles, barons,[2] and burgesses, was to choose its own representatives.

This time the Parliament as well as the Assembly had challenged the King, and in the late summer of 1640 Leslie again led an army towards the border. Charles was even less able to meet the challenge than he had been in 1639, though he had summoned the 'Short' Parliament earlier in the year. He had quarrelled with it at once and dissolved it without obtaining any money from it.

The ill-trained and disorderly troops that Charles got together were worse than useless. Ten days after crossing the Tweed the Scots captured Newcastle; four days later they were in Durham. As they could now cut off the coal supply of

[1] Name given to the nobleman who acted as the King's representative in Parliament or in the General Assembly.

[2] The name usually given to the country gentlemen who were Commissioners for the Shires.

London, the King had no choice but to open negotiations with them, and, as they declared that they would accept no treaty of which the English Parliament had not approved, he was forced to summon the famous 'Long' Parliament. Commissioners from both countries met in London to settle the terms of the treaty, but, as the English Commissioners knew that the presence of a Scottish Army in the northern counties was a check on the King, a year passed before the treaty was at last completed. It gave the Scots all that they wanted; the King promised to approve of the Acts of the Scottish Parliament of 1640, including the obnoxious Acts abolishing Episcopacy and limiting the powers of the Lords of the Articles; and, in addition, to give Parliament the right to challenge the actions of his ministers. At the same time the English Commons voted an indemnity of £300,000 to the Scots.

But much had happened in England between the opening of the negotiations and the signing of the treaty. Against his will, the King had been forced by the Long Parliament to surrender what he considered inalienable rights: he could no longer summon or dismiss Parliament just when he thought good ; he could no longer raise money to supplement his ordinary revenues without first consulting Parliament, and worst of all, as the execution of Strafford proved, his goodwill could no longer protect from the vengeance of Parliament a minister who carried out his policy. If he wanted to win back what he had lost, or even to keep what he had got, he would have to fight. Why then not make sure of the support of the Scots in the coming struggle ? With this purpose in view he visited Edinburgh in the autumn of 1641, but, though he made concession after concession, though he scattered titles broadcast, no one trusted him ; his visit was a failure. Of those who had appeared against him, the only one whom he won over to his side was the young Earl of Montrose, who had led the Scottish vanguard across the Tweed in 1640. Montrose was still a

Presbyterian, but he had begun to suspect that some of his fellow Covenanters, like the great Marquis of Argyll, were more interested in pulling down the monarchy than in setting up Presbyterianism.

So when the Civil War broke out in England the Scots at first held aloof. They were not interested in the political question, in the attempts to decide where the King's authority ended and where the authority of the Parliament began: they were almost wholly occupied with the ecclesiastical problem. The King, it is true, had consented to the establishment of Presbyterianism in Scotland, but reluctant consent to the establishment of Presbyterianism in only one part of his dominions was not sufficient to make the Scots come into the war on his side. They wanted a much higher price for their assistance— nothing short of the establishment of Presbyterianism and the suppression of Episcopacy in England, Scotland, and Ireland.

One would have thought that men who had fought so bitterly against interference with their modes of worship and system of Church organization would have been slow to interfere with the religion of other people. But this was not so. When they demanded freedom for the Church they demanded freedom for one Church only. Just as Charles thought that a Church which was not governed by bishops was no Church at all, and that therefore it was his duty to force all his subjects, in Scotland as in England, to become Episcopalians, so the Scots thought that a Church which was not governed according to the Presbyterian system was no Church at all, and that therefore it was their duty to make a Presbyterian, not only of every Scotsman, but, if they could manage it, of every Englishman too.

It seemed as if they might succeed. One royalist victory had followed another, and in the summer of 1643 the English Parliament, confronted with the prospect of utter defeat, appealed to Scotland for help. At the same time they summoned an Assembly of Divines to Westminster, to remodel the doctrines and ritual of the national Church, and to this Assembly representatives from Scotland were invited. By the Solemn League and Covenant, signed in the autumn of 1643, the Scots agreed to intervene on the side of the Parliament, and the Parliament undertook to establish Presbyterianism in England. So at the beginning of 1644 Alexander Leslie, now Earl of Leven, crossed the frozen Tweed at the head of 26,000 men.

At the battle of Marston Moor, in July 1644, the battle which lost the north of England to the King, the Scottish contingent played an important part. We are often told of the irresistible charge of Cromwell's Ironsides; we are not told that when Cromwell was wounded and his horsemen thrown into temporary confusion, David Leslie saved the situation by hurling the Scottish cavalry against Rupert's victorious squadrons, that, in the rout of the Parliamentary infantry, the Scottish regiments alone stood firm, or that, in the last triumphant charge which ended the battle, Cromwell's cuirassiers and Leslie's light horsemen rode side by side.

A few weeks later the tables were turned. Montrose, now a Marquis, made his way to the Highlands and got together an army composed mainly of Highlanders, with an Irish contingent, and a sprinkling of Lowland gentlemen and their retainers. With this motley host, destitute of artillery and almost destitute of cavalry, he proposed to win back Scotland for King Charles. It seemed a crack-brained scheme—to make the clans forget their feuds and jealousies and leave the security of their glens to fight for a distant King, for whom they cared nothing, in a quarrel which they could not understand. Yet it succeeded. The clansmen somehow knew that Montrose was not like other leaders, and that, if they followed him, they would have a chance of booty on a scale of which they had never dreamed.

Scotland soon learned how formidable these undisciplined,

A SOLEMN LEAGUE

AND

COVENANT

FOR

REFORMATION,

AND

Defence of RELIGION, The Honour
and Happines of the KING, and the Peace
and Safety of the three Kingdoms

OF

Scotland, *England*, and *Ireland*.

Appointed to be renewed

By the Acts of the COMMISSION of the
GENERALL ASSEMBLY, and the
COMMITTEE of ESTATES of the
sixth and fourteenth dayes of this
moneth of *October*.

Jer. 50.5. *Come, let us joyn our selves to the Lord in a perpetu-*
all Covenant, that shall not be forgotten.

Prov. 25.5. *Take away the wicked from before the King, and*
his Throne shall be established in righteousnesse.

2 Chron. 15.15. *And all Iudah rejoyced at the Oath, for they*
had sworn with all their heart, and sought him with their
whole desire, and he was found of them: and the Lord gave
them rest round about.

EDINBURGH,
Printed by *Evan Tyler*, Printer to the Kings most
Excellent Majestie, 1648.

THE TITLE-PAGE OF THE SOLEMN LEAGUE AND COVENANT
AS RENEWED IN 1648

impetuous fighters could be. At the beginning of September Montrose advanced against Perth, but found his way barred at Tippermuir by a Covenanting army twice as large as his own. The Highlanders fired one volley, then, flinging aside their muskets and their plaids, swept down with a wild yell on the wavering ranks of the Lowland infantry. The Covenanters lost their nerve and fled in terror, only to be cut down mercilessly by the pursuing Highlanders. Less than a fortnight later Montrose appeared before Aberdeen. Again the forces that tried to stop him melted away before the fierce onslaught of the Highlanders, who followed them up, and plundered and slew at will in the streets of the town. Then he disappeared into the Campbell country, where his great rival, the Marquis of Argyll, was wont to exercise a more than kingly authority, and plundered and burned at his pleasure till, in February 1645, he concluded his campaign in the west by swooping down on Argyll's army at Inverlochy, after a forced march through snow-blocked passes, and completely defeating it.

March saw him at the other side of Scotland, taking the walled town of Dundee by storm, then hustling his tipsy soldiers out by the East Port as the Covenanting army, under General Baillie, hurried in at the West Port. In May he utterly smashed an army commanded by Hurry, Baillie's second in command, at Auldearn, near the Moray Firth. In July he routed Baillie himself at Alford. Baillie escaped, and was put in command of another army, but at Kilsyth, in the following month, Montrose defeated Baillie a second time and occupied Glasgow.

It was a glorious record, a record that no other general living at that time, not even Cromwell himself, could have equalled. But Montrose had gained nothing but honour. He had failed to win over the Lowlands to his side, for the Lowland Scot could not forgive the man who had let his wild Highlanders and

Irishmen loose on Aberdeen to slaughter defenceless burgesses. He had failed to reinforce the hard-pressed Royalist armies, and though he had given Alexander Leslie some anxious moments, he had failed to divert a single regiment from the Scottish army in England. What could he do with an army which threatened

THE MARQUIS OF MONTROSE
According to the narrative on the back of the original,
the portrait was painted in 1640

to dissolve after every victory, with troops who went home after every battle, and did not return till they had seen their booty safely stowed away? Even if he could have invaded England after Kilsyth he would have been too late, for the King's hopes of victory had been destroyed a month earlier, in the crowning disaster of Naseby.

Now that the power of the King was shattered, the Scottish army in England could be used to deal with Montrose. David Leslie crossed the Tweed at the head of four thousand veterans and, on a misty September morning, surprised the remnants of the Royalist army at Philiphaugh, near Selkirk.

In vain Montrose galloped out from the town and charged at the head of his cavalry ; the battle had been lost before it was well begun.

Montrose's friends hurried him from the field. It was well, for the victors, remembering Aberdeen, showed no mercy to the prisoners. The bulk of them, including the women and children who had followed the army, were butchered on the battle-field. Those who were spared were spared only for trial and execution.

Meantime the Scots were sore perplexed. They had entered into an alliance with the English Parliament because they wanted to establish Presbyterianism in England, and because the English Parliament had promised to establish it. Further, as if to show that the Parliament was sincere, the Westminster Assembly still continued its deliberations, and still showed itself anxious to defer to the wishes of the Scottish representatives. But it was evident that the English Parliament could not keep to the bargain which it had made in the Solemn League and Covenant ; the destinies of the country were controlled no longer by Parliament, but by the Army, and the Army did not favour the establishment of Presbyterianism in England. Many of the officers and men were, like Cromwell, Independents, who thought that each congregation should manage its own affairs and mind its own business. They would not dream of interfering with the Presbyterians, if the Presbyterians left them alone, but that the Presbyterians should compel any Protestant to become a Presbyterian was intolerable to them.

The perplexity of the Scots grew deeper when, in 1646, the vanquished King threw himself on the mercy of the Scottish army. Since the English Parliament had disappointed them, they were ready to fight for the King, if he would undertake to

establish Presbyterianism in England. Charles refused. Reluctantly, in 1647, the Scots handed him over to the English
Parliament, and withdrew beyond the Tweed.

So the attempt to establish Presbyterianism in England,
through the co-operation of the King or of the English Parliament, had utterly failed. But though the Westminster Assembly
failed to transform the Church of England into a Presbyterian
Church, it has left its mark upon the Church of Scotland: to
this day Presbyterian services follow the order prescribed by
that Assembly. The Longer and Shorter Catechisms were
framed by it, and, what is stranger still, the metrical psalms,
which make the exiled Scot think of the 'clinkum clank o'
Sabbath bells' at home, were composed by a Cornishman, and
recommended to the use of a somewhat unwilling Church by
that same Westminster Assembly.

Meantime, some of the Scots began to think that they had
been in too great a hurry to give up their King; though they
objected to his ecclesiastical policy, they did not wish to see
his lawful authority diminished, and now it seemed that the
Parliament and the Army between them were doing their best
to deprive him of every shred of kingly power. Before the end
of 1647 the representatives of the Scottish Parliament signed
a treaty—the Engagement—by which they pledged themselves
to send an army into England to support the King, in return
for his promise to give Presbyterianism a three years' trial in
England. The Engagement split the country into two; the
more bigoted Presbyterians were furious because the Commissioners who negotiated the treaty had not insisted on Charles
signing the National Covenant and undertaking to establish
Presbyterianism for good. For their leader they had that
statesman who had been suspect to Montrose, the Marquis
of Argyll. The prophets of woe were justified: at the end of the
following summer the Duke of Hamilton led an army across the
border, but Cromwell came upon the Scots when they were

strung out from Preston to Wigan, and, in a three days' battle,
drove them out of Preston through Wigan, and finally rounded
them up at Winwick, about two miles from Warrington.

The remnants of the army surrendered. Hamilton himself
escaped death on the battle-field only to be executed a few
months later. Preston was an unmitigated disaster; it extinguished the King's last hopes of safety, for the army leaders
now hardened their hearts against him, and it led to civil strife
in Scotland. The Anti-Engagers in the West, the Whiggamores,[1]
as they were called, marched on Edinburgh and overthrew the
Government: Argyll was now master of Scotland.

But it soon became apparent that Cromwell was master of
Argyll. When he visited Edinburgh he was entertained as if he
had been a Scottish General who had triumphed over a foreign
army, not an English General who had vanquished a Scottish
army, and before he left he insisted that no one who had
fought for King Charles was to hold any office in Scotland.
A subservient Parliament hastened to obey him by passing the
Act of Classes in January 1649. But the execution of the King
a few weeks later horrified even those Scots who had hitherto
been the King's bitterest opponents, and swung the whole
country round into opposition to Cromwell and the Commonwealth. There was all the difference in the world, they felt,
between opposing the King's policy and laying violent hands
upon the King. That Scotland should be without a King was
unthinkable; now that Charles I had been slain, the only thing
to do was to proclaim his son as King in his stead.

To proclaim Charles II as King was one thing: to invite the
exiled monarch to Scotland and defend him against the
inevitable attacks of the Commonwealth armies was a very
different one. The Scots, however, were willing to do it, but for
a price. Charles must sign both Covenants. Charles did not

[1] They got their name because West-Country carters were supposed to
cry 'Whiggam!' when they wanted to encourage their horses.

wish to sign if it could possibly be evaded, and in 1650 he commissioned Montrose to invade northern Scotland. Montrose knew from the start that his enterprise was hopeless; his force of unwarlike Orcadians and foreign mercenaries was routed at Carbisdale in Ross-shire, and he himself was captured, taken to Edinburgh, and executed. He met disaster as he had

THE SCOTS HOLDING THEIR YOUNG KINGES NOSE TO Y GRINSTO
Come to the Grinstone Charles tis now to late
To Recolech tis presbiterian fate
You Counant pretenders must Thee
The subiect of Jouer Tradgie Comedie
Jockie
Stoope Charles

CHARLES II AND THE KIRK
From a satirical print of 1651

met triumph; on the day of his execution his calm and simple dignity silenced the brawling Edinburgh mob, and brought tears to the eyes of those who had wept for sons slain at Kilsyth or Tippermuir.

There was no help for it now: Charles undertook to observe both Covenants, and about midsummer he appeared in Scotland. A month later Cromwell crossed the border. The independence of Scotland was at stake now, but by the Act of Classes the privilege of fighting for his country was denied to the man who had followed Montrose or Hamilton, and so thousands of the bravest and most experienced soldiers were excluded from the army with which David Leslie confronted Cromwell. Even then the Scots outnumbered the English by two to one. Their commander, too, had made up his mind to play a cautious game, and give no opening to Cromwell. He kept him marching and countermarching, through country from which all food-stuffs had disappeared, in a vain attempt to get between the Scottish army and Edinburgh; then, when Cromwell, finding his army weakened by sickness and starvation, retreated to Dunbar, Leslie promptly occupied Doon Hill, about two miles to the south of the town. The northern slope of the hill is defended by a deep ravine, through which the Brocksburn flows to the sea. Cromwell was at his wit's end: though his confidence seemed unshaken, he admitted to one of his friends that he could not escape 'without almost a miracle'.

The miracle happened: Cromwell could hardly believe his eyes when, on the afternoon of the second of September, he saw the Scottish infantry descend the slopes of Doon Hill and take up their position on the plain. 'The Lord hath delivered them into our hands,' he cried. The Scots made no attempt to continue their advance. When the night came on with wind and rain they bivouacked on the southern side of the stream, confident that no one would be fool enough to fight in such dirty weather. But it was dangerous to make such an assumption when Cromwell was in the neighbourhood. In reality, his whole army was standing to on the other side of the ravine, for he was resolved to attack before dawn the next day. While it was still dark, fighting began away on the left of the Scottish position. As a wan light broke over the North Sea, the cannon began to thunder against the Scottish centre, and the trumpets sounded the advance. Under cover of the artillery fire detached bodies of red-coated cavalry and infantry, with shouts of 'The Lord of Hosts', forced their way across the stream. At first the Scottish centre stood fast, and the Scottish cavalry on the right charged and drove the advancing English back towards the ravine. But the counter-charge of Cromwell's second line hurled back the horsemen upon their own infantry in the centre. The centre held for a little and then gave way, and soon the whole Scottish army was rolling back in wild confusion. As the red-coated troopers clove deeper and deeper into the ranks of their despairing enemies, as the blue banners of St. Andrew were trampled underfoot, as the cries of 'God and the Covenant' grew fainter, the sun shone out over the North Sea. Cromwell accepted the omen: 'Let God arise,' he shouted, 'let his enemies be scattered!' Scattered they were; of the army of 23,000 men, three thousand fell on the field of battle and another ten thousand were made prisoners. Cromwell had lost barely a score of men.

But the upholders of the Covenant did not know when they were beaten. Cromwell followed up his victory by occupying Edinburgh. Argyll and his associates still refused to have anything to do with a man who was ready to allow every Protestant to cleave to his own special form of Protestantism. They turned instead to the prince who believed in his heart that Presbyterianism was no religion for a gentleman, but professed himself willing to impose it on his English subjects, and on 1st January Charles was crowned at Scone. They had learned some sense, however. Despite the protests of the stricter Presbyterians,[1] the Act of Classes was rescinded. No man was now debarred from fighting for Charles II because he had fought for Charles I. So the small force of famished and disgusted men, with which Leslie had guarded the approaches to Stirling throughout the winter, had grown to be a formidable army in the summer of 1651. And Leslie seemed to have learned his

[1] Known as Protesters: those who were willing to co-operate with the former followers of Charles I were called Resolutioners.

lesson; he refused to be lured from his position in front of Stirling. But Cromwell was too clever for him; he moved his army over into Fife, and marched on Perth, thus at the same time threatening to take Leslie in flank and leaving the road to England uncovered. The little stratagem worked beautifully; when Cromwell reached Perth, he heard that Charles and the whole Scottish army had left Stirling and were bound for the border.

Leaving Monk behind to deal with Stirling and Dundee, Cromwell hurried after the Scots, collecting reinforcements as he went, till his army had swelled to 31,000 men. The 3rd of September had come round again, and it was not among the gorse and bracken of some Scottish moorland, but where the spires of Worcester look down on the meadows watered by the Teme and the Severn, that the last scene of this grim tragedy was enacted. For five hours the Scots fought bravely against foes who outnumbered them two to one. They were forced over Severn Bridge and into the town on the west side only to sally from it gallantly on the east side, but they were beaten back, their guns captured and turned upon them, and they themselves forced to surrender. The King escaped, but not many more.

Five days earlier one of Monk's officers had captured the Committee of the Estates,[1] the last remnant of the Scottish Parliament; two days earlier Monk's troops had stormed and sacked the town of Dundee, next to Edinburgh the wealthiest town in Scotland.

The spirit of the Scots was completely broken. In a little over three years they had raised three armies, only to see each of them ground to powder by Cromwell, and now they could do no more. The English garrisons in their chief towns, the great new fortresses at Leith, Perth, and Ayr, reminded them that

[1] The committee of the Scottish Parliament which met when Parliament was not in session.

they belonged to a conquered country. They were not treated harshly. They were treated rather as children—but as children who might blunder into mischief if they were not carefully watched. A Committee of eight English officials replaced the old Privy Council, seven English judges, 'kinless loons', replaced the old Court of Session, but did not inherit that weakness for taking bribes which the 'Auld Fifteen'[1] had manifested. Finally, when Cromwell became Protector in 1653 the Scottish Parliament was absorbed in the English Parliament; thirty representatives, the majority of them Englishmen, went from Scotland to Westminster.

In return for her loss of independence, Scotland gained trading privileges that had hitherto been reserved for Englishmen. Scottish captains were allowed to bring goods from foreign harbours into English ports and ports in the English colonies. She gained too, what she did not value, a respite from religious strife. But the Presbyterians had not yet learned their lesson. They would still have refused to others the freedom which they claimed for themselves. They were to learn it soon, and in a hard school.

[1] The fifteen judges of the Court of Session.

CHAPTER XXIII

THE COVENANTERS

About the graves of the martyrs the whaups are crying.

STEVENSON.

Charles II .	.	.	.	.	1649–1685	William III	.	. .	1689–1702
James II & VII	.	.	.		1685–1688	Mary II	.	. . .	1689–1694

THE Scots greeted the Restoration of Charles II in 1660 with a delight untroubled by any forebodings of evil; defeat and humiliation were over ; Scotland was an independent kingdom once more—a kingdom, moreover, ruled over by a Covenanting King. But the bells which clanged their welcome from the Edinburgh steeples were ringing in years of even deeper misery and humiliation. For Charles had no intention of being bound by the Covenant, or of letting the Scottish Parliament enjoy the powers which his father had been forced to concede to it. In defiance of a statute of 1641, he chose his Privy Council and the great officers of state without ever consulting Parliament. And the Parliament, in its first raptures over the return of the King, came pretty near to signing its own death-warrant. It passed a Rescissory Act, annulling all Acts passed by its predecessors since 1633, thus automatically re-establishing the Committee of the Articles. It agreed that the King was supreme governor of his kingdom, over all persons and all causes ; it again gave bishops a place in the House, and it restored the old method of choosing the Committee of the Articles which James VI had introduced, which made it practically impossible for a member of whom the King did not approve to be appointed to the Committee.

But most people were less concerned about the changes in Parliament than about the rumours of changes in the Church.

Different people looked forward to different things: the nobles and country gentlemen, for example, in their relief at the passing of the long years of war and banishment, were set only on enjoying themselves; they bitterly regretted their short-lived alliance with the Presbyterian ministers against Charles I, and were ready to go to any length to help his son, Charles II, to put them in their place.

In the north-east of Scotland, too, the people honestly preferred Episcopacy to Presbyterianism; but in the greater part of the Lowlands the burgesses and country folk hoped and expected to see Presbyterianism again established as the national faith of Scotland. Dunbar and Worcester had taught them the folly, however, of attempting to impose Presbyterianism on England, or to hold Charles II to a Covenant which he had accepted under compulsion. In the south-west it was different. The spirit of the Protesters was still strong; ministers and people alike were out and out 'Covenanters', that is, they would be satisfied with nothing less than the establishment of Presbyterianism in Scotland and England, as required by the Solemn League and Covenant.

But in 1661 it was discovered that when Charles spoke of protecting the Church as established by law, he meant the Church as established by Charles I in 1633, and further, that the Presbyterian champion, James Sharp, who had been sent to London to persuade the King to support it, had himself been persuaded to become Archbishop of St. Andrews. The subservient Parliament not only consented to the reintroduction of bishops into the Church; it deprived congregations of the right of choosing their own ministers, and declared that ministers who had been so appointed must resign their charges, and receive them again from the hands of the bishop of the diocese.

Most of the ministers gave in for the sake of peace. They did not want the bishops, but they had to admit that the bishops made no attempt to interfere with the doctrines or services of the Church. No prayer-book was used; the worshippers still stood throughout the lengthy prayers, instead of kneeling, as they would have done in the Anglican Church; they still sang the psalms as appointed by the Westminster Assembly, droning them out line by line after the precentor.

About three hundred ministers, however, most of them from the south-west, left their churches rather than have any dealings with the bishops. Their places were filled by young men from the north, of little learning and less piety. But the people refused to listen to the 'curates', as the new ministers were called. They stayed away from church, to go to some secluded spot among the hills, where they could listen to their own banished minister. The Government retaliated by imposing heavy fines on all who ventured to attend these conventicles or even stayed away from church, and by sending dragoons into the west to collect the money at the sword's point. This severity, instead of frightening the enthusiasts for the Covenant in the west, only goaded them into rebellion. In 1666 some hundreds of them marched to Edinburgh, but, finding that the citizens did not mean to support them, they turned about and began to retreat homewards. They were overtaken, however, at Rullion Green in the Pentlands, by Sir Thomas Dalziel and his dragoons, and completely defeated. More than thirty of the prisoners were hanged; the remainder were sent to work as slaves in the sugar plantations of Barbados.

The Earl of Lauderdale, to whom Charles had entrusted the direction of Scottish affairs, now attempted a policy of conciliation. By his advice, Letters of Indulgence were issued in 1669 and 1672, giving permission to the banished ministers to return to their churches without submitting themselves to the bishops on condition that they remained in their own parishes. Many ministers availed themselves of the Indulgences, but a remnant refused to give way, and although in 1670 attendance at conventicles had been declared to be a treasonable offence, they did not lack for congregations. The worshippers were more careful now; they came to the conventicle fully armed, and posted sentries to keep watch while the preaching went on. Their attempts to avoid arrest only made the Government all the more anxious to arrest them. Lauderdale and Charles looked with suspicion on these musterings of armed men, and guessed that another rebellion was afoot. So the screw was tightened; in 1678, 3,000 Lowland militia men and a 'Highland Host' of 6,000 clansmen were sent into the south-west. The Highlanders were not cruel, but their habit of helping themselves to whatever they fancied in the houses where they were billeted did not endear them to their unwilling hosts.

These measures for preventing a rebellion only made a rebellion inevitable. At the beginning of May in 1679 Archbishop Sharp was dragged from his coach as he was crossing Magus Muir, near St. Andrews, and brutally murdered. A month later Captain John Graham of Claverhouse rode out from Hamilton with three troops of horse to disperse a conventicle. When he reached Drumclog, however, a stretch of marshy ground near Loudoun Hill, he found that he had to deal with a formidable body of armed men. His life guards and dragoons could not withstand the furious onslaught of the blue-bonneted country folk; they galloped pell-mell for Glasgow, leaving more than thirty of their comrades dead on the field. A few days later Glasgow itself was in the hands of the rebels. Their triumph was short-lived; they could not agree on what they were fighting for, and a fortnight after they had entered Glasgow they were completely defeated by the Duke of Monmouth at Bothwell Brig. Fourteen hundred prisoners were taken to Edinburgh to be herded into Greyfriars Churchyard. A few were executed, but most were released on condition that they promised never again to take up arms against the King; almost three hundred, however, refused to make this promise, and were shipped off to the West Indies. Only some forty reached their place of exile; the remainder were drowned.

Scotland, for the most part, had now sunk into a sullen acquiescence in the episcopal system. Some of the Covenanters, however, refused to be taught anything by defeat. In 1680 a few of them, headed by the preacher Richard Cameron, rode into Sanquhar, and at the Market Cross declared war against the King and all who supported him. Unfortunately, Lauderdale's successor, the Duke of York, could see nothing ludicrous in the sight of one minister and a few score of west-country rustics 'taking on' the whole British Empire. Cameron himself was killed in a skirmish at Aird's Moss; his followers were hunted down and shot. They were declared rebels, men who had drawn the sword against the King, and so could not complain if they perished by the sword of his officers. Grim, unlovable men these Cameronians must have been, immovable in their opinions, certain that they were right and that the rest of the world was hopelessly wrong. Yet, if we cannot admire their intolerance, we must admire that splendid courage which made them continue in a hopeless venture long after they knew it to be hopeless, and, when tortured by the thumb-screw or the boot, refuse to utter the word that would have saved their lives.

The more tolerant and peaceable Presbyterians, however, began to discover that there was no salvation in a middle course; the Government would be satisfied with nothing but complete surrender. In 1681 a 'Test' was imposed upon all ministers and all who held office: they were required to renounce the Covenants, and to treat of no matter, civil or ecclesiastical, without the King's consent. In 1684 those Presbyterian ministers who had been allowed to preach under the Indulgences of 1669 and 1672 were expelled from their parishes, and required to promise that they would never preach again. Most of them refused to promise, and were thrown into prison.

After the death of Charles II in 1685 and the accession of the Catholic James VII—James II of England—the plight of the Presbyterians became worse than it had been before. Parliament declared that the taking of the Covenants was a treasonable offence, and made preaching at any kind of conventicle, or mere attendance at a field conventicle, punishable by death.

It was in vain that the Earl of Argyll, the chief of the great Clan Campbell, returned from his exile in Holland to head a rebellion against King James. Disputes broke out among his followers; he disbanded his army, was captured, taken to Edinburgh, and executed. His attempt, indeed, brought fresh misery upon the Covenanters: when word of his coming arrived, the prisoners who had been confined because of their religion—two hundred in all—were packed off to Dunottar Castle and lodged in a miserable dungeon, open to the sea wind and the east coast 'haar'. Their guards made them pay, not only for their food, but even for their drinking-water. If they refused, their portion of water was spilt on the prison floor. Many died, and some who tried to escape were tortured by having pieces of lighted tow tied between their fingers. After Argyll's rebellion had collapsed, those who agreed to accept the Test were released; the remainder were transported to the American Colonies.

Yet nothing was farther from the King's wishes than the maintenance of Episcopacy: he meant, after he had undermined it by granting freedom of worship to all his subjects, to establish Roman Catholicism in its place, as the national religion. Though everybody knew the purpose which lay behind the Letters of Indulgence issued in 1687, most of the Presbyterians, wearied out with persecution, were in no mood to look a gift horse in the mouth, and gladly accepted the King's permission to go on with their worship in their own way. Only the followers of Cameron remained obdurate. They would accept no favours from a King who had not taken the Covenant.

The flight of James at the end of 1688, and the arrival in England of William of Orange, brought the long nightmare to an end. The Convention of the Estates which met in Edinburgh early in 1689 declared that James had forfeited the crown, and offered it to William and Mary. One condition was attached. The King was informed that Episcopacy must be abolished. Meantime, in many parishes the Presbyterians had taken their revenge on the Episcopal clergy by 'rabbling' them—driving them out by main force.

But the cause of James was not yet lost. Graham of Claverhouse, now Viscount Dundee, had ridden from Edinburgh to his Castle of Dudhope with sixty horsemen, resolved to go 'whither the spirit of Montrose should direct him'.

A few weeks later he disappeared. He had gone to the Highlands to raise the clans for King James. A force of regulars, commanded by General Mackay, was sent after him. The royal troops threaded the dangerous Pass of Killiecrankie unmolested, but when they emerged on the open ground at the head of the Pass they found Dundee waiting for them. It was the story of Tippermuir over again. One crashing volley, and then, before the soldiers could fix their bayonets, they saw, breaking through the smoke, a horde of half-naked Highlanders, yelling and brandishing their claymores and leathern shields. It was too much for them. They wavered and broke under the impetuous charge. Mackay, with a remnant of his troops, escaped, but hundreds of his soldiers lay dead on the battle-field or in the black pools of the Garry.

The victory of Killiecrankie availed James nothing, for Dundee was among the slain, and without a leader the Highlanders were useless. It is true that they advanced to Dunkeld, but Dunkeld was garrisoned by warriors as fierce as they were and far more obstinate—the Cameronians, who had been formed into a regular regiment. The Highlanders outnumbered them by four to one, but they held on after their colonel was killed, after their ammunition was exhausted, till finally Lowland 'dourness' prevailed against Highland fire and dash, the attacks ceased, and the clansmen melted away.

The fear of rebellion in the Highlands had not altogether disappeared when in 1690 the Scottish Parliament attempted a final settlement of the ecclesiastical problem, and established the Church of Scotland that we know to-day. The doctrine that the King was supreme ruler over the Church was repudiated ; the Presbyterian system of Church government was re-established, and the right of each congregation to choose its own minister was acknowledged. Presbyterian ministers who had been expelled during the two previous reigns were brought back to their parishes, and commissioners were appointed to exclude ministers whose life and doctrines seemed to be unsatisfactory. King William was not satisfied ; the settlement seemed to threaten further strife. It seemed to him that the triumphant Presbyterians were persecuting the Episcopalians, as the Episcopalians had persecuted them, and he did not see why an Episcopalian clergyman should not remain undisturbed in his parish as long as he took the oath of allegiance, and kept his ideas about Church government to himself. But King William's plan for a really comprehensive Church broke down. The Presbyterians were afraid that if the numerous Episcopalian clergymen were allowed to remain in the Church they would recapture it and make it an Episcopal Church once more, and were not sorry when most of the Episcopal clergy shut themselves out of the national Church by refusing to take the oath of allegiance, or to acknowledge King William as the rightful king.

The days of religious persecution were gone for ever. Though poverty was the lot of most of the Episcopalian clergy, they did not suffer imprisonment or death. And the mad dream of making England Presbyterian had become only a memory—except to the Cameronians, and, protest as they liked, they could persuade no one but themselves.

CHAPTER XXIV

DARIEN AND THE UNION
THE END OF THE SCOTTISH PARLIAMENT: 1690–1707

The End of an Auld Sang.
EARL OF SEAFIELD.

William III 1689–1702   Anne 1702–1714

NOW that the fear of persecution no longer troubled either Presbyterians or Episcopalians, now that both England and Scotland were governed by a wise and tolerant prince, there seemed no reason why Scotland should not become a prosperous and contented country. But prosperous and contented it certainly was not. For one thing, the Union of the Crowns had not removed the danger of disputes with England. To all appearance, that union left Scotland a completely independent country, with its own Parliament and Privy Council, its own laws and law-courts. To all appearance, allegiance to the same sovereign was the only tie that bound the two countries together. But had that independence been as complete as it seemed, it would have involved both countries in serious difficulties. Suppose England wanted to enter upon war with France or Holland, and suppose Scotland was determined to stay out—what then? As a matter of fact Scotland never could stay out of a war in which England was involved. The war between England and France which broke out in the reign of Charles I resulted in the loss to Scotland of her one colony—Nova Scotia, and though the Dutch had granted valuable trading privileges to Scottish merchants, though the bulk of the Scottish exports to the Continent passed through the Dutch port of Veere, Scotland was twice dragged into war with Holland in the reign of Charles II. For Scotland was not really independent: James VI and his successors chose and dismissed their ministers without consulting the Scottish Parliament, nor did Parliament object, for the control which the sovereign exercised over the election of the Lords of the Articles made it a most obliging and accommodating body.

At last, in the year 1690, King William consented to the abolition of the Committee of the Articles, though he refused to surrender the right of appointing what ministers he pleased. At last the Scottish Parliament seemed free to do something really useful— to encourage trade and so diminish the appalling poverty of the country— but it could do nothing.

The hardships of colonization in Nova Scotia. From a satiric playing-card

England was the obstacle. In 1651 the English Parliament passed the Navigation Act, which forbade goods to be imported into England and its colonies unless they were carried in English ships or in ships belonging to the country in which the goods were produced. The complete union of the two countries two years later shielded the Scottish merchants from the evil effects of the Act, but the Restoration made them aliens once more and deprived them of the privileges which the English merchants enjoyed. The captain of a Scottish ship could no longer bring French silks and wines into an English port; he could take Scottish goods only, and on these he had to pay higher customs dues than his English rival. He might, if he chose, take Scottish linens and woollens into a port in the North American Colonies, but he did not choose, for he knew that though he was allowed to bring Scottish goods in, he was not allowed to take Colonial goods out.

To make matters worse, the powerful English trading companies considered that they had the sole right of trading with certain regions; a Scottish merchant who attempted to trade with India must expect the implacable hostility of the East India Company, if he thereupon took his goods to any part of Africa he would be warned off by the African Company. Turn where he might, the Scottish merchant found his English rival blocking the way. Meantime his country sank deeper and deeper into the mire of poverty.

One might have expected a wise and conscientious ruler like William III to grapple with the problem, but, as we shall see, the black business of Glencoe and the blacker business of Darien seemed to prove that William did not care what happened to his Scottish subjects.

Since, in spite of the failure of the Killiecrankie campaign, many of the Highland chiefs still remained faithful to the exiled King, a proclamation was issued ordering every chief to take the oath of allegiance to King William before January 1st, 1692. All the chiefs but two, MacDonnell of Glengarry and MacIan of Glencoe, took the oath before the appointed date. Glengarry was head of a formidable clan and master of a powerful fortress; MacIan was the chieftain of a small sept or branch of the Clan MacDonald, and dwelt in a narrow glen four miles long, the outlets from which could easily be blocked. William, advised by Sir James Dalrymple, the Master of Stair,[1] sent a letter to the general commanding the royal forces in the Highlands, ordering him to give Glengarry a second chance

[1] Master: the title given to the eldest son of some Scottish noblemen.

but adding, 'If MacIan of Glencoe and that tribe can be well separated from the rest, it will be a proper vindication of public justice to extirpate that sect of thieves.'

Dalrymple was aware, and perhaps William was aware too, that MacIan had really meant to take the oath and had made his way to Fort-William before the end of the year, only to be told by the officer there that he should have gone to the Sheriff at Inveraray, that he had struggled through snow-blocked passes and arrived at Inveraray three days late, but three days in front of the Sheriff, and that when the Sheriff did appear on the 6th of January he was so much moved by the old chieftain's tears that he allowed him to take the oath. It mattered nothing to Dalrymple, he had intended to make an example of MacIan all along, and now MacIan had delivered himself into his hands. William, his mind full of weightier matters, did not trouble to find out precisely what Dalrymple meant to do.

At the beginning of February 1692 the inhabitants of Glencoe were alarmed by the appearance among them of a company of soldiers. They soon recovered from their alarm, however, when they discovered that the commander of the royal troops was Captain Campbell of Glenlyon, whose niece was the wife of MacIan's second son. The soldiers were billeted in the cottages scattered up and down the glen, and soon made friends with the clansmen. Glenlyon spent much of his time drinking with old MacIan or playing cards with his sons, and when MacIan invited him to bring two of his officers with him to dinner on the 13th of February he did not refuse.

MacIan little knew that his guest had just received a letter containing the following words: 'You are hereby ordered to fall upon the McDonalds of Glencoe and put all to the sword under seventy; you are to have a speciall care that the old fox and his sons doe on no account escape your hands.' He little knew that four hundred soldiers were being moved up to block the southern end of the glen, and that another four hundred were making for the northern entrance.

Very early in the morning of the 13th the work of slaughter began. Parties of soldiers went from house to house, shooting the sleeping or half-awakened occupants, driving off the cattle and setting fire to the thatch. MacIan was shot down by one of the officers whom he had invited to dinner; a soldier tore the rings from his wife's fingers with his teeth. Among the slain were three or four women and a boy of six, who clung to Glenlyon's knees and offered to be his slave if only he would spare his life. As if to add to the terrors of the morning, snow began to fall heavily. But the snow acted as a screen to the dwellers in the more remote cottages, who, warned by the sound of firing, escaped by the unguarded outlets from the pass. For the plot had miscarried: the soldiers who should have guarded the northern end failed to arrive in time. Mischief enough had been done, twenty-five or thirty people were slain by the soldiers and others escaped for a time, only to perish in the snow.

At first no one in the Lowlands bothered his head about the massacre. Most of the soldiers were Campbells, the inhabitants of Glencoe were MacDonalds, so the average Lowlander looked on the affair as nothing more than an ordinary clan fight— something over which pity or indignation would be wasted— and refused to listen to the Jacobite pamphleteers who insisted that William was at the bottom of the business. But William's reluctance to order an inquiry, his strange action in pardoning Dalrymple after being compelled by the Scottish Parliament to dismiss him from office, and his neglect to send the guilty soldiers home for trial, made the average Lowlander feel that there must be some truth in the accusations of the Jacobites. Still he did not worry himself; if the King chose to exterminate a turbulent thieving Highland clan, no great harm was done.

But soon the Lowlander too had cause, or thought he had

DUNCANSON'S LETTER TO GLENLYON

cause, to curse King William's lack of regard for his Scottish subjects. So far the Scottish merchants had complained bitterly of the privileges which English traders and trading companies

THE BANK OF ENGLAND
The early building

enjoyed, but they had done nothing more. Now in 1695 there appeared in Edinburgh a man who claimed to have found a remedy for Scotland's worst ills. This was William Paterson, the roving financial genius who in the previous year had founded the Bank of England. Paterson's plan was a simple one: the English Parliament had granted monopolies to English trading companies; let the Scottish Parliament therefore grant a monopoly of trade with Africa and the Indies to a Scottish trading company. The Scottish company must then make haste to gain what Paterson called 'the Door of the Seas, the key of the Universe'— the unoccupied Isthmus of Darien. For Paterson was confident that sooner or later Darien would become the centre of the world's commerce, that goods destined for India, instead of being sent round the Cape of Good Hope or the more perilous Cape Horn, would simply be shipped to some port on the eastern side of Darien, then carried across the narrow isthmus to a port on the western side, where ships that had come from India would be waiting. Thus the merchandise of Europe and the merchandise of Asia would be exchanged, not in Europe or Asia, but in Darien.

To plant a settlement like this, with its harbours and roads, forts and fleets, would be an expensive business, too expensive for a poverty-stricken country like Scotland; but Paterson knew that there were other English merchants besides those who were members of the African or East India Company who wanted to trade with Africa and India, and he knew that these unprivileged merchants would be glad to become members of a Scottish trading company.

In June 1695 the Scottish Parliament passed an Act establishing 'the Company of Scotland Trading to Africa and the Indies', or the Darien Company, as it is usually called. Its capital was to be £600,000, but only half that sum was to be subscribed by the Scottish shareholders.

At first everything went well; English investors speedily subscribed the £300,000 which was their share of the capital. Meantime the directors of the English East India Company saw that if they did not act their monopoly would be broken and their Company ruined—already the price of its stock was falling with disastrous rapidity—so they set to work, and soon the English Parliament declared that it meant to impeach the leading English members of the Scottish Company. The threat was enough; the English investors at once withdrew their money. William himself frowned on the scheme. 'I have been ill-served in Scotland,' he declared, 'but I hope some remedies may be found.'

The opposition of the King and of the English Parliament raised the enthusiasm of the Scots to a veritable frenzy; £400,000 of the necessary £600,000 they would find themselves, the remainder they would get on the Continent. But though agents of the Company crossed to Hamburg they found that the representative of the English Government had been there before them; the foreign merchants would not subscribe a penny unless they could get a definite assurance from King William that he approved of the Scottish Company, and this assurance the King was careful not to give.

Though it was hopeless to go on with insufficient capital, national pride would not permit the scheme to be abandoned. A great effort was made, the whole of the £400,000 was subscribed, and in July 1698 the ships *Caledonia*, *St. Andrew*, and *Unicorn* with twelve hundred emigrants on board, freighted besides with the hopes of a whole nation, set sail from the port of Leith. Paterson himself accompanied the expedition.

In November Darien was reached. The emigrants were enchanted by the first prospect of New Caledonia, as they had decided to call their settlement. 'The Soil is rich,' said one of them, 'the Air good and temperate, the Water is Sweet, and everything contributes to make it healthful and convenient. . . . We are certainly much bound to Providence in this affair.' The natives were not unfriendly, the gift of a hat laced with gold won them the good favour of the most important chief, a pompous little Indian called Andreas, who appeared before them in a gay scarlet coat, but with no shoes or stockings. They built a fort, to which they gave the name of Fort St. Andrew, on a little promontory, and busied themselves in putting up huts and in making clearings in 'the legion of monstrous plants', where they tried to grow yams and maize.

The glamour soon faded from the scene, they grew tired of the chattering monkeys, and the brilliant but songless birds which flashed through the gloom of the tropical forests. The captain of the *St. Andrew* might declare that the harbour beside the fort could easily contain a thousand of the greatest merchantmen in the world; what did that matter when only one or two ships appeared—ships whose business was not to trade but to spy ? The Indians were willing to accept presents, but showed no anxiety to buy the wigs, stockings, and Bibles which the colonists tried to sell to them.

The prospect of financial ruin was bad enough, but the prospect of starving to death in a foreign land was worse. The colonists had been sent off with only six months' provisions, instead of the supplies for nine months which had been promised them. They tried to get provisions from Jamaica, but in vain ; King William had published a prohibition forbidding the English colonists in America to have any dealings with the Scottish settlers. And behind the spectre of Famine loomed the spectre of Pestilence ; fever broke out and slew one out of every four among the wretched adventurers. There was nothing for it but to abandon the colony, and in July 1699 the survivors re-embarked. But they took the fever aboard with them, and little more than half of those who set sail from Darien put into port in the English colonies.

News travelled slowly in those days, and so it came about that a few weeks after the survivors of the first expedition had left, a second contingent of three hundred colonists arrived. They could do nothing but turn about—not, however, before one of their two ships was burned—and make for Jamaica.

At the end of September, just when a third expedition of 1,300 settlers was ready to sail, vague rumours of the disaster reached Scotland. The commander of the expedition, however, started off without waiting to find out what truth was in the rumours and involved the third expedition in a bigger disaster than had befallen the first.

Hitherto the unhealthy climate had been the worst enemy that the settlers had to contend with, but now they had to reckon with another foe. Though the Spaniards knew better than to attempt to settle in this extremely unhealthy part of the coast, they were firmly resolved that no other European colonists must be allowed to establish themselves there. So,

soon after they landed and reoccupied the deserted Fort
St. Andrew the colonists learned that a Spanish army and fleet
were moving against them. In vain the gallant Campbell of
Fonab attempted to delay the Spaniards by storming their
encampment; Fort St. Andrew was soon blockaded both by
land and sea. Already the fort was no better than a pest-house,
but the Scots stubbornly defended it for more than a month;
only when the number of men able to handle a musket was
reduced to three hundred did they surrender.

The Spaniards had admired their bravery, and allowed them
to march out as if in triumph, with drums beating and colours
flying, but they had to leave Darien. The sorry history of the
first expedition was repeated; fever slew them by the hundred
on their voyage to the English colonies.

The Darien Scheme had ended in complete and disastrous
failure. Two hundred thousand pounds, and what was worse,
the lives of more than two thousand men, had been flung away.

It is easy for us to apportion the blame, to say that people
who knew nothing about tropical medicine—who tried to fight
yellow fever with whisky—had no right to complain if they
fell mortally ill when they went to a tropical country. But to
the Scotsman of the time the villain of the piece was not
Stegomyia fasciata—the mosquito that carries the yellow fever
germ—but William the Third. It would have been so easy for
William to have given his approval and support to the scheme.
Why did he not do it?

To William himself it did not seem so easy; he could not
support the Scots Company without breaking the monopoly of
the English companies. But the privileges which the English
merchants enjoyed, though unjust, were not illegal; he could not
disregard the rights conferred by the English Parliament without
creating a storm of indignation in England. And William knew
something to which his Scottish subjects never gave a thought:
he knew that at any moment Europe might be plunged into war,

a war in which Britain and Holland would be fighting for their very existence against the forces of Louis XIV of France. It was of the utmost importance that he should have Spain on his side, but if he had supported a scheme for planting a Scottish colony in territory claimed by the Spanish Government, if he had sent British men-of-war to protect it, he would certainly have driven Spain into the ranks of his enemies. No, the only way to avoid the confusion caused by the Scottish Parliament granting to Scottish merchants privileges which the English Parliament had already granted to English merchants, the only way to keep the Scottish Parliament from ruining his carefully calculated foreign policy was to unite the Scottish Parliament to the English Parliament. He made an attempt to get the English Parliament to consider a scheme for union, but the Commons would have nothing to do with it.

The disaster of Darien had moved William more than his Scottish subjects thought; even when he lay on his death-bed, in the early weeks of 1702, he sent a second appeal to the English Parliament, but again no heed was paid to his request. Queen Anne's appeals were more successful, but though in the first year of her reign representatives of the two countries met at Whitehall to draw up a treaty of union, nothing came of the negotiations; the Scots would accept the Union only if they were to be admitted to the trading privileges which the English enjoyed, privileges which the English representatives obstinately refused to part with.

It is little wonder that the Scottish Parliament which met in 1703 showed rather an ugly temper. Two years previously the English Parliament had declared in the Act of Settlement that if Queen Anne died without children the crown was to go to the Electress Sophia of Hanover; now the Scottish Parliament passed an Act of Security, which declared that unless Scotland received the same trading privileges as England, the Scots would choose a sovereign of their own after the death of Queen

Anne. This Bill, which would have effected the complete
separation of the two kingdoms, the Queen naturally refused
to accept, whereupon the Scottish Parliament refused to vote
supplies, and forced her to give her assent before the end of
1704. But intimidation was a game that two could play at. In
February 1705 the English Parliament passed the Aliens Act,
which prohibited the importation of cattle, linen, and coals—
almost the only commodities which the Scots could export—
from Scotland into England, and declared that if at the end of
the year the Scottish Parliament still refused to fall into line
with the English Parliament about the question of the succession, then all Scots would be treated as aliens.

Meantime English interference with Scottish trade continued.
After the settlement on the Isthmus had been abandoned the
Darien Company attempted once or twice to send merchant
ships to Africa and India, but one of these, the *Annandale*, was
captured and retained by the English, and another, the *Speedy
Return*, disappeared. So when the English merchant ship
Worcester was driven into the Firth of Forth in August 1704 it
was promptly seized to compensate for the *Annandale*. That
was not all. The rumour spread that the apparently innocent
merchant ship was a pirate, and that it had sunk the *Speedy
Return*. As a matter of fact there was not a word of truth in the
story; the *Speedy Return* had itself turned pirate. It made no
difference; the captain and crew were arrested, and though
there was not a shred of evidence to justify the verdict, they
were found guilty. The knowledge that two of the crew of the
Speedy Return had actually landed in England, the Queen's
orders that a reprieve should be granted, weighed less with the
judges than their fears of the Edinburgh mob; in April 1705
Captain Green and two of his men were hanged on the sands of
Leith, between high and low water mark.

This was nothing less than murder, though murder disguised
under the forms of justice, and for a time it seemed as if war

could be its only sequel. But though the English people were furious, the English Government did not want war with Scotland at a time when it required all its resources for the struggle with France. The alternative to war was a closer union, so in summer the Duke of Argyll—'Red John of the Battles' as the Highlanders called him—was sent down to Edinburgh as High Commissioner to persuade the reluctant Scottish Parliament to open negotiations for a treaty of union. After more than a month of fierce debate the Scottish Parliament consented; it was arranged that thirty-one Scottish Commissioners should be appointed by the Queen to meet an equal number of English Commissioners.

With the repeal of the Aliens Act at the end of the year the relations between the two countries became less strained, and in April 1706 the representatives of the two countries met at the Cockpit at Whitehall. Though each side wanted some sort of a union, each side was determined to keep as much and to give away as little as it could. The Scots, for example, contended that the union of the two countries need not involve the disappearance of the Scottish Parliament, that questions which affected both nations might be settled either in a joint session of both Parliaments, or by a body of members drawn from both Parliaments. They demanded, in other words, a federal union, and many Scotsmen to-day think that this demand was just and sensible, that even now Scotland should have a Parliament at Edinburgh to deal with purely Scottish affairs, and at the same time send representatives to an Imperial Parliament at Westminster. But the English contended that this was too small a price for the Scots to pay for complete commercial equality with England, and demanded an incorporating union. It was agreed, therefore, that there should be one Parliament for the whole of Great Britain, and that to it Scotland should send sixteen Peers and forty-five members of the House of Commons. On the death of Queen Anne, the Electress Sophia of Hanover and her descendants were to be sovereigns of this now United Kingdom. In return for the loss of their Parliament the Scots would be granted 'full freedom and intercourse of trade and navigation', but with equality of privileges went equality of burdens, customs duties in Scotland would be raised to the English level. On the other hand, a sum of £398,095 10s.—the Equivalent as it was called—was to be paid over by the English Government, mainly as compensation to the shareholders in the Darien Company. Further, there was to be a common coinage—at this time the pound Scots was worth only twenty pence in English money—and a common system of weights and measures. But the smaller country was not to be entirely absorbed into the greater : it was still to have its own law courts and its own code of laws; the private law courts of the great nobles—abolished at the Restoration in England—were to be retained in Scotland, and the royal burghs were to keep their peculiar privileges.

The Treaty had obvious defects; for example, in the new House of Commons England would still have her five hundred and twelve members, Scotland would have only forty-five, yet the population of England was little more than five times larger than the population of Scotland. And the Presbyterians saw at once that the Treaty made no provision for maintaining the Church of Scotland as it had been established in 1692. But the great majority of Scotsmen did not stop to find out by a careful examination whether the merits outweighed the defects; the Union for them meant simply the loss of national independence and they wanted to have nothing to do with it. The smaller burghs were all against it; only in the large towns, and there only among the merchants, was there any real enthusiasm for the Union.

At the beginning of October 1706 the Scottish Parliament met to consider whether it should accept or reject the Treaty. Rejection seemed more probable than acceptance, for the

THE INTERIOR OF PARLIAMENT HOUSE
From an engraving

Country Party or Opposition outnumbered the Court Party or Government Party, and the clamorous mob which filled Parliament Square every day did their best to make rejection certain. Even the Duke of Queensberry, the High Commissioner, was not safe; the mob on one occasion tried to attack him and chased his coach down the Canongate to Holyrood. Not till three regiments of soldiers had been called in to keep order in the city were the members of Parliament able to go on with their deliberations without fear of disturbance. Things were worse in Glasgow, where a minister had wound up his sermon on the Treaty with the words, 'Up and be valiant for the city of our God'. As a result of his eloquence a riot broke out; the Provost, far from being able to control the disturbers of the peace, was forced to hide in a box-bed, and the town remained in the hands of the mob for more than a month.

But the Opposition was not really united. One section, the Jacobites, would not have the Treaty at any price; another, the 'Squadrone Volante', had hovered in the past between the Court Party and the Country Party, and had committed itself to neither. When at the beginning of November the first article of the Treaty was discussed, Lord Belhaven's stately rhetoric, his impressive description of 'our ancient mother Caledonia . . . sitting in the midst of our senate . . . waiting for her own children to deal the fatal blow' moved the house less than the short speech of Lord Marchmont which followed it: 'Behold, he dreamed, but lo! when he awoke, he found it was a dream.' When the article was put to the vote, the 'Squadrone Volante' went over to the Government side and voted for acceptance.

The Opposition, however, could not see that they were beaten; they insisted on a lengthy discussion of every one of the twenty-five articles in the Treaty. Meantime the passing of an Act of Security, giving a definite assurance that no alteration in the Church of Scotland would be attempted, removed the fears of the Presbyterians, and in January 1707 the High Commissioner touched the Act with his sceptre, in token of the royal approval.

From Edinburgh the Treaty, in which the Act of Security was now embodied, went to Westminster, but it met with no opposition in the English Parliament, and on 6th March, 1707, the royal assent was given.

A few days later, on the 25th of March, 1707, to be exact, the Scottish Parliament met for the last time. There were no displays of stately oratory, no moving farewells, only the transaction of a few trivial pieces of business. Why should the members feel shame for what they had done and shed tears over it ? They were not traitors who had been bribed by English gold to sell the independence of their country, but practical men confronted with the task of extricating their country from an exceedingly perilous position. Perhaps they had conceded too much to the English Government, but they could console themselves with the thought that the terms were the best that could be obtained in the circumstances. And if there was no impassioned eloquence, there was cold common sense in the words with which the High Commissioner brought the Session— and the Parliament—to a close.

'The public business of this session now being over, it is full time to put an end to it.

'I am persuaded that we and all posterity will reap the benefit of the Union of the two kingdoms, and I doubt not . . . that you will promote an universal desire in this kingdom to become one in hearts and affections, as we are inseparably joined in interest with our neighbour nation.'

CHAPTER XXV

AFTER THE UNION: 1707–1744

God bless the King!—I mean the Faith's Defender;
God bless (no harm in blessing) the Pretender!
But who Pretender is, or who is King,
God bless us all!—that's quite another thing.

                                        J. BYROM.

Anne 1702–1714   George I 1714–1727
           George II 1727–1760

THE Union did not bring immediate prosperity to Scotland; its first effect was to depress, not to stimulate, the trade of the country. Before 1707, for example, the Scottish woollen manufacturer was protected from his more skilful English rival by a stiff import duty on English cloth. After 1707, of course, this duty was removed, English cloth was imported into Scotland, and drove the Scottish cloth, which was of inferior quality, out of the market altogether. Similarly, in 1712, the Scottish fisheries were almost ruined by an increase on the salt tax, designed to bring it up to the English level. Then, as now, the prosperity of the fishing industry depended on the export of cured salt fish to the Continent, and the increase in the tax made salt so dear that the fish-curers could not afford to buy it.

It is true that if Scotland had the same burdens as England it had now the same privileges, yet though Scotland was now free to export her goods to the Colonies, it profited her little, since she had no goods to export. The Colonies did not want hides, only the West Indian slave owners wanted salt fish—not for themselves but for their slaves; what they wanted were the articles which they could not manufacture for themselves. The Scots, indeed, like the Dutch, could have become the carriers of goods manufactured in other countries, but for this they required ships, and the Scots seemed to have lost the skill in ship-building which they displayed in the sixteenth century.

Most of the ships which sailed to Darien had been built in foreign yards; at the time of the Union there was not one ship on the register of the port of Glasgow that was capable of sailing across the Atlantic.

So the Scots blamed the Union for what was due really to their own lack of enterprise, and they grew all the more discontented with it, because it seemed to them that it was a case of 'heads you win, and tails I lose', that the English statesmen, though they usually insisted on sticking to the letter of the Treaty regardless of the loss that it inflicted on Scotland, were quite ready to set it aside when it suited themselves.

In 1709, for example, an Episcopal clergyman, called Greenshields, was thrown into prison by order of the Court of Session, because he had used the English Book of Common Prayer. He appealed from the Court of Session to the House of Lords;[1] his appeal was sustained, and he was released. The Scots were furious: that the decision overturned was intolerably harsh counted for nothing with them; all they saw was that the decision of the supreme Scottish court had been overturned by an English court. Yet the Treaty had not really been broken: as appeals from the Court of Session to the Scottish Parliament had been made before the Union, there was no reason why, after the Union, they should not be made to the British Parliament, in which the old Scottish Parliament was now incorporated. So, in spite of the protests of the Scots, litigants who considered that they had not got satisfaction from the Court of Session continued to take their cases to the House of Lords.

[1] The English Parliament, like the Scottish Parliament, had two functions: to make laws, and to try cases sent to it from inferior courts. But just as the Commons secured a monopoly of all the legislation dealing with finance, so the Lords secured a monopoly of the judicial work of Parliament. Consequently, appeals from an inferior court are made, not to Parliament as a whole, but to the House of Lords. This judicial work is now entrusted to a small committee of the House of Lords, composed of peers who have already had experience as judges.

A more serious blow to the Church of Scotland followed. The supporters of the Presbyterian system had always maintained that no minister should be forced on a congregation without its consent, that on the contrary he should be elected, either by the whole congregation, or by a body which really represented it. It is true that during the greater part of the seventeenth century the minister was chosen by a lay patron, usually a nobleman or county gentleman who had gained possession of the lands from which the revenues of the parish church had been derived before the Reformation, but in 1690 Lay Patronage was abolished; in every parish the right of selecting a minister was given to a body consisting of the elders and the Protestant heritors or landowners. In 1712, however, the British Parliament reversed the policy, and by restoring Lay Patronage again, laid itself open a second time to the charge of the flouting of the Treaty of Union.

So, if the Act of Union had been repealed at the end of Queen Anne's reign, no tears would have been shed over it in Scotland; and repealed it almost was. In 1713 the Earl of Marchmont, infuriated at the proposal to place an unfairly stiff tax on Scottish malt, retaliated by proposing in the House of Lords that the Act of Union should be repealed. His motion was lost by only four votes.

There were some people who drew comfort from this discontent; to the Jacobites it seemed a sure sign that Scotland was ready to fight for the exiled Stewarts. When James II had died in 1700, Louis XIV of France had promised to support the cause of his son—James III, as the Jacobites called him, the 'Pretender', as he was known to his enemies. Why, then, should the old plan not be tried once more? Why should not the Pretender, with a French army at his back, land in Scotland, rally his faithful Scottish subjects to his standard, and at the head of a great Franco-Scottish force, make his way across the border, and recall England to its allegiance? An excellent plan;

but there were two obstacles in the way of its fulfilment: the British Fleet, and the reluctance of the Lowland Scot to fight for a Catholic king. A French fleet did indeed escort the Pretender to the coast of Fife in 1708, but when British war-ships were sighted at the mouth of the Firth of Forth, it slipped back to France without landing its royal cargo. And though the craftsman or merchant might grumble about the Union, he was not prepared to risk his life for its repeal; though he might sing scurrilous songs, and repeat scandalous stories about the German Prince who, in 1714, was proclaimed as King George the First, his contempt for George I was not to be construed as respect for King James. He remembered the last King James and the 'Killing Time'. King George, with all his faults, had at least promised not to make any alteration in the Church of Scotland. Certainly the Pretender was not altogether without support in the Lowlands: in Angus, Aberdeenshire, and the south-west, most of the country gentlemen were enthusiastic Jacobites, who drank valiantly to the health of the exiled king every night. Since the majority of them were Episcopalians, they could not sympathize with the fears for Presbyterianism which held back their tenants; since they were landowners, they could not understand the fear of an interruption of the trade with England or the Colonies, which held back the douce burgesses. So they had no following in the Lowlands, except among those tenants who were bound to them, either by a feeling of loyalty, or by a dread of what might happen to them if they disobeyed a superior who still wielded the powers of a feudal baron.

More was to be expected from the Highlands, which had changed little since the days of Montrose. The average High-land chief had grown more like an ordinary Lowland gentleman. He was better educated, and had travelled more than his predecessor of eighty years before, but his relations to his clan remained the same. Clan feuds had grown less fierce, clan battles on a large scale had become only a memory. Partly because of the more peaceful times, the population of the Highlands was increasing rapidly. But though the population increased, the soil remained as sterile, the rain fell as heavily on the water-logged valleys. And so the old problem remained —only it had become more difficult of solution than ever— what was to be done with this great multitude of half-starved Highlanders? Let us see how the problem presented itself to the ordinary sensible Glasgow merchant.[1]

'Now, sir,' said Bailie Nicol Jarvie to Francis Osbaldistone, 'it's a sad and awfu' truth, that there is neither wark, nor the very fashion nor appearance of wark, for the tae half of thae puir creatures . . . let them work as lazily as they like, and they do work as if a pleugh or a spade burnt their fingers. . . . Ye hae . . . the tae half o' the population employed and maintained in a sort o' fashion, wi' some chance o' sour-milk and crowdie,[2] but I wad be glad to ken what the other five hunder are to do?'

'What *do* they do, Mr. Jarvie?' asked Francis Osbaldistone. 'It makes me shudder to think of their situation.'

'Sir,' replied the Bailie, 'ye wad maybe shudder mair if ye were living near-hand them, for, admitting that the tae half o' them may make some little thing for themsells honestly in the Lowlands by shearing in harst, droving, hay-making and the like; ye hae still mony hundreds and thousands o' lang-legged Hieland gillies, that will neither work nor want, and maun gang thigging and sorning[3] about on their acquaintance, or live by doing the laird's bidding, be't right or be't wrang. And mair especially, mony hundreds o' them come down to the borders of the low country, where there's gear to grip, and live by stealing, reiving, lifting cows, and the like depredations— a thing deplorable in any Christian country! . . . And the lairds are as bad as the loons; for, if they dinna bid them gae reive and

[1] See *Rob Roy* (Chapter XXVI).   [2] brose.   [3] obtaining alms by threats.

harry, the deil a bit they forbid them; and they shelter them,
or let them shelter themselves, in their woods, and mountains,
and strongholds, whenever the thing's dune. And every ane
o' them will maintain as mony as can in ony fashion, fair or

THE EARL OF MAR

foul, mainteen themselves—and there they are, wi' gun and
pistol, dirk and dourlach,[1] ready to disturb the peace of the
country whenever the laird likes; and that's the grievance o' the
Hielands, whilk are, and hae been for this thousand years by-
past, a bike[2] o' the maist lawless, unchristian limmers that
ever disturbed a douce, quiet, God-fearing neighbourhood.'

[1] knapsack.   [2] hive.

It was not simply a feeling of loyalty and gratitude that bound the clansmen to their chiefs. Parliament still allowed the chief to retain the powers of deciding disputes and imposing penalties which his ancestors had enjoyed. So if the clansman refused to obey his chief, he would probably find that his cattle disappeared, and that his house was set on fire; yet he could not ask for redress, for the only judge to whom he could appeal was the chief—the man who was responsible for his troubles.

In 1715 the Pretender, having persuaded himself that the time had come to start a rebellion in Scotland, wrote from France to the Earl of Mar, urging him to raise the clans at once. It was a curious time to choose, for the Treaty of Utrecht, ending the war between France and Britain, was only two years old, and James could no longer count on the help of the Regent of France, or, indeed, of any of the continental princes. And Mar was a curious leader, a great Highland nobleman with nothing of the Highland dash and fire, a trimming politician who had taken a long time to discover which side he should stick to.

The Pretender almost immediately repented of his rashness, and sent a letter to Mar, countermanding the expedition, but he was too late. Mar for once had acted speedily; he had hurried north to Scotland and issued invitations for a great tinchal or hunting-parting. But the invitations went only to those chiefs and lairds whom he considered to be staunch Jacobites. The real business of the meeting was the discussion of plans for a rebellion; the guests dispersed, only to assemble a few days later with their tenants and clansmen at Castletown in Braemar. Here the old Scottish standard was raised as a sign that the struggle had begun, but the fall of a golden ball from the top of the flag-staff damped the enthusiasm of the superstitious Highlanders. For a time, however, everything went well; most of the northern towns declared for King James, and Mar occupied Perth without the slightest difficulty.

Between him and England there was now only a force of two thousand government troops, under the Duke of Argyll, in the neighbourhood of Stirling. Yet having reached Perth about the middle of September, only twelve days after the campaign had begun, Mar refused to advance farther until he was joined by the clans from the West Highlands.

At the beginning of October the news that the border Jacobites were astir roused him from his inactivity. Lord Kenmure on the Scottish side, and Lord Derwentwater and Mr. Forster on the English side, had each gathered a small force of a few hundred horsemen, and, having got them, began to ask what they should do with them. Mar resolved to send some two thousand men southward under Mackintosh of Borlum to co-operate with them, while he himself stayed at Perth with the main part of the army. But 'Red John of the Battles' barred the road to the south at Stirling; the only alternative route to England was across the Firth of Forth, and this was no safer, for the Forth was patrolled by British warships. It was this second route, however, which Mackintosh decided to take.

Mackintosh was no amateur in war like Mar; he had learned his business in an excellent school—the French army. He marched a small detachment of his force ostentatiously to Burntisland, where it was bombarded by the fleet. Meantime, the rest of his men had slipped across Fife undiscovered, occupied the little towns near the mouth of the firth, and helped themselves to such fishing-boats as they required. In these they crossed under cover of darkness to the Lothian coast. Mackintosh, instead of making straight for the border, turned westward and marched upon Edinburgh. Everything seemed in his favour, for Argyll was still in Stirling, more than thirty miles away, and had very few horsemen in his little army. Yet he was prompter than Mackintosh; he mounted two hundred of his infantrymen on cart-horses, and with these, and a body of three hundred cavalry, he clattered into Edinburgh. Mackintosh

promptly retired to an old fort at Leith originally erected
by Cromwell's troops, and now, though half ruined, still a formidable stronghold. The volunteers who had rallied to Argyll's
standard urged him to attack the fort at once, even though he
had no artillery, but when he told them that, as volunteers,
they would have the honour of leading the attack, their martial
ardour suddenly disappeared. Mackintosh, however, fearing
that he would be trapped behind stone walls, led his men out
when darkness had fallen, flitted silent and unobserved along
the shore of the firth, and then struck southward for the
border, where the forces of Kenmure and Forster had already
effected a junction. He found his allies at Kelso, disputing
what they were to do next. Forster's plans for an advance into
Lancashire were accepted in place of Mackintosh's more sensible
scheme for co-operating with Mar, and at the beginning of
November the motley force crossed the Tweed. Five hundred
of the Highlanders, however, deserted, rather than follow
Mackintosh into what they considered a foreign country.
Meantime, Mar lingered irresolute in Perth. He had advanced
on Dunblane when Argyll dashed to rescue Edinburgh, only to
withdraw again to Perth when Argyll returned to Stirling. In
the second week of November, after the western clans had come
in, he discovered that he had no longer any excuse for delay,
and advanced on Stirling. Argyll had advanced too, and on the
morning of the 13th November the two armies blundered into
each other at Sheriffmuir, a mile or two north of Dunblane,
where the 'heighs and howes' on the heathery moorland made
it difficult for the commanders to see what was happening
except in their immediate vicinity.

'Gentlemen, this is a day we have long wished to see,' said
the chief of the Clan MacLean to his followers, who formed part
of the right wing of the Jacobite army. 'Yonder stands
MacCallummore for King George—here stands MacLean for
King James; God bless MacLean and King James! Charge,

gentlemen!' The Highlanders, after their custom, flung off their plaids, fired one volley, then, throwing away their muskets and grasping their claymores, they rushed, yelling like wild beasts, on the ranks of the regular troops. A volley which crashed into them and mortally wounded one of their chiefs made them waver, but when they heard MacDonnell of Glengarry cry: 'Revenge! Revenge! To-day for revenge, and to-morrow for mourning!' they charged with redoubled fury, broke the ranks of the hapless regulars, and slew them without mercy.

The Jacobite left wing had to do, not with an incompetent subordinate, but with Argyll himself. The Highlanders charged, but while they were in mid-career, before they had reached the red lines of the waiting infantry, they were thrown into confusion by the sudden cavalry charge which Argyll launched against their flank. Seizing his opportunity, the Duke ordered the whole right wing to advance, and drove the Highlanders back to their camp on the Allan Water.

It was an absurd situation, if not an uncommon one in battles of those days. The right wing of each army had been victorious, the left wing had been defeated. Who, then, was the real victor? As the old ballad writer put it:

> There's some say that we wan,
> Some say that they wan,
> Some say that nane wan at a', man:
> But one thing I'm sure,
> That at Sheriffmuir,
> A battle there was, which I saw, man.

There was really no doubt about it. Mar's retreat to Perth immediately afterwards converted a drawn battle into a victory for King George's men; Argyll still remained in front of Stirling, the road to the south was still closed to the Jacobites.

Meantime the Jacobites in the north of England had occupied Preston, where, on the day before the battle of Sheriffmuir, they were attacked by the Government troops. They beat off the small force which tried to drive them from the town, but reinforcements arrived, and two days later they surrendered unconditionally. The seemingly indecisive battle of Sheriffmuir had really decided the campaign. Mar's Highlanders, tired of inactivity, and disappointed in their hope of plunder, slipped off to their native glens by dozens and scores every day, while Argyll's army, reinforced by some regiments from Holland, and by the troops that had been employed against the Jacobites in northern England, now outnumbered that of his opponent by almost three to one. But Mar's lethargy seemed to have infected Argyll himself.

And now, at the end of the year, when all hope of a Jacobite victory had disappeared, the Pretender himself arrived in Scotland. Alas! this too clear-sighted prince was not the leader who could rekindle a dying enthusiasm, and convert defeat into victory. 'For me it is no new thing to be unfortunate,' he declared to his officers, 'since my whole life from my cradle has been a constant series of misfortunes.' The Highlanders were puzzled by his cold, reserved manner. 'Can he speak?' they whispered to one another.

Their bewilderment turned to rage when, at the end of January 1716, they learned that, though Argyll was at last advancing to attack them, their leaders had decided to abandon Perth and to retire to the north.

It was useless to point out to them that Argyll's army was superior in numbers and equipment, and that there was no sense in waiting to be defeated. 'What can we do?' asked one of the officers. 'Do?' was the indignant answer. 'Let us do what we were called to arms for, which certainly was not to run away.' When the officer urged that the King's safety had to be considered, he was silenced by the reply: 'Trust his safety to us, and if he is willing to die like a prince, he shall see that there are ten thousand men in Scotland willing to die with him.'

James was not willing to die like a prince: he consented to

Perth being abandoned, and to the northward march being begun; what was more, when he reached Montrose, he gave his followers the slip, and, along with Mar, embarked on a ship which was bound for France. The Highlanders marched on to Aberdeen, where a message from the Pretender was read to them. They got scanty comfort from it, for he simply thanked them and advised them to shift for themselves. With rage in their hearts, they straggled on to Ruthven in Badenoch, where they dispersed. The 'Fifteen' Rebellion was over.

Obviously the danger of a similar rebellion was not over as long as each clan was a private army, taking orders from its chief. On the very eve of the 'Fifteen', the Government had made an attempt to weaken the power of the chiefs by passing the Clan Act, which declared that the lands of any chief who rebelled would be forfeit to the Crown, while, if his tenants remained loyal in spite of his orders to rebel, they would be excused the payment of rent for two years. Immediately after the Rebellion, a Disarming Act was passed, but it disarmed only the loyal clans: the clans who still preferred King James to King George did indeed hand over a curious assortment of obsolete weapons, but anything that was really serviceable they usually managed to keep.

In 1719 the hopes of the Jacobites again rose high: Cardinal Alberoni, the all-powerful Spanish minister, had come forward as champion of the Pretender. It was arranged that while the Earl Marischal, with two frigates and some three hundred Spanish soldiers, attempted a landing on the west of Scotland, a large expedition, consisting of five warships and twenty-two transports, with five thousand soldiers on board, should sail for England. But a storm scattered the larger expedition, and though the Earl Marischal and his three hundred Spanish landed in Loch Alsh and marched into Glenshiel, they soon found their advance barred by the Government troops, and their retreat cut off by the fleet. The Spaniards surrendered, the Earl Marischal and the Scottish Jacobites who had joined him scattered, and lived to fight another day.

This 'Nineteen' Rebellion, then, had been easily snuffed out, and, when General Wade undertook to pacify the Highlanders in 1724, it seemed as if another attempt at a rebellion would be impossible. A more stringent Disarming Act was passed in 1725, and General Wade congratulated himself that the High-

General Wade's bridge over the Tay at Aberfeldy

lander no longer went to kirk and market armed with claymore and pistols, but was content with a stick. The Highlander had learned caution, that was all; he had his claymore and pistols, dirk and target still, though he did not swagger abroad with them.

But Wade was not content with the Disarming Act. He saw that while the Lowlands could easily be invaded from the Highlands, the absence of roads and bridges made a counter-invasion of the Highlands very difficult—absolutely impossible in fact for an army equipped with artillery. He therefore set his soldiers to construct a network of roads—roads such as had not been made since the Romans left Scotland, where once there had been only rough tracks or no trails at all. In eleven years two hundred and fifty miles of road and forty-two bridges were constructed. The Highlands were being conquered by pick and spade.

In 1739, however, the outbreak of war between Britain and Spain aroused the old hopes and the old fears, and when, a year or two later, the relations between Britain and France became strained, nothing seemed more certain than that the restoration of the Stewarts by a French army of invasion would be attempted. An invasion was indeed planned, but nothing came of it. The warships and transports which had been collected were scattered by a tempest when they left their harbours at Brest and Dunkirk, and in 1744 the French Government, convinced that the Scottish and English Jacobites were too weak to co-operate effectively with an invading force, abandoned the scheme altogether.

Without help from France—and very substantial help—it would be madness to attempt anything; of that all the most experienced Jacobite leaders, from the Pretender downwards, were firmly convinced. The trouble, it seemed, had blown over. And then, in the autumn of 1745, news reached the capital that Prince Charles Edward, the Pretender's eldest son, had landed in the West Highlands, and that the clans were flocking to his standard.

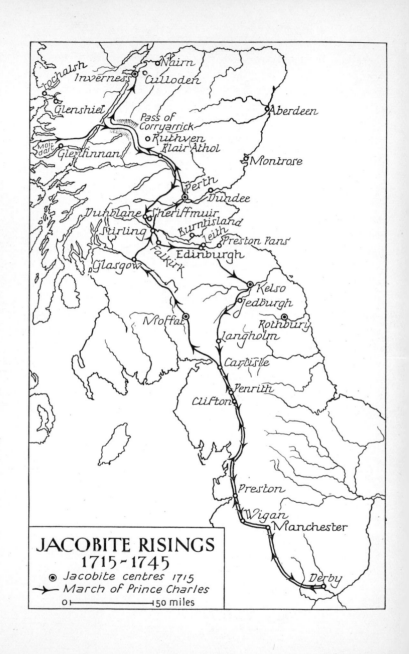

Lochaish
Nairn
Inverness
Culloden
Glenshiel
Aberdeen
Pass of
Corryarrick
Ruthven
Moidart
Blair Athol
Glenfinnan
Montrose
Perth
Dundee
Dunblane
Sheriffmuir
Stirling
Burntisland
Leith
Preston Pans
Falkirk
Edinburgh
Glasgow
Kelso
Jedburgh
Rothbury
Moffat
Langholm
Carlisle
Penrith
Clifton
Preston
Wigan
Manchester
Derby

JACOBITE RISINGS
1715 ~ 1745
⦿ Jacobite centres 1715
➤ March of Prince Charles
0 ├──────────────┤ 50 miles

CHAPTER XXVI

'THE "FORTY-FIVE" AND AFTER': 1744–1800

O that he'd bidden awa',
He's turned their heads, the lad,
And ruin will bring on us a'.
Anti-Jacobite Song.

George II 1727–1760   George III . . . 1760–1820

CHARLES EDWARD, moved partly by the persuasions of Irish exiles like Sir Thomas Sheridan and Scottish plotters like Murray of Broughton, who had everything to gain and nothing to lose, but mainly by his 'young adventurousness', had resolved 'to put it to the touch, to win or lose it all'. To him it seemed that at such a time only boldness could command success. The French Government, he knew, would do nothing, because the Jacobites in Britain would not move. The Jacobites in Britain would not stir until the French had done something. The only way, then, to get this all-important help from France was to go to Scotland, win over the clans, not by appealing to the common sense, but to the honour and loyalty of the chieftains, sweep through the Lowlands into England, and thus show the hesitating French statesmen that the Scottish Jacobites were no mere backboneless intriguers, but formidable warriors, and that it would profit France to give them generous support.

At his own expense he fitted out a battleship, the *Elizabeth*, and a frigate, the *Du Tellier*, and in the summer of 1745 he set sail from France. The *Elizabeth* was intercepted by a British warship, and so badly battered that she had to put back to harbour. The *Du Tellier*, however, evaded her pursuers, and at the beginning of August Charles landed on the island of Eriskay, in the Outer Hebrides. There MacDonald of Boisdale advised him to go home. 'I am come home,' said the Prince, and ordered his ship to set sail for the mainland. He landed in

Moidart with seven followers. But here all was uncertainty. Some of the chiefs flatly refused to have anything to do with the expedition, others hung back and would not commit themselves.

While the whole affair hung in the balance, Lochiel, the head of the great Clan Cameron, one of the most faithful supporters whom the exiled Stewarts possessed, made up his mind that he would see the Prince and convince him that it was his duty to abandon the enterprise and go back to France. His brother, knowing his romantic and chivalrous disposition, advised him not to venture into the Prince's presence, but to carry on the debate by letter. Lochiel refused to take his advice, was granted an interview with the Prince, and explained to him why the expedition was certain to fail.

'Be the issue what it will,' said the Prince, 'I am determined to display my standard, and take the field with such as may join it. Lochiel, whom my father esteemed the best friend of our family, may stay at home, and learn his Prince's fate from the newspapers.'

'Not so,' cried Lochiel. 'If you are resolved on that rash undertaking, I will go with you, and so shall every one over whom I have influence.'

With Lochiel and his seven hundred Camerons behind him, Charles knew that he could go on; a few days later he raised his standard at Glenfinnan before a small army of MacDonalds and Camerons. Clans which had hung back now joined him, and soon he found himself in command of a force of over two thousand five hundred men. It was true that they were not as well equipped as the regular soldiers; though the men in the front ranks bore not only a musket, but a sword and dirk and a target—a leather shield studded with nails—the men in the rear rank would probably have only a single weapon, and often no weapon at all, except a scythe blade stuck straight in a pole.

But the regular troops in Scotland were few in number, not

more than three thousand altogether. Many of them were raw recruits, and their commander—Sir John Cope—an unenterprising, over-methodical officer, was no match for Lord George Murray, the clear-headed, scientific soldier, whom Charles had made his chief of staff. Reinforcements for the royal forces, too, would be hard to get, for Fontenoy had just been fought, and the bulk of the regular army was still on the Continent.

Cope, hearing that the Jacobite army was moving eastward, making for Perth and the Lowlands, marched his troops into the Highlands, meaning to bar the advance of the Jacobites at the Pass of Corryarrick. He changed his mind, however, and went on to Inverness.

Thus the road to the capital was open: the Highlanders captured Perth, crossed the Forth by the Fords of Frew, a mile or two above Stirling, and got to Coltbridge, within two miles of Edinburgh, before any opposition was offered to them. Here two regiments of dragoons were drawn up to do battle with them, but as soon as the valiant horsemen heard the bullets from the Highland muskets whistle past their ears, they turned about, fled along the country road which is now George Street, and did not draw rein till they had reached Leith. Even there their halt was a brief one; the cry that the Highlanders were at hand sent them galloping in headlong haste to Prestonpans and beyond.

In Edinburgh itself, panic reigned. The old walls and gates which had not stopped the Porteous mob,[1] would not stop an army, and the garrison consisted only of a few decrepit veterans of the City Guard, and a regiment of volunteers which melted away when it was ordered to march out and meet the rebels. A message from the 'Young Pretender', demanding the instant surrender of the city, found the Town Council in two

---

[1] In 1736 an armed mob entered the city, broke into the Tolbooth, and hanged Captain Porteous, the commander of the City Guard, in the Grassmarket.

minds. The councillors knew that their present defenders could not be trusted, but they also knew that Cope's transports had been sighted off Dunbar. In the end, late at night, they sent three of the bailies in a coach to the Pretender's head-quarters, to ask for time to consider the demand.

Meantime, after darkness had fallen, the Camerons made a detour to the south of the city, and, creeping in silently, took up their position in the wynds leading up to the Canongate, just outside the well-guarded Netherbow Port. Back to the city and through the West Port rumbled the coach with the three bailies, disconsolate because their request had been refused. The gates clashed behind them, they dismounted and made their way back to the Council, while the coachman whipped up his horses and drove down the street towards their stable in the Canongate. The sentinels at the Netherbow Port recognized him and opened the gate, but as the coach lurched out, the Camerons rushed in, and made themselves masters of the sleeping city. Next day the unwilling heralds proclaimed James the Eighth at the Market Cross, and Charles Edward entered the palace of his ancestors.

To some at least of those who knelt to kiss his hand, this tall handsome youth with the light of triumph in his eyes, must have seemed like a prince out of a fairy tale. The spell was lifted from the dark forsaken palace; again lights gleamed from the windows; again one heard the strains of music and the tap of dancing feet. But the revels in Holyrood were interrupted by the news that Cope had landed, and was approaching Edinburgh from the east.

Charles led out his men and came upon Cope's army near Prestonpans, drawn up at the western end of a stretch of level ground. Cope had chosen his position well: his front was protected by a series of high walls, on his right was the firth, and on his left an apparently impassable marsh. He had, moreover, six pieces of artillery with him, and two regiments

of cavalry, the heroes of Coltbridge. But, led by a Lowland
volunteer who knew a path through the marsh, the rebels filed
across it in the darkness, and took up their position on the level
ground in the rear of Cope's army. When it was too late, Cope

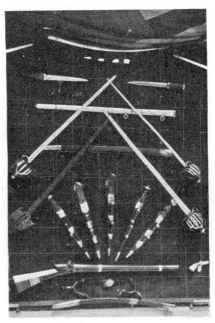

A COLLECTION OF HIGHLAND ARMS

discovered what had happened, and in the grey light of dawn
he made his army turn about, so that it now faced the east.
The artillery he moved to his right flank: as before, the infantry
were drawn up in line in the centre, with a regiment of cavalry
on each flank.

When the morning mists suddenly lifted and revealed the
glittering scarlet ranks of the regular infantry, the hearts of the
Highlanders sank for a moment, but after muttering a prayer,

they pulled their bonnets down over their brows, and then, at the word of command, they rushed wildly at the royal troops, firing their muskets as they ran. They formed a splendid target for Cope's artillery, but the gunners had lost their nerve when they saw the hordes of plaided warriors bearing down upon them, yelling and waving their claymores; they fled without firing a shot. The two cavalry regiments followed their example, and left the flanks of the infantry unsupported. The infantry fired one volley, but before they could fire a second, the Highlanders were among them, slashing them with their claymores, and warding off the bayonet thrusts with their leathern targets. Soon the thin line was broken in half a dozen places by the weight of the Highlanders' onslaught. Retreat was impossible; behind the royal troops stretched the line of high walls, so they had no choice but to surrender or die fighting. Most of them chose to surrender.

Cope's army had ceased to exist. Cope himself galloped to Berwick with news of the disaster—'The first general in Europe', said a wit, 'who had brought the first tidings of his own defeat!' He is not forgotten. To this day the impudent strains of the Jacobite ballad, 'Hey, Johnnie Cope, are ye wauken yet?' are played in Scottish regiments immediately after reveille, to arouse the sleeping troops.

But Charles made no use of his spectacular victory. He lingered in Holyrood while regular troops poured into English harbours from the Continent. Not till the beginning of November did he cross the border and advance on London by the western route.

Disappointment followed; though the Prince captured Carlisle and advanced as far as Derby without meeting with any opposition, it was plain that the English did not want him. He obtained in England only three hundred recruits. Every day, too, the number of the Government troops was increasing. Wade, with one army, watched Charles's rear from Newcastle;

the Duke of Cumberland was marching through the Midlands to meet him with a second; a third was encamped at Finchley for the defence of London—altogether thirty thousand regular troops were ranged against his five thousand Highlanders. And though the French Government had at last definitely promised to support him, its promise mattered little as long as the British fleet had command of the seas; a body of a few hundred Irish soldiers enlisted in the French army was the only force that it succeeded in sending to Scotland.

Charles's officers pointed out to him that it was folly to advance farther, and with London only a hundred and thirty miles away, the Highlanders reluctantly turned about and trudged back by the way that they had come. They succeeded in outmarching Cumberland's army; at Clifton, however, Cumberland's advance-guard of cavalry blundered into the Jacobite rear-guard, which was commanded by Lord George Murray himself. The Highlanders, instead of retreating or remaining on the defensive, charged the dismounted troopers in their usual fashion, and drove them back with heavy loss. After this the royalist vanguard kept at a respectful distance from the Jacobite rear-guard.

At mid-winter the Highlanders, arm-in-arm, struggled across the flooded Esk, and stood once more upon Scottish soil. All was not lost. If England would not be conquered, Scotland at least might be held: other clans had declared for the Prince in his absence, and so he now found that he had at his disposal a force almost twice as large as that with which he had invaded England. At the beginning of 1746 he advanced to Stirling, but his siege operations against the Castle were interrupted by the news that General Hawley was marching from Edinburgh at the head of nine thousand regular troops. The two armies met near Falkirk; the Highlanders fired one volley which turned the advance of Hawley's cavalry into a panic-stricken flight, then, flinging away their muskets, they drew their swords and hurled themselves upon the long red line of infantry. The elements seemed to fight on their side; they were whirled along by a great storm of wind and hail which blinded and confused their antagonists. It was Sheriffmuir over again: on the right, one or two of the regular regiments stood firm, fired steadily, and repulsed every attack of the clansmen; on the left, the infantry gave way before the tremendous onslaught of the Highlanders, and fled in confusion. But in the tempest and gathering darkness the Highlanders could not follow up their advantage, and Hawley withdrew unmolested to Linlithgow, where some of his men set fire to the noble palace.

A few days later Charles abandoned the siege of Stirling and retired to the regions beyond the Tay, where in the late winter and early spring his followers captured a number of posts garrisoned by Government troops. But these minor successes could not stop the flow of deserters from the Jacobite army, or delay the day of reckoning. In April, Charles learned that Cumberland had led an army of nine thousand men up the east coast to Aberdeen and was advancing on Inverness, where the Jacobite head-quarters were. At once the stragglers were summoned, but only five thousand Highlanders assembled on Drummossie Moor, near Culloden House, about five miles to the east of Inverness.

The royal forces soon forced the passage of the Spey and encamped outside the town of Nairn, about twelve miles from Culloden. Lord George Murray, seeing that victory was impossible by ordinary means, proposed that a night attack should be made on Cumberland's camp. The plan miscarried; though the night march was begun, the men, weary and half-starved, dragged themselves along at such a pace, that, if they had reached the enemy's camp at all, it would have been in broad daylight. There was nothing for it but to order the dispirited troops to turn about and march back to Culloden. They struggled back to their camp, which they reached just as dawn was breaking, flung themselves on the ground, and at once fell asleep.

They were roused two hours later by the drums beating to arms; Cumberland's army was at hand. Half asleep, they moved forward to their battle positions. Their right flank was protected by a wall which ran southward to the River Nairn, a few hundred yards to the south, their left flank by the walls enclosing the grounds of Culloden House. Cumberland was confident of success. Not only were his troops twice as numerous as the Jacobites, they had been carefully trained, and knew now what to do when they had to meet the headlong charge of the Highlanders. He put only seven of his fifteen infantry battalions in the front line, and between each battalion he placed two pieces of artillery. Should the Highlanders break through the front line, they would find themselves confronted by a second line consisting of six more battalions drawn up three deep, flanked by guns to right and left.

And now Cumberland's artillery thundered out, and the grape-shot whistled through the air. The rebel guns replied, but did little damage, while the Highlanders began to grow restive as they saw their comrades go down beside them, groaning horribly or ominously silent. Meantime, the Argyll Highlanders, who were fighting for the Duke, crept up to the wall on the left flank of the regular infantry and began to pull down the stones to make a passage for the royal cavalry.

After the cannonade had lasted for an hour, the Prince told Lord George Murray to give the word to charge. The clans on the right swept down into a storm of snow, that at once changed into a storm of grape-shot and musket bullets. It seemed as if nothing could stop them; they broke through the first line of the stubborn infantry and advanced upon the second. Their valour availed them nothing, for a battalion from the Duke's reserve advanced on the left flank of the second line and formed up at right angles to it. The Highlanders as they surged forward were caught between two fires; they crumpled up as volley after volley was poured into them, not only by the troops facing them but by the regiment on their flank.

The left wing advanced too, but something seemed to be amiss. It was composed of MacDonalds, and the MacDonalds, it is said, were indignant because they had been removed from the post of honour on the right wing, a position which they claimed had been theirs since the Battle of Bannockburn. Thrice they rushed forward, but thrice, as they looked at the long rows of levelled muskets, they hesitated and retired. The third time they noticed that the right of the army had been broken and was streaming back in disorder. There was nothing for them now to do but join in the general flight.

Meantime, Cumberland's horsemen had made their way through the gaps in the wall and fallen upon the flank and rear of the retreating army, which, indeed, could hardly be called an army any longer. The survivors had passed the limits of what men could endure. Though some of the clans kept together and retired in good order, it was for the most part a panic-stricken mob that fled westward, begging in vain for quarter from the pursuing dragoons.

The Prince watched the rout of his army with tears in his eyes. It would have been better for him if his had been the fate of James the Fourth at Flodden, but when one of his Irish officers laid hold of his horse's bridle, he allowed himself to be led from the field. Soon after he separated himself from his officers, and made his way to South Uist, in the hope that from that remote island he might be able to escape to France. But his chances seemed ridiculously small, for the island was overrun by hundreds of soldiers, every one of whom knew that a reward of £30,000 would be his if he captured the Prince, while the surrounding seas were patrolled by innumerable small war vessels.

From his perilous plight he was rescued by the quick wit and courage of a lady, Flora MacDonald, who disguised him in woman's clothes, obtained a passport for an imaginary maid-servant called 'Betty Burke', and so succeeded in smuggling him over to the Isle of Skye. There 'Betty' attracted a dangerous amount of attention. 'I have never seen such a tall, impudent jaud in all my life,' said a genuine maidservant to Flora MacDonald; 'see what lang strides she takes.'

But Skye, like Uist, was too hot to hold the Prince. He was forced to cross to the mainland, where he hid for a time in a cave occupied by seven robbers, till he was able to make his way to 'Cluny's Cage', a hut hidden in a tangle of brushwood on the side of Ben Alder, where he dwelt some time with Mac-pherson of Cluny, the owner of the cage, and Cameron of Lochiel. Not till September 1746, five months after Culloden was fought, did he succeed in embarking on a French frigate and escaping to France.

It would have been well for him had he fallen 'when the clans faced the bayonets and died on the guns'. Though he lived on for another forty-two years, 'the name died before the man', the gallant and chivalrous adventurer was forgotten in the querulous, drink-sodden voluptuary. Long before his death in 1788, the most devoted of his followers knew that he would never—could never—be their leader again. His younger brother, Henry, had renounced all secular ambitions and had entered the Church. He died in 1807, a Cardinal and a pensioner of King George the Third.

Long before the death of the last Stewart prince, peace had descended upon the Highlands. The victorious Cumberland resolved to terrorize the Highlanders; not only did he instruct his troops to give no quarter to the fugitives fleeing from the battle-field, he ordered detachments of his soldiers to march into the country occupied by the rebel clans, burn their houses, destroy their corn, and drive away their cattle. He was backed up by the Government. Of the three thousand five hundred prisoners taken during the campaign, one hundred and twenty were executed, over eleven hundred were transported or banished, and almost seven hundred died as a result of their confinement in filthy and overcrowded prisons.

The Government went further. It was convinced that the clan system was the source of all trouble. In 1746 Parliament passed a Disarming Act—one which, this time, really did disarm—and an Act prohibiting the wearing of the kilt or plaid, or, in fact, any garment made of tartan. In 1748 the Act abolishing Heritable Jurisdictions completed the destruction of the clan system, and extinguished the last relics of feudal authority in the Lowlands. The chief ceased to be a judge and became only a landowner; the old inefficient hereditary sheriff was replaced by a competent lawyer appointed by the Crown, and the disappearance of tenure by military service loosened still further the hold which the landowner had over his principal tenants.

But, though one problem that had perplexed Scottish kings and statesmen for centuries had been solved—a very few years after the rebellion the Highlands had become as peaceful and law-abiding as any part of Britain—another equally formidable problem still remained: how were the inhabitants of these sterile regions to provide themselves with the bare necessaries of existence ?

The pacification of the Highlands after the Forty-Five Rebellion did not impoverish the Highlands: they were miserably poor already. As we have seen, it was the pinch of hunger rather than sheer love of mischief which made the Highlander drive off the cattle and sheep of his Lowland neighbour. The best of the houses—with the exception of the dwellings of the chiefs—were miserable hovels, like the one which Dr. Johnson and Mr. Boswell visited on the shores of Loch Ness in 1773. The thick low walls were built of unmortared stone, with a core of turf or earth, and loose thatch covered the roof, held in place by ropes of heather or straw, weighted by stones, which rested

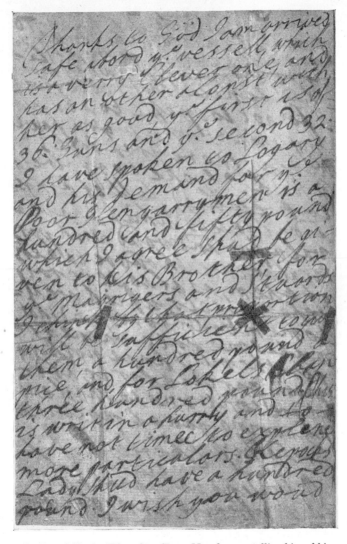

Letter of Charles Edward to Cluny Macpherson telling him of his safety and of his embarkation on board the ship *L'Heureux*

on the top of the wall. As the thatch left the core of turf uncovered, the rain soaked in between the inner and outer surfaces of the walls, and kept the house damp even in the rare spells of dry weather. Often there was neither window nor chimney; at best, the window was a hole in the wall, closed by a piece of turf in stormy weather, and the chimney a hole in the roof. Within, a fire of peat smouldered night and day on the flat hearth-stone placed in the middle of the earthen floor, and, as the occupants of the house always refrained from placing it directly under the hole in the roof, the hut was always full of the odour of peat smoke. But the inhabitants did not mind. On the contrary, they wanted the interior of their houses to be properly smoked, for every few years they pulled down the sooty thatch and spread it on their fields as manure.

Unfortunately there were less pleasant odours in the hut than that of 'peat reek'; one end of the house served as a shelter for the sheep and cattle, which in those days were kept under cover all winter. They entered by the same doorway as the human occupants, from whom they were separated, in the more care-fully arranged houses, by a flimsy wicker-work partition. A similar partition sometimes separated the living room from a bedroom at the other end of the hut, where the bedsteads were wooden boards, and the spring mattresses closely packed bunches of heather.

Such were the houses that Cumberland's soldiers burned or pulled to pieces. But the Highlanders did not know or did not want any other type of house. They continued to be built for more than a century after Culloden; even to this day, the 'white house', with its walls of stone and mortar and its slated roof, has not altogether displaced the old-fashioned 'black house' in many of the remoter western islands. And the lot of these hut-dwellers was not absolutely miserable. As long as they had enough food to keep body and soul together, they would live nowhere else. After all, if their feet were on the dunghill their heads were in the stars. They were far from being insensitive to the beauty of the great hills or the desolate moorlands, of the brown, birch-fringed Highland rivers or the lonely lochs and sounds of the west. The glamour of the long-delaying northern spring, of the endless summer days, when the sunset passes imperceptibly into the sunrise, had entered into their

'BLACK HOUSE' AND 'WHITE HOUSE'

hearts. Even in winter, when they crouched about the glowing peats in their malodorous hovels, music and romance were their guests. They would tell about the heroes of old, or about the fairies who, they believed, still dwelt in the neighbouring green knoll, and sing old songs, songs which echoed the wail of the sea-wind and the surge of the wave on the Hebridean beaches.

All this time they were living on the verge of starvation, working not too energetically—for in winter and summer alike, the rain-laden winds of the Atlantic prevented that—and with no special skill. But even if they had used the new iron swing plough instead of the spade or the old wooden plough, even if they had learned all the new lore of drainage and manure and the rotation of crops, they could have expected only a trifling increase from the crops grown on their sterile and rain-sodden soil. There were few places in the Western Highlands or the Hebrides where a farmer in his senses would attempt to grow corn for profit. To people in this position, a single bad harvest meant not only scarcity but actual starvation. Before the 'Forty-Five', however, they knew that they had the chief behind them. He counted his wealth, not in money, but in men; his rents were paid for the most part in kind, so that he got far more food than he or his family could consume. It was only natural, then, that he should keep open house, and in times of scarcity see that his clansmen had sufficient food. But Culloden and the Act abolishing heritable jurisdictions changed all this. The chief became a landowner, to whom the existence of a multitude of half-starved dependants was a perplexity and not a pleasure. There was nothing now to bind him to the grim old feudal keep in which he had spent his boyhood, and so he often became an absentee, living in Edinburgh or London, and drawing his rents from tenants whom he never saw. Sometimes he sold his estates altogether, to a Lowland or English proprietor.

It was seldom, before the 'Forty-Five', that the poorer tenant paid his rent directly to the chief, or that the chief received the whole of his rent from the poor tenant. Large estates were usually leased to tacksmen, petty magnates, who were often kinsmen of the chief. Each tacksman paid an annual rent to the chief, but the rent which he paid to the chief was much less than the rents which he in his turn received from the sub-tenants among whom his portion of the estate was divided. These sub-tenants, though their fathers, and their fathers' fathers, might have cultivated the same amount of ground, had no security of tenure. Their land was let to them from year to year, and if the chief or the tacksman chose to raise their rent or put another tenant in their place, they would have no remedy.

The changing attitude of the chiefs towards their tenants and their estates is shown by three great changes which took place in the second half of the eighteenth century and the earlier part of the nineteenth century. The Highland landowners found that the system of running their estates with the help of tacksmen was extremely extravagant, so, by refusing to renew a tacksman's lease when it expired, they gradually eliminated the tacksmen altogether. They had discovered, too, that the only way to make money out of their estates was to encourage sheep-farming, but sheep-farming required large stretches of land. Those the landowner obtained by transforming a group of small farms into one large farm, which he offered at a rent sometimes six times as much as that which the tenants had formerly paid. Sometimes there was no tenant on the estate who could pay the new rent, and so the dreamy, improvident Highlanders were often elbowed aside by some hard-headed Lowlander, who had enough money in his purse to enable him to stock the farm properly, and to pay the rent without difficulty. Often one of the original tenants, more provident and enterprising than his fellows, would take over the new farm, and at the end of a very few years live in comfort suc has his fathers had never known, in a 'white house', with wooden floors, glazed windows, and plastered walls.

So the introduction of sheep-farming benefited—apart from the landlords—only a small fraction of the population. Some of the dispossessed tenants, but only a few, found occupation as shepherds on the new farms, others moved from the inland glens to the sea-coast, where they were placed on crofts or small farms by their landlord. Others drifted south to Edinburgh and Glasgow, where they bent their spirits to such menial tasks as carrying sedan-chairs. Thousands of the more enterprising crossed to America, or enlisted in the new Highland regiments which were raised during the Seven Years' War.

The third change to be chronicled, beside the disappearance of the tacksmen and the appearance of the big sheep farms, was the introduction of the crofting system. Hitherto, the arable land had been let out, not to individuals but to groups of men. Now the residue that was not transformed into sheep-walks was divided into crofts or compact holdings, each of which was assigned to a single tenant. When this arrangement was first made, it was calculated by the landowners that each croft should support a household, for, though they had only a few acres of arable land, they were still allowed to graze sheep and cattle on the hill pastures around their crofts, and as they were usually not far from some sea loch, they could combine fishing with agriculture.

But in spite of the diminution of the amount of land available for agriculture, in spite of the departure of soldiers and emigrants, the population of the Highlands and Islands increased steadily through the century which followed Culloden. Crofts were divided and divided again, and cultivated year after year without a respite, till they yielded to their cultivators, at the best of times, only enough to keep body and soul together. It is true that the cultivation of the potato, introduced soon after the middle of the eighteenth century, enabled the country to support a far greater population than it otherwise would have been able to do. It is true that the development of fishing and of the kelp [1] industry, the cutting of the Crinan Canal and the Caledonian Canal [2] in the early years of the nineteenth century, and the construction of hundreds of miles of roads in the same period, gave work and wages to many Highlanders who otherwise would have starved. The fact remained, however, that the population was increasing far faster than its means of subsistence, and that the inhabitants of the Highlands were in a desperate plight, from which only desperate remedies could extricate them.

[1] Kelp was a kind of seaweed from which soda was prepared.
[2] The Crinan Canal was constructed between 1793 and 1817, and the Caledonian Canal between 1803 and 1822.

CHAPTER XXVII

THE INDUSTRIAL REVOLUTION: 1750–1830

The minds of men were excited to new enterprises; a new genius, as it were, had descended upon the earth, and there was an erect and outlooking spirit abroad that was not to be satisfied with the taciturn regularity of ancient affairs.—JOHN GALT, *Annals of the Parish*.

George III 1760–1820   George IV . . . 1820–1830

AFTER Culloden the noise of battle rolls far away from our shores; never again shall we see Scotland distracted by invasion or civil war. It is true that Highlanders and Low-landers still met on the field of battle, but now they fought side by side. Before the ' Forty-Five ' only one Highland regiment—the Black Watch—occupied a place in the Army List, and it had been embodied no later than 1739. Now, urged by Pitt, the Government raised regiment after regiment in the over-popu-lated glens, and so at one and the same time removed from the Highlands its most turbulent and adventurous spirits and put at the service of the regular army that fierce valour which had lately been used against it.

The exploits of the new Highland regiments, like those of the old Lowland regiments, like the achievements of generals of Scottish birth, Sir John Moore, who forged the weapon used by Wellington, and Craufurd, the most daring of Wellington's lieutenants in the Peninsula, belong to the history of the British Empire, rather than to the history of Scotland. So you must read elsewhere how in 1797 a Scottish admiral, old Adam Duncan, leaving a mutinous fleet behind him, put to sea with two ships of the line to do battle, if necessary, with the whole of the Dutch fleet, by what tricks and stratagems he kept the Dutch-men in harbour till the mutiny had blown over, and how, when he was at last able to meet the enemy on equal terms, he shattered the naval power of Holland in the hard-fought Battle

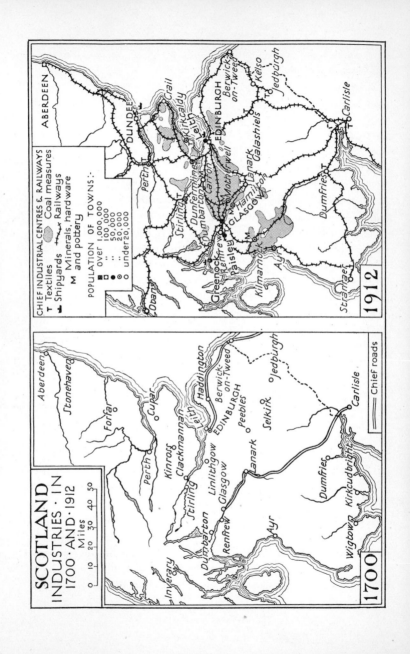

SCOTLAND
INDUSTRIES · IN
1700 · AND · 1912

Miles
0 10 20 30 40 50

1700

Chief roads

Aberdeen
Stonehaven
Forfar
Perth
Cupar
Kinross
Clackmannan
Stirling
Dumbarton
Linlithgow
Leith
Haddington
Renfrew Glasgow EDINBURGH
Berwick-on-Tweed
Lanark Peebles
Inverary
Ayr Selkirk
Jedburgh
Dumfries
Wigtown
Kirkcudbright
Carlisle

CHIEF INDUSTRIAL CENTRES & RAILWAYS
T Textiles   Coal measures
‡ Shipyards   — Railways
M Minerals, hardware
        and pottery

POPULATION OF TOWNS:-
■ over 1,000,000
■   100,000
□   50,000
●   20,000
○   under 20,000

1912

ABERDEEN
DUNDEE
Crail
Kirkcaldy
Perth T
Leith
Stirling T
Dunfermline
Carron
Dumbarton
Greenock
Renfrew T
Paisley
Kilmarnock
GLASGOW
Hamilton
Motherwell
Lanark
EDINBURGH
Berwick-on-Tweed
Kelso
Jedburgh
Galashiels
Dumfries T
Ayr
Oban
Stranraer
Carlisle T

of Camperdown. It is with another warfare that we are now concerned, the warfare waged by the home-keeping Scot against a stubborn soil, in a land where 'it girned a' summer and grat a' winter'.

So far he seemed to have been fighting a hopeless battle; there was little to distinguish the Scottish Lowlands in 1750 from the Scottish Lowlands of the early sixteenth century, described in Chapter XV. One saw the same bare, treeless landscape, the same marshes by the river bank, the same pools in the low-lying meadows. In the little farms of twenty-six Scots acres,[1] arranged in groups of four or six, which were held jointly by four or six tenants, the old methods of cultivation still prevailed: on the 'in-field' barley and oats, oats and barley, was grown every year without intermission; portions of the 'out-field', the inferior land, would be cultivated for two or three years on end and then used as pasture for another two or three years, but, unlike the in-field, it was never manured. If you visited such a cluster of farms in spring you would see a strange sight—three or four men tenderly leading out emaciated cattle from the low-roofed cottages, where they had spent the winter, and harnessing them, with ropes made of plaited straw, to a clumsy wooden plough. Though the plough-team seldom contained fewer than eight oxen, it often stuck fast; and sometimes the oxen collapsed altogether and had to be lifted out of the deep furrows by the ploughmen. The poor beasts were starved. The problem of the winter feeding of cattle was still unsolved; oil-cake was unknown, turnips were usually planted only in gardens, though after 1747 they were grown in the open field by one or two innovating lairds; no farmer was bold enough to grow crops of clover and lucerne along with the orthodox crops of oats and barley, whereby he might have increased his too scanty supply of hay. No, every year when Martinmas (11th November) came round, there was

[1] About thirty-two ordinary acres.

a great slaughter of 'marts'—superfluous cattle—and the survivors had to exist as best they could on a meagre diet of hay and chopped straw.

The carcasses of the marts were salted; indeed, during the winter it was difficult to obtain any meat that was not salted. Little fresh meat was eaten at any time, unless one counted as fresh meat 'braxy' mutton—the flesh of a sheep that had died a natural death. Only the largest towns boasted a 'flesher' or butcher; in the smaller burghs the bellman was sent round on the rare occasions when a cow or a sheep was slaughtered.

In the houses of the country folk little improvement was to be noted. Cottages built of unmortared stones like those described in Chapter XXVI, with a hole in the thatched roof to serve for a chimney, and a hole in the wall to serve as a window, were by no means confined to the Highlands. In some parts of the Lowlands the houses were built of turfs stripped from the pasture; these low-roofed huts interested the poet Gray when he visited Forfarshire in 1765. Though he did not know it, a boy who was destined to be a greater poet than himself was at that time living in an equally humble dwelling in Ayrshire. Robert Burns spent his boyhood in a 'clay biggin'—a cottage with thatched roof and walls made of clay mixed with straw— which his father had built with his own hands. 'There', he wrote,

> . . . lanely by the ingle-cheek,
> I sat and ey'd the spewing reek,
> That fill'd, wi' hoast-provoking smeek,
>   The auld clay biggin;
> An' heard the restless rattons squeak
>   About the riggin.

Long before the end of Burns's brief life in 1796, the transformation of rural Scotland had begun. Already about the middle of the eighteenth century great landowners like the Duke of Argyll were planting larches by the thousand on bare hillsides, already in the Lowlands one could see rows of young

'THE AULD CLAY BIGGIN'

The interior of Burns's cottage at Ayr

ashes or beeches lining the country roads, or clustering about the laird's mansion house. It was not an absence of all trees, but only an absence of old trees, that moved Dr. Johnson to scornful speech when he visited Scotland in 1773.

Other, more important changes were taking place in the rural districts. Large farms became the rule; not only would four or six little farms be thrown together to form one big one, but land once regarded as good for nothing would be included in the new-fashioned farmer's holding. Shallow lochs and marshy hollows and flat green carses by the riverside were drained and brought under the plough, loose stones were collected from land hitherto untilled—and from much of the tilled land as well—and piled up to form 'dry stane dykes'. For in Scotland, as in England, enclosures came in with the new methods of farming; the days of the unfenced corn-rigs, of the pasture shared by the cattle of half a dozen owners, were at an end; farms, big and little, were rearranged as compact parcels of land, which had to be fenced off from neighbouring farms by a march dyke or boundary wall. So the go-ahead farmer was freed from the interference of stupid or lazy neighbours; he was freed, too, from the fear of being hustled out of his farm before he had time to carry out the improvements that he had planned, for he now held his farm on a lease, not of two or three, but of nineteen or twenty-one years.

So instead of growing oats and barley year after year on the in-field, and letting the out-field lie fallow for three or four years on end, exhausting the one and not getting nearly enough from the other, the new-fashioned farmer increased the yield from his acres by manuring the land more heavily and by varying the crops in different fields from year to year; after oats he might sow, not more oats, but turnips, after turnips, wheat, after wheat, clover, then in the fifth year he would return to oats again. As soon as he could he got rid of the old-fashioned wooden plough, and adopted the new swing plough, invented by John Small of Dalkeith in 1750, which required only one man and one pair of horses. The flail followed the old wooden plough into oblivion; in 1787 Andrew Meikle, a millwright of Dunbar, invented a new threshing machine, and soon threshing machines, driven by horses or by water-power, were installed in every up-to-date farm. The sleds and the 'tumblers' with their solid wooden wheels which had satisfied the farmers of an earlier day no longer satisfied the up-to-date farmer; he insisted on the 'wricht' supplying him with carts like those which are in use to-day.

Change produced change; the introduction of crops like turnips, clover, and lucerne enormously increased the supply of fodder for cattle, and so made the wholesale slaughter at Martinmas unnecessary. But the new-fashioned farmer was not content with a mere increase in the numbers of his sheep and cattle; he wanted an improvement in the quality, and he did not rest till he had succeeded in rearing animals that were far larger and healthier than their predecessors.

So, in spite of the enormous increase in his rent, the new-fashioned farmer made money, especially in the war years, when the price of corn rose to dizzy heights. His prosperity was shown in the changed appearance of the farm buildings. Not for him now the 'auld clay biggin' with its thatched roof; the tenant of two or three hundred acres must live in a substantial stone house of two or three stories, as big as the manse, and three or four times bigger than the schoolhouse. And the farm-house was only one of a group of massive stone buildings, a 'farm town' that looked down on the rolling cornfields like a medieval fortress. Thatched roofs, too, had gone out of fashion with walls of turf and unmortared stone; in Fife and the Lothians the red-tiled roofs of farm steading and cottage added a new note of colour to the landscape, while in the south-west, and north of the Tay, slate roofs gave a somewhat chilly and forbidding look to the new stone buildings.

So the new-fashioned farmer prospered exceedingly, nor did increasing prosperity make him lose his spirit of enterprise. Even before the year 1830 the tall brick chimney rising from the farm steading showed that some of the farmers had installed steam-engines to drives their threshing-mills, while others were experimenting with the primitive reaping machine which an Angus minister had invented. But what of the old-fashioned farmer? If six small farms were conjoined to form one big one, then only one farmer out of the six could remain. Then what happened to the other five? One or two might remain on the farm, not as tenants, but as farm-servants, hired by their former co-tenant for a term of six or of twelve months, and living in a cottage which they must leave if they left his service. They were still working the land that their fathers had tilled, but now that they were working it for another man they could no longer feel, as they had once done, that they were all but rooted to the soil.

We must not think that the transition from small-scale farming was complete at the end of the eighteenth century. The change was a gradual one, affecting different parts of the Lowlands in different degrees, and in many districts small farms, worked by the tenant and the members of his family, were numerous long after the year 1830. Still, the small farmer was fighting a losing battle, though there were certain factors which tended to postpone his inevitable defeat.

In a rural parish in twentieth-century Scotland we expect the inhabitants to be engaged in farming and in nothing else. But in a rural parish in eighteenth-century Scotland other occupations were carried on. On the rare occasions when the countryman wanted a new suit, he handed the wool which he had sheared from his own sheep to his wife or his daughter, who carded it and spun it on her own spinning-wheel. Next he took it to the local webster, who wove it into hodden grey cloth on the handloom which stood in his cottage. Even now he did not go to the tailor; he waited for the tailor to come to him. For the country tailor had no shop; he wandered from house to house, staying a day here and a day there, cutting out and sewing together the homespun garments. In the same way the careful housewife filled her linen-cupboard; she spun the thread from flax gathered in the fields about her house, then made the

SPINNING DURING THE TIME OF THE DOMESTIC SYSTEM

webster weave it into sheets and tablecloths. Just as the old-fashioned farmer contented himself with growing only as much corn as his family could consume, so the old-fashioned house-wife spun only as much yarn as her household would require. In the closing years of the eighteenth century, however, a demand sprang up outside Scotland for the once despised Scottish linens and woollens, and the women in the country districts discovered that they could make money by selling the yarn which they had spun to the cloth merchants in the burghs. So the earnings of his womenfolk often stood between the old fashioned farmer and ruin. Noticing, too, that the burgh merchant was ready to take as much cloth as the village webster could weave, the dispossessed farmer often set up a handloom in his cottage and turned weaver too.

The yarn and cloth were often carried to town in creels slung on the backs of pack-horses, for in many places no ordinary wheeled vehicle could negotiate the muddy or boulder-strewn tracks that did duty for roads. It is true that by an old Act of Parliament every householder was compelled either to pay a small sum of money for the upkeep of the roads that ran through his parish, or to work on the roads for six days every year; in spite of this the Lowland roads at the middle of the eighteenth century were far inferior to the military roads which Wade had built in the Highlands. In consequence, even the big towns were almost isolated from one another. Not till 1763, for example, did a stage-coach ply regularly between Edinburgh and Glasgow. Even with four or six horses it required twelve hours for the journey, and it ran only three times a week. Twice a month ever since 1753 a stage-coach had left Edinburgh for London, covering the 393 miles in ten days in summer and twelve days in winter; not till 1788, however, did stage-coaches run directly from Glasgow to London.

Yet all through the second half of the eighteenth century and the first quarter of the nineteenth century old roads were being improved out of recognition and new roads opened up. In 1750 the first of some hundreds of private Turnpike Acts were passed. These Acts empowered landowners to construct new roads with borrowed money, and to repay the money out of tolls levied on the drivers of vehicles who made use of these roads, and so the toll-house and the white toll-gate became familiar features of the Scottish landscape. Nor was the traveller on these new roads compelled to trust himself and his horse to treacherous fords or overloaded ferry-boats, for this was the age of the great bridge-builders Rennie and Telford. In every part of

Scotland rose the stately and beautiful structures that they had planned. And though at this time Scotland could boast only one or two short lengths of railway over which trains of wagons drawn by horses slowly rumbled, the opening of the Forth and Clyde Canal in 1790 made it possible to transport heavy goods across central Scotland. At one time it seemed as if the horse-drawn barges would be replaced by speedier

KELSO BRIDGE

Built by Rennie. On the right can be seen the ruins of Kelso Abbey

vessels. In 1801 the people of Kirkintilloch were astonished to see a strange monster, breathing smoke and steam, churning its way through the water at the rate of almost six miles an hour, and pulling two barges after it. Their wonder was pardonable, for they were looking at the first steam-boat, the *Charlotte Dundas*, which William Symington had designed after years of experiment. But the *Charlotte Dundas* was allowed to make only a few voyages, for the owners of the canal were afraid that the waves which the vessel made would undermine the banks, and it was not till 1812, when the *Comet*, built by another Scotsman, Henry Bell, began to ply on the

Firth of Clyde, that people realized the importance of the new invention.

The graceful bridges, the cosy-looking red-roofed cottages and farm-houses, the woods that covered the once bare hills, in 1830 had brought a new beauty into the Scottish countryside. The same could not be said of the towns ; no one could maintain, for example, that the Glasgow of 1830 was a more beautiful place than the Glasgow of 1750.

Eighty years had changed Glasgow out of all recognition. For one thing, ever since 1770 engineers had been busy deepening the channel of the Clyde below Glasgow, and so the biggest sea-going ships could now lie off the new piers and jetties. And the changes which had affected Glasgow could be paralleled in many a smaller Scottish burgh. In Lowland Scotland, as in England at the same period, trade and manufactures were becoming more important than farming, and though the population of the country districts continued to increase, the drift of the country folk to the towns had already set in. It was easier to find work there. The cloth merchants in the burghs, for example, found that they could produce goods much more quickly and cheaply if, instead of buying their yarn from spinners scattered up and down half a score of parishes, they set up spinning-mills of their own, equipped, not with old-fashioned spinning-wheels, but with the machinery driven by water-power which Crompton and Arkwright had lately invented. The spinning-wheel could not compete with the new machine ; the spinners in the country districts found that the price which the merchants offered for their homespun yarns sank lower and lower, till they had no longer any hope of making a living from their work. For many there was only one thing to do, go to the town and get employment in the mills, where one was lucky if one did not have to work more than twelve hours a day. The same fate hung over the weavers ; but though an effective power-loom had been invented before the end of the eighteenth century, in 1830 the great bulk of the cloth manufactured in Scotland was still woven on the old-fashioned handloom, either in small weaving-shops or in the weaver's own home.

So in once sleepy little burghs by some burn or river the new many-windowed buildings sprang up; flax mills in the north-east, woollen mills on the Tweed and its tributaries, cotton

CROMPTON'S MULE

This machine, completed in 1779, and worked by hand, was the fore-runner of that machine which was turned by water-power in 1790

mills on the Clyde and the Cart. Not for long were the new mills dependent on water-power; as early as 1774 James Watt had succeeded in making a really effective steam-engine, which was used for pumping water from mines, and he was not content till, in 1782, he had made one that could turn the wheels of machines. In the early years of the nineteenth century steam-engines were introduced not only in most of the new mills and factories, but, as we have seen, on some of the larger farms. Steam-engines required coal; so new shafts were sunk, and the amount of coal produced began steadily to increase. And as the new machinery was made, not of wood, but of iron or steel, it was inevitable that hitherto untouched deposits of iron-stone should be opened up and that engineering works should spring up in the new industrial centres. The increasing dependence of the new industries on coal and iron had another consequence; factories and engineering works which were within easy reach of the mining areas had a tremendous advantage over those which were farther away, and so we shall witness throughout the nineteenth century a steadily increasing drift of population and industry from the north and south to the centre of Scotland, where alone coal and iron are to be found.

The changes which have been described in this chapter, changes startling enough to deserve the name of the Industrial Revolution, were not, we know, confined to Scotland. The Industrial Revolution had originated, if anywhere, in England, and in time it affected the whole of Western Europe. But nowhere were the changes more sudden and startling than in Scotland; in no other country did the ordinary workman reach a higher level of efficiency, and even in that age of invention there was no achievement which could be placed beside that of James Watt. For the first time in its history Scotland had become a wealthy and a busy country. Whether it had also become a happier country we shall discover in the next chapter.

THE COMET

CHAPTER XXVIII

PARLIAMENTARY AND BURGH REFORM:
1789–1833

> They, an' be damn'd ! what right hae they
> To meat or sleep or light o' day,
> Far less to riches, pow'r or freedom,
> But what your lordship likes to gie them ?
> BURNS.

George III 1760–1820   George IV . . . 1820–1830
William IV . . . 1830–1837

A SINGLE walk through the newer streets of a town like
Edinburgh in the earlier part of the nineteenth century
would have convinced the inquirer that the inhabitants were,
if not happier, at least much more comfortable than their
fathers and grandfathers had been. Down to the closing years
of the eighteenth century the prosperous merchant or shop-
keeper had been content to live above his shop, in a flat that
contained at the most four rooms. One might admire the carved
stone fireplace, the panelled walls, and the graceful lines of the
new mahogany furniture ; still one had to admit that a house
lighted at night by one or two flickering candles, a house without water-pipes or drains, left much to be desired.

Water could be got only by sending one's servants for it to
the public well in the street below or else by waiting till the
water caddie appeared with his water-cart. Household refuse
had to be thrown from the window after dark, and woe betide
the benighted wayfarer who did not have presence of mind to
shout 'Haud your hand' when he heard the warning shout of
'Gardyloo !' [1] from a window above.

Such a house, with its tiny windows which were seldom opened,

---

[1] *Gardez l'eau*—look out for the water.

with the cavernous box-beds in every room, would have seemed dark and stuffy even if it had stood in the middle of a ten-acre field. But it was hemmed in on every side by tall 'lands' or blocks of flats, which in Edinburgh became veritable sky-scrapers, often reaching a height of ten or eleven stories. For down to the closing years of the eighteenth century additional accommodation was found for the increasing population by building higher, and by packing the houses more tightly, within the old boundaries of the town. The 'closes', the gardens which had once brought a country fragrance into the very heart of towns like Edinburgh and Glasgow, disappeared altogether under the great bulks of stone and mortar, or survived only as dark passages leading into narrow and sunless courtyards.

It was in a flat in one of these tall 'lands', approached by a malodorous common stair, that not only prosperous merchants, not only ministers, lawyers, and doctors, but judges and lords and ladies 'wi' a lang pedigree' were content to dwell. This shortage of accommodation had one curious consequence: the fashionable doctor prescribed for his patients, the busy lawyer interviewed his clients, not in his own house, but in the tavern at the close end.

In the closing years of the eighteenth century, however, a big change took place. It was most marked in Edinburgh, where merchant and minister, doctor and lawyer, judge and lady of high degree, forsook their cramped and lofty quarters in the Old Town and settled in the 'New Town' of broad streets and stately houses that had sprung up on the farther side of the Nor' Loch. The change was not confined to Edinburgh; in Glasgow, in Dundee, in Aberdeen the prosperous manufacturer or merchant built himself a roomy villa, set in a spacious garden, on the outskirts of the town. The new houses had their disadvantages; water, for example, had to be drawn from a well in the garden, the architect, in his anxiety to make the

CHARLOTTE SQUARE, EDINBURGH
Designed by Robert Adam in 1791

house look dignified, tucked the kitchen and scullery away underground, at night the light of the candles scarcely revealed the design of the new wall-paper—for wall-paper had taken the place of the old-fashioned wood-panelling. Still, they were a great improvement on the old insanitary dwellings. And in 1823 gas was introduced into some of the more up-to-date houses, though many people declared that they preferred the old-fashioned candles. 'The blaze and glow, and occasional odour of gas,' said Sir Walter Scott's son-in-law, 'when spread over every part of a private house, will ever constitute a serious annoyance to the majority of men—still more so of women.' But the 'blazing stars of gas' of which Lockhart complained had come to stay; soon, too, they replaced the dim uncertain oil lamps in the public streets.

So long as we kept to these stately terraces and squares, these white villas set among new planted trees, we should have seen nothing but signs of increasing prosperity and increasing comfort. But if we had turned to the unfashionable quarters of the town, abandoned by the owners of these new houses, we should have found that they had a very different story to tell. They were far more dirty, crowded, and uncomfortable than they had been a generation before. The population of the ordinary Scottish industrial town was growing at a tremendous rate—Glasgow for example had 77,385 inhabitants in 1801, and 202,420 in 1831; Dundee, fewer than 27,000 in 1801 and over 45,000 in 1831. This increase was caused largely by an influx of strangers—not only country folk from the neighbouring parishes, but immigrants from the Highlands and from Ireland, lured thither by the hope of work. The new-comers had to live somewhere, and accommodation was found for them in these old 'lands' which had recently been abandoned by their more prosperous tenants. The old dwelling-houses were divided and sub-divided; few Scottish working men could boast of a house containing more than two rooms; many had to be content with one. And though the town broke through its ancient boundaries in more directions than one, though the villas on the west were balanced by row after row of grim tenements on the east, 'these additional suburbs', as a Dundee minister remarked, 'were built without any general plan, and

The good Effects of CARBONIC GAS.!!!

From a satiric print of 1807

without the least regard to health, elegance, or cleanliness'. Here, as in the older quarters of the town, one-roomed and two-roomed houses were the rule.

It was inevitable that in these crowded 'lands', some of them looking on to sunless and malodorous lanes or courts, all of them without drains and without a proper water-supply, should be the breeding grounds of disease. Typhus always lurked there; more terrible still were the rarer visitations of cholera and small-pox.

You may ask why self-respecting Scotsmen should have been content to live in dwellings like these. Some were quite satisfied; they did not understand—most doctors even did not understand—how closely connected dirt and overcrowding were with disease, and if you had found fault with them they would at once have quoted the proverb 'the clartier the cosier'. Higher wages would do such people no good, it was argued, they would simply drink the increase. But though there was a great deal of unnecessary drinking in early nineteenth-century Scotland— it was said in 1835 that Glasgow could boast one public-house for every fourteen families—the hardships which the majority of Scotsmen had to endure were not self-inflicted. Low wages and long hours were the rule everywhere, and, strange as it may seem, the conditions were worst in some of the most prosperous industries. The older generation of linen weavers, for example, found it more and more difficult to make both ends meet. The boom in the linen industry had attracted new-comers, many of them starving Irishmen who were willing to accept a lower wage than the Scot could live on; women, too, who had once worked only in the spinning-mills made their way into the weaving sheds in larger and larger numbers. So with a superabundance of workers to choose from the manufacturer could reduce wages and disregard the protests of the old-fashioned weaver. A weaver was lucky if he got ten shillings a week; he might have to be content with seven, while many of the women had to accept five. Nor was that all, hours of work were intolerably long; in Dundee, for example, the spinners and weavers began work at half-past five in the morning, winter and summer, and finished at seven in the evening. They were not pent up in the factory all the time it is true; they were allowed one interval of half an hour for breakfast and another half-hour for dinner. Nowadays we should count it an intolerably hard day's darg for a grown man; then it was not thought too hard for boys and girls; hundreds of these mill and factory workers had not reached the age of fourteen.

The plight of the miners was even worse than that of the factory workers. Till 1799 many of them were serfs, bound for life to the mine in which they worked, as their fathers and grandfathers had been before them. The Act of 1799, which abolished serfdom in the Scottish mines, did not remove the worst of the evils connected with these mines. The very worst were too hideous for description; one may say, however, that women and girls—some of the girls only six years old—were employed to do the work which later was done by pit ponies, and that the hours of work for all, men, women, and children, were cruelly long. A fifteen hours' spell of work was common; a twenty-four hours' spell was not unknown.

Many a douce, hard-working Scotsman pondered over the desperate position in which he and his children found themselves. It was hard to discover a way out. He and his friends might have formed a union and refused to work unless their wages were increased and their working day reduced, but in 1800 Parliament declared such Trade Unions to be illegal, and though in 1824 the ban on Trade Unions was removed, they were only tolerated, they had little real power.

Another way of escape, however, offered itself. The great majority of these harassed and over-driven workmen believed that they would get fair treatment only when Parliament was reformed and made a really representative body. At the beginning of the nineteenth century it was hard to say whom the forty-five Scottish members represented. Fifteen of them were supposed to represent the sixty-six royal burghs, but only one of these burghs, Edinburgh, had a member all to itself. The remaining burghs, irrespective of their size, were divided into groups of four or five, to each of which one member was allotted. Glasgow, for example, joined with Renfrew, Rutherglen, and Dumbarton to send one member to Parliament; though it had a population of over 200,000 it could claim only one-quarter of a member. The little Fifeshire village of Kilrenny, with a population of two hundred souls, was also a royal burgh; it joined with the neighbouring fishing hamlets of Crail, Anstruther Easter, Anstruther Wester, and Pittenweem to send its representative to Parliament. If Edinburgh was entitled to one member, Glasgow should have had two; if Kilrenny was entitled to a fifth share in a member, Glasgow should have had two hundred.

To make matters worse, a member was chosen not by all the burgesses in his group of burghs; each town council in the group nominated one delegate, and these four or five delegates elected the member. And who elected the town council? Not the burgesses, but the town council of the previous year. In Aberdeen, for example, the old town council met every year about Michaelmas [1] and elected four of their own number, thirteen members of the merchant gild, and two of the six deacons of trades or craft gilds, to form the new town council. The old and new council then united to elect the provost, the four bailies, and the other burgh officials.

So in Scotland the problem of reforming the representation of the burghs in Parliament was bound up with the problem of reforming the burghs themselves. But those lucky burgesses within the charmed circle from which the magistrates and council were chosen did not want any change. Under the existing system they could do what they liked with the town and its revenues, knowing that their voteless fellow townsmen could not drive them from office. Again and again a provost or bailie would help himself to a big slice of the common land of the burgh, paying either a ridiculously small price or no price at all, and his comrades on the council, instead of protesting, lay low till they could follow his example. And to sins of commis-

[1] 29th September.

sion they added sins of omission; the rapidly expanding towns
were allowed to grow anyhow, without plan or arrangement;
it was none of their business if houses and factories were mixed
up in hopeless confusion, if new tenements were planted in
already over-crowded areas, and if green spaces in the heart of
the town disappeared under masses of stone and lime. Every
big Scottish town, even Edinburgh, even Aberdeen, glittering
in all the splendour of granite, has its story to tell to-day of
opportunities wasted through the short-sightedness, the lack
of imagination of those who ruled it in those critical years.

The system by which the thirty county representatives were
elected was equally absurd. The only persons entitled to vote
were those landowners whose estates were held directly of the
Crown and were valued at not less than £400 Scots [1] a year. A
sub-tenant, whatever the extent or value of the lands which he
occupied, could not claim a vote. This arrangement put too
much power in the hands of the landowners, and, to make
things worse, a landed proprietor would often multiply voting
power by the creation of 'parchment barons'. He would go
through the form of handing over portions of his estate, of an
annual value of £400 Scots, to friends and dependants whom he
could trust to vote exactly as he told them. Still, even though
their numbers were swelled by over thirteen hundred parchment barons, there were fewer than three thousand county
electors in the whole of Scotland at the end of the eighteenth
century.

Even if the burgh councillors and county electors had always
been honest and disinterested, their fellow countrymen would
still have grumbled at being excluded from any part in the
choice of members of Parliament. Most of them, however, were
'but indifferent honest', ready, if the Government made it
worth their while, to vote only for such candidates as would
support the party in power. And it was made worth their

---

[1] £33 6s. 8d. sterling.

while; since there were so few of them it cost the Government very little to buy their votes.

Though the office of Secretary of State for Scotland had been abolished in 1746, the Prime Minister always entrusted some member of the Cabinet with the management of Scottish affairs, including the management of the elections. The most famous of all these Managers was the colleague and friend of Pitt, Henry Dundas, who between 1783 and 1805 was successively Treasurer of the Navy, President of the Board of Control of India, Home Secretary, and Secretary for War, and so, in those days when entrance to the public service was not guarded by competitive examinations, he became a dispenser on a large scale of comfortable little Government jobs and of posts in the East India Company Service. Many a poor Scots youth owed his start in life to this genial despot, who, even after he became Viscount Melville, remained faithful to the homely Scottish speech. But his patronage was limited to faithful Tories and their kinsfolk; Whig electors soon learned that the 'uncrowned king of Scotland' would do nothing for them unless he was assured that they would vote Tory at the next election. They usually took the hint, and, so long as Dundas remained in power, he could assure the Prime Minister of the support of thirty-nine out of forty-five Scottish members, pledged to resist any attempt to alter the existing system of government.

In this they differed from the great majority of their countrymen, who thought that parliamentary reform was long overdue. Some, the Whigs, who belonged mainly to the middle classes, would have been content if the worst absurdities of the existing system had been corrected, others, the Radicals, the root and branch reformers, most of whom were working men, declared that Parliament could not really be representative until every householder had a vote, and until the introduction of secret voting or voting by ballot would make threats and bribes alike of no avail.

The outbreak of the French Revolution in 1789 seemed at first as if it would hasten the coming of parliamentary reform in Great Britain; Whigs and Radicals alike were filled with enthusiasm when they marked how the French people, while

HENRY DUNDAS

remaining to all appearance loyal to their king, had succeeded in establishing a really representative assembly; even peers and lawyers joined the Friends of the People, a society which advocated immediate political reform. Soon there came a change; in 1792 King Louis was deposed, and his execution in 1793, followed by the outbreak of war between

Britain and France, caused all reformers, Whig and Radical
alike, to be regarded with suspicion. Had not those who began
the French Revolution, it was argued, been respectable middle-
class people just like these plausible Whig lawyers, and had not
their apparently reasonable and moderate demands led to
wholesale confiscation and massacre ? The Whigs bowed to the
storm ; the question of reform, they recognized, must wait till
the war was over. Their less cautious allies were bullied into
silence by the political trials of 1794, when packed juries found
Thomas Muir, an advocate, Fysshe Palmer, a minister, and
three other Radical agitators guilty of sedition, and when
Braxfield, the Lord Justice Clerk, gleefully dealt out sentences
of fourteen years transportation to them.

Peace came in 1815, but not a word of parliamentary reform.
The Dundas despotism was still unbroken, for though Viscount
Melville had been compelled to resign in 1805, his son had
succeeded to his place as manager of Scottish affairs. In 1820
the whole of Glasgow went on strike, and fighting took place
at Bonnymuir between a handful of Radical weavers and a
detachment of cavalry, but this ' Radical War ', as it was
called, simply confirmed the Government in its opposition to
any change. Three of the Radical leaders were executed. Not
till 1830 did the resignation of Wellington, the Tory Prime
Minister, give the Whigs a chance to carry out their long-
meditated scheme of moderate reform.

The story of the two years battle over the Reform Bills
belongs to British rather than to Scottish history. Its fluctua-
tions were followed with intense—almost too intense—interest
by the unenfranchised Scot, who illuminated his own windows
when the Whigs scored a victory and broke the windows of his
Tory neighbour when they were defeated. At last, in June 1832,
the English Reform Bill passed the House of Lords and obtained
the royal assent, and a month later the Scottish Reform Bill
became law.

The Reform Act of 1832 increased the number of Scottish members in the Commons from 45 to 53. The number of county representatives was left unaltered: Edinburgh and Glasgow were each given two members, and Dundee, Aberdeen, Paisley, Perth, and Greenock, one apiece. The smaller burghs were still arranged in groups, but eight new burghs were added to their number. It was no longer possible, however, for the small burghs in a group to outvote a large one, for the system of indirect election by delegates from the burgh councils was abandoned; henceforward all householders paying an annual rent of £10 a year or more were entitled to vote. In the counties the Act enfranchised only the actual proprietors of land or houses worth more than £10 a year, and tenants paying a rent of more than £50 a year who held their farms on a lease of more than seven years. The dismal prophesies of the Tories, the exultation of the Radicals over the passing of the Bill, seem alike strange to us nowadays. For the 1832 Reform Act enfranchised only the middle classes; few even of the highly-skilled workmen could afford to pay £10 a year for house rent; [1] the £10 qualification shut out the great bulk of the working classes. But the change was startling enough; under the Dundas despotism, as we have seen, all but half a dozen of the forty-five Scots members were Tories; in the first reformed Parliament, which met in 1833, all but nine of the fifty-three Scots members were Whigs.

Parliamentary reform brought burgh reform in its train; before the end of 1833 the Scottish Burgh Reform Bill placed the power of electing town councils in the hands of those householders who were already entitled to vote in parliamentary elections.

[1] In Dundee in 1835 the wages of masons were from seven shillings and sixpence to fifteen shillings a week; carpenters earned from ten shillings to thirteen shillings, and weavers from seven shillings to ten shillings a week.

CHAPTER XXIX

MODERN SCOTLAND: 1832–1929

Sunk, sunk in life more dead than sleep,
  And silent when thou shouldst be loud,
Still do thy faithful sentinels keep
  Their patient watch and service proud.
Awake! for all thy hills rejoice
To hear again the Muses' voice. . . .

Awake, thou! Bless the eager faces,
  The hearts that hunger for thy sake,
Come from thy dream in sleep's far places,
  Before the eager hearts shall break;
And on the hill and down the glen,
Indifferent night fall dark again.

GEORGE RESTON MALLOCH.

IN July 1832 the Scottish Reform Bill became law; in September 1832, his last hours troubled by fears for his country, died the greatest of Scotsmen. Though Sir Walter Scott was only sixty-one when he died, the Scotland of his youth, the Scotland which he loved, already existed only in the pages of his novels, and he found himself moving in a world that grew stranger and more inexplicable every day. He turned away his eyes from the gaunt new mills that were springing up by Tweed and Teviot, Ettrick and Yarrow, to the crumbling towers that rose above those haunted streams; he saw nothing of the festering squalor of the old town of Edinburgh, only its grim mysterious splendour; he remembered the plaided warriors, sallying forth from their glens to fight for Montrose or Dundee or Prince Charlie, and forgot the Highlander of his own day sharing his hovel with his cattle, half-starved, with complete starvation waiting for him if ever blight should get into his potato patch.

So, to Scott, who saw nothing but good in the old strictly-ordered Scotland, bound together by the memories of feudal loyalties, every change wrought by the political reformers was a change for the worse. We may laugh at his fears; still we must admit that, if much has been gained, something hard to replace has been lost.

In the hundred years that have passed since his death, Scotland has steadily become less Scotch. The very speech of the people shows the change: down to the end of the eighteenth century Broad Scots had been the language of high and low alike; ministers used it when they were out of the pulpit, judges even when they were on the bench. Now the ploughman or the town-bred artisan, though he refuses to speak English except with a strong Scots accent, reads nothing but English newspapers and English books, and has forgotten, or rather, has never known, the pungent, expressive words and phrases which his grandfather used every day. The old festivals, too, have been forgotten or have changed out of all recognition; the 'fasts' have become public holidays; the 'guisers' no longer enact their mystery play in the farm-house kitchens at Yule, and though they still appear in the darkening streets as Hallowe'en draws near, it is only to beg for halfpennies.

Even Edinburgh has become less dignified and self-sufficing, less of a capital city. At the beginning of the nineteenth century the Scottish nobleman, the laird whom the new methods of farming had enriched, had his town house not in London but in Edinburgh. To-day, London is the magnet which draws the ambitious Scot who wants to be a great artist or a man of letters; at the beginning of the nineteenth century, he turned his steps to the city where Raeburn, the greatest portrait-painter of his time, and Scott, whom most people then regarded as the greatest imaginative writer in Europe, were content to make their homes. But already the drift southwards had begun: Scottish architects like Robert Adam,

the designer of the most stately square in the New Town, found in London an opportunity that was denied them in Edinburgh; and though in his troubled and tempestuous youth Thomas Carlyle had looked down on Edinburgh from a lofty attic window, just as the hero of his *Sartor Resartus* looked down on the city of Weissnichtwo, the books which in the mid-nineteenth century made him the most famous Scottish man of letters were written in a red-brick villa in Chelsea.

For, as Henry the Seventh said more than four hundred years ago, 'the greater will draw the less'. The larger and richer country offers more to a man ambitious of either fame or wealth. It was difficult for the greater to draw the less, however, as long as the

From an advertisement in *The Liverpool Mercury*, 23 August 1816

old lumbering stage-coach was the only means of communication between the two countries. But in 1821 steamships began
to ply between Leith and London. 'The convenience of
going to London by the steam-packet,' wrote Scott to
Southey in 1824, 'which carries you on whether you wake
or sleep, is so much preferable to a long land journey, that
I took it. . . . The extreme rapidity of communication . . .
is like to be attended with a mass of most important consequences—some, or rather most of them, good, but some also
which are not to be viewed without apprehension. . . . Formerly
in Edinburgh and other towns . . . the cry which was raised
in the great mart of halloo and humbug (London) was not
instantly echoed back, as it may be in the present day and
present circumstances, when our opinion, like a small drop of
water brought into immediate contiguity with a bigger, is
most likely to be absorbed in, and united with, that of the
larger mass.'

After the steamboat came the railway. In the year of Scott's
death there were only two locomotives in the whole of Scotland;
eighteen years later—in 1850—the construction of the Royal
Border Bridge at Berwick-on-Tweed linked up the Scottish and
the English railway systems and brought Edinburgh within
half-a-day's journey of London.

Though the bonds which bound the two countries together
were being drawn tighter every day, the Scotsman still declared
proudly that in two things he was still far superior to the
Englishman. One was thrift. The new Poor Law, passed by
Parliament in 1834, did not apply to Scotland; so, north of the
border, there was neither workhouse nor compulsory poor-
rate: in some parishes there was a voluntary poor-rate; in
most, the kirk-session doled out miserable sums from the
collections in the parish church to such of the members as were
known to be too old or too feeble to work. Thrifty to a fault
the Scottish workman was, but in those days when wages were

3437.2   D d

low, when the wildest Radical had never dreamed of insurance against sickness or unemployment, he often found that thrift alone was of little avail. And if in the rural parishes in the Lowlands the machinery of poor relief creaked and groaned, in the Highlands and in the over-crowded city parishes it had broken down altogether.

Then in 1843 came the Disruption, when the Church of Scotland was rent in two over the question of Lay Patronage. One party in the Church, led by the eloquent and impetuous Thomas Chalmers, demanded that Lay Patronage should be abolished—that no minister should be appointed to a church without the consent of the congregation. When it could not have its way, it separated from the Church of Scotland to form the Free Church, leaving all the property and endowments of the once united Church to the rival party.

It was the Disruption that dealt the final blow to the anti-quated system of poor relief: now that the majority of the inhabitants of Scotland had no longer any connexion with the State Church, it seemed hardly fair that its kirk-sessions should retain the exclusive right of administering relief to the poor. So in 1845 the new Poor Law was passed. It replaced the kirk-sessions by elected boards, and made it almost impossible for unwilling parishes to evade the levying of a Poor Rate.

If the Scotsman was more thrifty, he was also better educated than the average Englishman. Though it was long before John Knox's dream of a school in every parish came true, as early as 1696 the Scottish Parliament had passed an Act ordering a school to be established in every parish not already provided with one. The school and the schoolmaster were both to be maintained by the heritors—those people who had land within the parish. This Act, however, was often disregarded, especially in the Highland parishes, and in 1803 a more stringent Act was passed. For one thing, it provided that no schoolmaster should be paid an annual salary of less than three hundred marks—

Scots; for another, it ordered the heritors to provide the schoolmaster with a 'commodious house'. But Parliament was not as generous as it seemed; though the mark Scots had once been worth thirteen and fourpence, in 1803 it was worth a little less than a shilling and three-halfpence, and, according to the Act, none of these 'commodious houses' was to contain more than two rooms. Still, many of the occupants of these 'palaces for dominies' were sound and enthusiastic scholars, willing to teach Latin and Greek to the son of the ploughman or of the village tradesman who aspired to enter the University. And many a 'lad o' pairts' did pass straight from the village school to the University. For the Scottish Universities, unlike the English Universities of that time, did not close their gates against the youth whose only wealth was a little learning: in November they welcomed men who had spent the months from April to October in the field or workshop, and who had come up to wear the student's red gown through the five months session.

The Disruption broke the monopoly of the control of educa-tion which had been enjoyed by the Church of Scotland since the Reformation. As no one who was not a member of the Church of Scotland could become a parish schoolmaster, the Free Church set about building schools of its own, and so doubled the number of schools in districts that hitherto had been inadequately supplied.

Though the Scottish school system was the wonder of Europe, it was wonderful only when compared with the systems which obtained in other countries: as late as 1867 more than a sixth of the children of Scotland succeeded in evading school altogether. The Education Act of 1872, how-ever, not only brought the existing schools under the control of the State, it compelled the ratepayers in each parish to build schools large enough to receive all the children of school age who lived in the parish, and compelled the parents to send their children to these schools.

Almost as important as a civilizing influence was the Public Health Act, passed in 1867—the first shot fired in the campaign against disease and dirt.

The abolition of the privileges of the trade and merchant gilds in 1846, the quality of the education which the average Scot received, each contributed to bring about an extraordinary burst of prosperity in mid-nineteenth-century Scotland. From his own country the head of one of the new engineering or textile firms could get an almost inexhaustible supply of well-educated and highly-skilled artisans; from Ireland came an almost inexhaustible supply of cheap, unskilled labour. For after the Potato Famine of 1846 the stream of Irish immigration became a flood: Irishmen by the thousand crowded into central Scotland, and since they were fleeing from starvation they were content to accept any wage that would put food into their stomachs, and to crowd into any hovel, however small and squalid it might be.

So in many industries the captains and non-commissioned officers, we might say, were Scotsmen, the rank and file Irishmen. And this combination produced marvellous results. To take one example : at the beginning of the nineteenth century the annual output of the Scottish blast furnaces was about 20,000 tons ; in 1838, thanks largely to Neilson's invention of the hot-air blast, the figures leapt up to over 147,000 tons ; before the middle of the century half a million tons had come to be the annual output ; in 1865 it was over a million, and at the end of the century it had risen to almost a million and a half, despite the fact that the Scottish iron fields were becoming exhausted, and the bulk of the iron ore had to be imported from Spain. In spinning and weaving the same story has to be told. In Dundee, for example, the amount of flax imported to be woven into canvas and coarse linen rose from 5,724 tons in 1821 to over 39,000 tons in 1871, and though the disappearance of the large sailing-ship led to a decreased demand for canvas, the rapid rise in the jute industry more than balanced the decline in the linen industry. In 1838, for example, 1,136 tons of raw jute came into Dundee harbour; in 1863 the figure had risen to 47,000 tons, and in 1883 it reached its highest point, a little short of 234,000 tons. We might take other industries: ship-building, coal-mining, what you like, it would make no difference; everywhere you hear the same tale of progress, of prosperity, of great fortunes accumulated by shrewd and thrifty Scotsmen who had begun with no capital but their brains.

Nowadays we cannot get rid of the suspicion that Scotland may have paid too high a price for this prosperity. For one thing, though the influx of Irishmen gave the Scottish employer an unlimited supply of cheap labour, it tended to lower the wages of the less highly skilled among the Scottish workmen. For another, this peaceful invasion of Scotland by people of a different race, with different traditions, different ways of looking at things, has created some rather difficult problems. There are regions in industrial Scotland which have practically ceased to be Scotch: their inhabitants may never have set foot in Ireland, but they regard themselves as Irish and look on Ireland as their home. The time will come when the descendant of the nineteenth-century Irish immigrant will look on himself as a Scotsman, just as the descendant of the invading Norseman or Anglo-Norman does to-day, but that time is, as yet, far off.

One part of Scotland, however, had no share in this abounding prosperity. Though the population of the Highlands continued to increase in the first four decades of the century, there had been no corresponding increase in the means of subsistence. It is true that at the beginning of the century the making of soda from kelp gave employment to fifty thousand Highlanders, but the kelp industry had grown up behind the shelter of an import duty on barilla—soda prepared in Spain from the barilla plant

—and a similar duty on salt, heavy enough to keep it from being used in the manufacture of soda. The reduction of the duty on salt in 1817, followed by the halving of the duty on barilla in 1822, killed the kelp industry. The completion of a long programme of road building and canal making about the same time meant further unemployment. Though in the fourth decade of the century landlords discovered that they could make money by turning the more barren sheep-runs into deer forests, the discovery did not alter the lot of their tenants either for better or for worse. Sheep had already driven men from the inland farms; now sheep in their turn were driven out by deer: a few score of hill shepherds had to go; a few score of ghillies and gamekeepers took their place—that was all.

Something far more serious happened in 1846: the potato crop failed. To people who lived on potatoes for ten months out of the twelve, the news of the disaster came as a sentence of death, and though the money which poured in from all parts of the island saved the inhabitants of the Highlands from actually dying of hunger, landlord and tenant alike began to realize that there was something far wrong with a country where the difference between potatoes and no potatoes was also the difference between life and death. There were far too many people in the Highlands—that was the chief cause of the trouble. Many of the Highlanders had already recognized it: ever since the 'Forty-Five' there had been a steady drift of population from the Highlands to the Lowlands, and a steady flow of immigration westward to North America, but many more had shut their eyes to it, and as a result the population of the Highlands was far larger in 1845 than it had been in 1745. Now, when none but the most obstinate could doubt the facts, the drift southward and westward became a rush: ever since 1846 the population of the Highlands has steadily declined.

To begin with, however, the movement was not altogether

a voluntary one. In many districts 'clearances' were made: the landlord ordered his tenants to leave, and, if they refused, pulled the thatch from their houses and made it impossible for them to stay.

When the exile had left the languid, moisture-laden air and sterile soil of his native glen he generally gained, if not wealth, at least comfort. To be owner of two hundred acres of good cornland in Manitoba was far better than to remain tenant of two or three or half a score acres in Skye or Sutherland. But it is hard to remember this when one looks at the roofless cottages, overgrown with nettles and foxglove, that are to be seen in every Highland glen, or, stranger still, when one comes on a whole village, once the home of two-score families, now as dead as Pompeii or Herculaneum. 'There has been no dance in Corodale for two generations. Still the crash of seas, and Corodale Loch in sunshine blue as an angel's eye: still the mountains, but never again the men!'[1]

The roofless cottage, the farm-steading tumbling into decay, is not unknown even in the Lowlands. Down to 1870 agriculture continued to flourish: the skill, enterprise, and driving-power of the hard-headed Lowland farmer had placed him in a seemingly impregnable position. Even the much dreaded repeal of the Corn Laws in 1846 did not affect him. Suddenly he was assailed from two quarters at once: with the autumn of 1872 began a ten years' series of bad harvests, and the importation of wheat from the new corn-growing countries forced down the price of grain. Only the farmer with capital behind him could weather the storm, and he found that it paid to grow wheat only in places where the soil was exceptionally fertile. In 1857, for example, almost a quarter of a million acres were under wheat; in 1877 this had shrunk to about 81,000 acres, and in 1928 to 58,000 acres. Other crops have not diminished in the same degree, still the tendency is for the Lowland farmer to

---

[1] Neil Munro, *Children of Tempest.*

devote less attention to arable farming and more to the raising
of sheep and cattle and to dairy farming.[1]

Just as the eighteenth-century landlord threw together half
a dozen small farms to form one large one, so his twentieth-
century successor welcomes the tenant who is willing to lease
two or more farms at once. And the enterprising tenant farmer
argues that he will be twice as well off with two farms as he is
with one. So to-day it is quite easy to find farmers who run
three or four farms from one farm-house. This development is
not altogether a change for the better: it squeezes out the
farmer who has little money behind him, and it widens still
farther the gulf that yawns between the farmer and the farm
labourer. Of the passionate attachment of the French peasant
to the soil which he tills you find not a trace in rural Scotland:
the Scottish ploughman 'flits', as he calls it, from one farm to
another at intervals of six months, or, at most, of a year; his
two-roomed cottage is an encampment rather than a home, and
his children may attend ten different schools in their seven
years of school life.

Why does he 'flit'? Because there is no special reason why
he should stay. Some of his children will probably migrate to
the towns, but he will never be anything but a ploughman, and
though he may strive to become a better ploughman, his
superior skill will not increase his wages or add another room
to his tiny house. If he does grow tired of going round and
round, like a squirrel in a cage, his only chance is to break away
altogether, and go to Canada, where the land that he ploughs
will be his own.

So we notice a movement of population in the Lowlands only
a little less striking than the movement in the Highlands, a
drift from the rural districts to the towns, from the smaller

---

[1] In 1877, 269,845 acres were under barley, in 1928, 117,369; in 1877,
1,024,882 acres were under oats, in 1928, 878,436. Pasture in 1928 occupied
over three million acres, as compared with two and a half millions in 1877.

towns to the larger towns, and another drift westwards across the Atlantic to Canada and the United States.

If you know the political history of England after the passing of the Reform Act of 1832, you also know the political history of Scotland. Though in the nineteenth century there was an Irish Nationalist Party at Westminster, no Scottish Nationalist Party has ever appeared in the House of Commons. In the nineteenth century the Scottish voter, like the English voter, voted either Conservative or Liberal; in the twentieth century, like the English elector, he may be Conservative, Liberal, or Labour. The Scottish voter, however, 'inclines to the left': if the English voter is in doubt he votes Conservative; if the Scottish voter is in doubt he votes Labour, though his 'swithering' grandfather would have voted Liberal. At only one general election since 1832 have the Scottish constituencies returned a Conservative majority.

The Reform Act of 1868 increased the number of Scottish members from 53 to 60, and gave a vote to all householders in the burghs, though in the counties the franchise was restricted to the owners of property worth more than £5 a year and tenants paying a rent of more than £14. The Act of 1885, however, besides raising the number of members to 72, gave the vote to householders in the rural districts; and the Act of 1918, besides admitting women to the vote for the first time, gave Scotland one additional member of parliament. In 1885, too, the office of Secretary for Scotland, abolished in 1746, was restored. The Secretary of State for Scotland, as he is now called, has a seat in the Cabinet; he is the official head of most of the Government departments in Scotland—of the Scottish Education Department, for example—and he is looked on as the person who is responsible for the proper management of Scottish affairs.

Another important innovation was the establishment, in 1889, of county councils, elective bodies whose authority has gradually extended, till, with the passing of the Local Government Act of 1929, they have acquired many of the powers once possessed by the councils of the smaller burghs.

Though the Scotsman may sometimes feel aggrieved because he is governed, not from Edinburgh, but from Westminster, he finds consolation in the thought that the head of the Government is, as often as not, a Scotsman. Of the nine Prime Ministers who have held office since Gladstone resigned in 1894, five have been Scotsmen,[1] and Gladstone, though born in England, was of Scottish descent. Nor is it only as statesmen that Scotsmen have served Great Britain and the whole Empire. If you visit the National Scottish War Memorial in Edinburgh you will find that among all the symbolical figures there is only one portrait—the portrait of Douglas Haig, Commander-in-Chief of the British Expeditionary force from 1916 to the end of the Great War. It was well for Britain that in her hour of trial she committed her fortunes to this soldier of the valiant heart and cool clear brain, whom no calamity nor treachery could shake, whom no jealous regard for his own name could deflect from the path of duty.

But while we remember Haig, do not let us forget those tens of thousands of Scotsmen, unknown to fame, who played their part in battles beside which Bannockburn and Flodden shrink to the dimensions of a playground scrimmage. 'All down the slopes towards Lens', says Mr. John Buchan in his description of the first of these battles, 'lay the tartans, Gordon and Black Watch, Seaforth and Cameron, like the drift left on the shore when the tide has ebbed.' And what was seen at Loos in 1915 might have been seen at the Battle of the Somme in 1916, after the fighting in front of Arras and the even more terrible struggle for Passchendaele in 1917, and after each desperate thrust and counter-thrust in 1918, for wherever there was hard fighting to

[1] Earl of Rosebery, 1894–5; Earl of Balfour, 1902–5; Sir Henry Campbell-Bannerman, 1905–8; Andrew Bonar Law, 1922–3; James Ramsay Mac-Donald, 1924 and 1929– .

be done, there would be found at least one of the famous Scottish divisions, the Ninth, the Fifteenth, the Fifty-first, and the Fifty-second.

Since the War, however, Scotland has been depressed and ill at ease: the ordinary Scotsman seems to have lost that

The plaque from the National Memorial

complacency which by turns annoyed and amused his southern neighbour. He is no longer proud, for example, of the 'but and ben', the two-roomed house which sentimental poets and novelists have celebrated ; he does not like to be reminded that one out of every twelve of his fellow-countrymen lives in a one-roomed house and two out of every five in a two-roomed house, whereas in England only one person in seventy-seven has to endure life in a one-roomed house and only one in eighteen

has to be content with a two-roomed house. And the houses
are overcrowded, most of the two-roomed houses, for example,
have at least four occupants. He knows that bad housing
means bad health—physical and moral—and a high death-
rate. It is not a fact commonly grasped, but it is a fact that
the average Scotsman does not live as long as the average
Englishman. It is true that since the War the worst of the old
houses have been cleared away and more than one hundred
thousand new houses have been built, but even now it remains
true that 'half Scotland is slum-poisoned'.

The slum is a legacy from an earlier generation. Another
problem bequeathed by an earlier generation—the problem
of the relations of the two great Presbyterian Churches, has
been happily solved. The abolition of Lay Patronage in the
Church of Scotland in 1874 failed to remove the old bitterness;
it died away, however, before the end of the century, and in
1929 the two Churches were reunited.[1]

But there are other, newer problems which perplex the
present-day Scot. You have noticed that the long-continued
advance in Scottish agriculture was followed by a decline. The
history of Scottish industry in general, and of the iron industry
in particular, is much the same: a long steady advance—an
advance which slowed down a little at the end of the nineteenth
century, and then a persistent decline.

Some Scotsmen blame the Union, and think that Scotland
will not prosper till a Scottish Parliament sits once more in
Edinburgh. But these troubles are not peculiar to Scotland;
from the north of England comes the same complaint. The
northward drift of industry, which set in at the end of the
eighteenth century, has been reversed: the tide is now flowing
to the south. And not only in England, but in France, one
hears the familiar story of rural depopulation, of fields aban-

---

[1] In 1900 the Free Church and a smaller body of Presbyterians, the
United Presbyterian Church, combined to form the United Free Church.

THE SHRINE
National War Memorial

doned which have been cultivated for centuries. A parliament in Edinburgh might do many things for Scotland which the Parliament at Westminster is unable to do, but it is hard to see how it could control these mysterious movements of population and industry. It is still harder to see how it could control the movements of the spirit. For even more disturbing than the decline in material prosperity is the decline in intellectual activity, the failure of modern Scotland to produce men of really commanding genius, men like Scott in literature, David Hume and Adam Smith in philosophy, or Clerk Maxwell in science.

At first this may seem a depressing picture, but, whatever it may not do, History does teach us to take long views, to see that this 'post-war depression' must be cheerfulness itself beside the gloom which settled down on Scotland after the death of Alexander III, after Flodden, after Worcester, after Darien. This is not the first time that Scotland has been 'stad in perplexity'; this will not be the last time that Scotsmen will fight their way out. To some of us, as to Scott, the real, essential Scotland lies buried deep in the past. We grumble because we cannot put back the hands of the clock; we move ill at ease in this new Scotland, muttering, 'This is no my ain hoose, I ken by the biggin' o't.' It is better to think of the Scotland we love as something that lies, not in the past, but in the future, something that may be lost for ever unless we ourselves help to make it real.

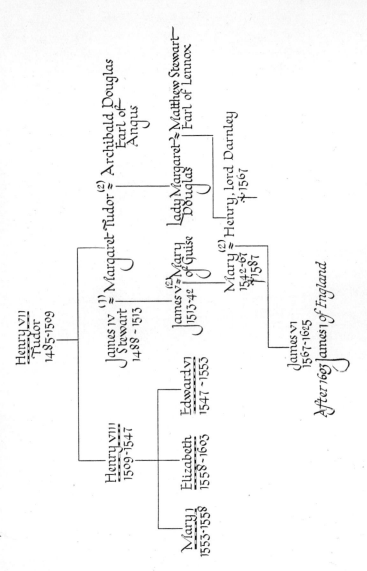

GENEALOGICAL · TABLE · THE · TUDORS · AND · STEWARTS

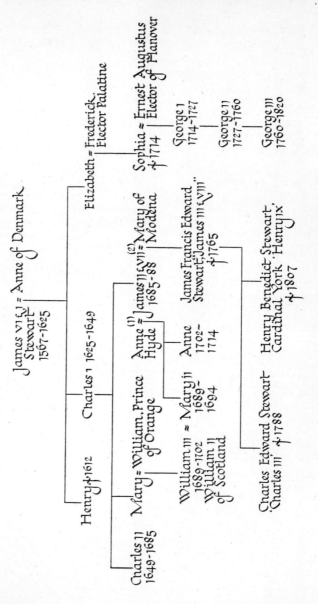

A CHRONOLOGY OF SCOTTISH HISTORY

c. 4000 B.C.	Beginning of Neolithic Age in Scotland.
c. 1800 B.C.	Beginning of Bronze Age in Britain.
c. 400 B.C.	Beginning of Iron Age in Britain.
80 A.D.	Agricola's invasion of Scotland.
85	Battle of Mons Graupius.
c. 115	End of First Roman Occupation of Scotland.
140	Antonine Wall built; beginning of Second Roman Occupation of Scotland.
c. 180	End of Second Roman Occupation of Scotland.
208–11	Invasion of Septimius Severus.
397	St. Ninian founds First Christian Church in Scotland.
501	Foundation of kingdom of Dalriata.
563–97	The mission of St. Columba.
664	The Synod of Whitby.
685	Battle of Nechtansmere.
794	Beginning of Norse invasions of Scotland.
843	Kenneth MacAlpin becomes King of Picts and Scots; formation of kingdom of Alba.
c. 874	Harold Harfagr, King of Norway, becomes overlord of Orkneys and Hebrides.
937	Battle of Brunanburh.
945	Malcolm I, King of Alba, becomes overlord of Cumbria.
c. 962	Indulf, King of Alba, gains northern part of Lothian.
1014	Battle of Clontarf; Malcolm II, King of Alba, regains Hebrides and Northern Scotland.
1018	Battle of Carham. Annexation of Lothian and Cumbria by Malcolm II completes unification of Scotland.
1040	Murder of King Duncan by Macbeth.
1070	Marriage of Malcolm III and Queen Margaret.
1092	William Rufus seizes Carlisle and southern Cumbria.
1093	Death of Malcolm and Margaret.
1098	Magnus Bareleg, King of Norway, regains Hebrides.
1124–53	Reign of David I.
1174	Treaty of Falaise; subjection of Scotland to England.
1189	Scotland regains its independence.
1230	Final pacification of Moray.
1235	Final pacification of Galloway.
1237	Alexander II abandons claim to northern counties of England.
1263	Battle of Largs.

1266	Hebrides ceded to Scotland.
1286	Death of Alexander III.
1290	Death of the Maid of Norway.
1292	Edward I awards crown of Scotland to John Balliol.
1296	Invasion of Scotland by Edward I; abdication of Balliol.
1297	Wallace defeats English at Stirling Bridge.
1298	Edward I defeats Wallace at Falkirk.
1306	Assassination of Comyn and coronation of Robert I (Bruce).
1314	Battle of Bannockburn.
1326	First appearance of Burgh Representatives in Parliament.
1328	Treaty of Northampton.
1332	Battle of Dupplin.
1346	Battle of Neville's Cross.
1370	Institution of Committee of Articles.
1385	French Expedition to Scotland.
1388	Battle of Otterburn.
1406	James I captured by English.
1411	Battle of Harlaw.
1412	Foundation of St. Andrews University.
1424	James I returns to Scotland.
1426	Establishment of the Session.
1437	James I assassinated.
1451	Foundation of Glasgow University.
1452	James II kills William, 8th Earl of Douglas.
1455	Battle of Arkinholm and Fall of the Douglases.
1474	Orkneys and Shetlands annexed to Scotland.
1482–3	First Rebellion against James III.
1488	Second Rebellion against James III; Battle of Sauchieburn and assassination of James III.
1495	Foundation of King's College, Aberdeen.
1496	First Education Act.
1503	Marriage of James IV and Margaret Tudor.
1513	Battle of Flodden and death of James IV.
1528	Patrick Hamilton burned.
1532	Foundation of College of Justice (Court of Session).
1542	Battle of Solway Moss and death of James V.
1544	Hertford's Invasion of Scotland; Edinburgh burned.
1546	Burning of George Wishart and assassination of Cardinal Beaton.
1559	John Knox returns to Scotland; opening of hostilities between Scottish Catholics and Scottish Protestants.

1560	End of Franco-Scottish Alliance and establishment of Protestantism in Scotland.
1561	The First Book of Discipline; arrival of Queen Mary in Scotland.
1567	Abdication of Queen Mary.
1568	Queen Mary's flight to England.
1573	Capture of Edinburgh Castle and end of Wars of Religion in Scotland.
1578	The Second Book of Discipline.
1582	Foundation of Edinburgh University.
1603	The Union of the Crowns.
1610	Episcopacy replaces Presbyterian form of Church Government.
1625	Accession of Charles I; Act of Revocation.
1638	The National Covenant; re-establishment of Presbyterianism.
1639	First Bishops' War
1640	Second Bishops' War.
1643	Solemn League and Covenant.
1644–5	Campaigns of Montrose.
1648	Battle of Preston.
1650	Battle of Dunbar.
1651	Battle of Worcester.
1653–60	The Cromwellian Union.
1660	The Restoration.
1661	Re-establishment of Episcopacy.
1679	Murder of Archbishop Sharp; Battles of Drumclog and Bothwell Bridge.
1689	Battle of Killiecrankie.
1690	Re-establishment of Presbyterianism; abolition of Committee of Articles.
1692	The Massacre of Glencoe.
1696	Education Act; schools to be established in every parish.
1698	The First Darien Expedition.
1704	The Act of Security.
1707	The Union of the Parliaments.
1712	Reintroduction of Lay Patronage.
1715–16	The Fifteen Rebellion.
1745–6	The Forty-Five Rebellion.
1746	Office of Secretary of State for Scotland abolished.
1748	Abolition of Heritable Jurisdictions.
1750	First Turnpike Act; Invention of swing plough.
1770	Deepening of Clyde begun.
1774	James Watt constructs first efficient steam-engine.

1782	James Watt invents rotary steam-engine.
1790	Forth and Clyde Canal constructed.
1794	The Political Trials.
1799	Serfdom in Scottish Mines abolished.
1801	First Steamboat—Symington's *Charlotte Dundas*.
1803	Education Act; schoolhouses to be provided in every parish.
1812	Bell's *Comet*.
1820	'The Radical War.'
1822	Caledonian Canal completed.
1832	First Reform Act.
1833	Burgh Reform Act.
1843	The Disruption.
1845	The Scottish Poor Law.
1846	The Potato Famine; abolition of privileges of Trade and Merchant Gilds.
1867	First Public Health Act.
1868	Second Reform Act.
1872	Education Act; introduction of compulsory education.
1874	Abolition of Lay Patronage.
1885	Third Reform Act; office of Secretary for Scotland restored.
1889	County Councils established.
1918	Representation of the People Act.
1929	Union of Church of Scotland and United Free Church; Local Government Act.

INDEX

INDEX

INDEX

ERRATA

Page 3, line 5, *for* twelve thousand *read* six thousand
Page 134, line 8, *for* Humphrey *read* Henry
Page 167, line 6, *for* boy of nine *read* boy of six
Page 196, line 2, *for* 1450 *read* 1451
Page 254, line 21, *for* James *read* John
Page 322, 3rd line from foot of page, *for* James *read* John
Page 374, 2nd line from foot of page, *for* Argyll *read* Atholl

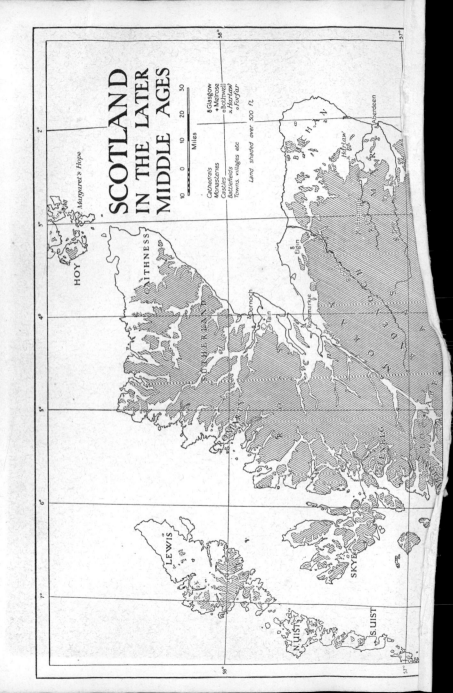

SCOTLAND
IN THE LATER
MIDDLE AGES

Miles

10   0   10   20   30

Cathedrals   δ Glasgow
Monasteries   + Melrose
Castles   ⬡ Bothwell
Battlefields   × Harlaw
Towns. villages etc   ○ Forfar

Land shaded over 500 ft.

Margaret's Hope

HOY

CAITHNESS

SUTHERLAND

Dornoch

Tain

Rosemarkie

Elgin

R O S S

MORAY

B U C H A N

Harlaw

Aberdeen

LEWIS

SKYE

N. UIST

S. UIST